British and Irish Butterflies

The complete Identification, Field and Site Guide to the Species, Subspecies and Forms

Adrian M. Riley

Brambleby Books

British and Irish Butterflies
©Adrian M. Riley, 2007

All Rights Reserved

No part of this book may be reproduced in any form by photocopying or by any electronic or mechanical means, including information, storage or retrieval systems, without permission in writing from both the copyright owner and the publisher of this book.

ISBN-13: 978 0 9553928 0 1

Published 2007 by
BRAMBLEBY BOOKS
Luton, Bedfordshire, UK
www.bramblebybooks.co.uk

Cover design and book layout by Tanya Warren, Creatix
Front cover photos by Adrian Riley

Dedicated to my friend and mentor
Bernard Skinner

Chalkhill Blue

Welcome by Butterfly Conservation

Butterfly Conservation is delighted to welcome this important new book on British and Irish butterflies. It contains a wealth of information about the butterflies of Britain and Ireland, which is essential to underpin our conservation efforts. It also imparts the enthusiasm and deep knowledge of a genuine butterfly lover. The book helps readers to understand butterflies more fully as well as encouraging them to help take action to conserve them for the future.

Butterflies have been in steep decline for over a century, but threats to their future have never been greater than today. Having suffered decades of habitat destruction and widespread changes in habitat management, they are now under new pressures from climate change and urban expansion. They need our help.

The conservation of butterflies is important in its own right but it has wider implications for wildlife and for we humans who share the planet with them. Butterflies are valuable indicators of the general health of the environment and help us understand the impacts of human activity on wildlife and the countryside. They also help us monitor the effect of factors such as climate change and pollution. By contributing to the study and conservation of these beautiful insects, we can help build a world where people and wildlife can better co-exist.

There are many practical ways readers can help conserve butterflies, including by contributing to our world famous recording and monitoring schemes or by becoming a Butterfly Conservation member and supporting our work. There are also many gaps in our knowledge of the life cycle and habitats of each species, which can be filled by careful observations and study. This book gives an authoritative starting place.

Further information on our activities and how to get involved can be found on our website: www.butterfly-conservation.org or by writing to Butterfly Conservation, Manor Yard, East Lulworth, Dorset BH20 5QP (Tel: 01929 400209).

Martin Warren

Dr Martin Warren
Chief Executive
Butterfly Conservation

About the Author

Adrian Riley was born in Birmingham in 1958 but spent his formative years amongst the glorious countryside of Shropshire. Surrounded by such splendour, it is perhaps not surprising that he developed an interest in natural history at an early age. His first forays were deep into the past as a fossil-hunter and, given Shropshire's diverse geology, he found many treasures. His extensive fossil collection was donated to his former grammar school in Wellington. He also took great excitement in fishing and caught 'specimen-sized' examples of tench, bream, roach, perch, carp and pike from waters in Shropshire, Hertfordshire, Buckinghamshire and Norfolk. However, until 2001, his main interest was butterflies and moths and he wrote a book on the Lepidoptera of Shropshire: *A Natural History of the Butterflies and Moths of Shropshire* (Swan Hill Press, 1991) which remains a key publication on the subject. He moved to Hertfordshire in 1979 and thereafter worked his way through the ranks and became the supervisor and chief taxonomist of the light-trap network of Rothamsted Research, Harpenden, the agricultural research station. He also wrote a rock album in 1982 (*All on One Side,* Ercall Wood (privately published)) and took his band on, as he says, a "reasonably unsuccessful" tour around the north London circuit.

Adrian Riley left Rothamsted in 2001, by which time he had written over 150 scientific papers and articles and three books. His book *British and Irish Pug*

The author and his constant companion (self portrait)

Moths (Harley Books, 2003) is now regarded as the standard work on the subject. He was also Membership Secretary for the *Cross-Keys Preservation Society* (Harpenden, Hertfordshire) – an ancient pub he still frequents and treats as his 'International Headquarters'. For Hertfordshire, his main contribution to lepidoptery was perhaps the publication of *The Macrolepidoptera of the Rothamsted Estate*[†] (1999) in which he describes the collecting methodology, time-series and results for a farmland estate in the county. Many of his other published articles describe the first records for moths for a variety of counties – one of which concerned the first mainland record for Britain of the Channel Islands Pug, *Eupithecia ultimaria* Boisduval. He has given several talks to the

About the Author

Hertfordshire and Shropshire Wildlife Trusts and always enjoys a pint or two afterwards with the many friends that he made over the years. He still sees Rothamsted as his 'home from home'.

In 2001, Adrian Riley left Hertfordshire and moved to Norfolk. His 'new-found' interest in birds (he and his grandfather bred finches, budgerigars and doves in the 1970s) took over his life. In 2002, he took on the 'twitching' world and won the annual competition for the largest number of birds seen in the British Isles in a calendar year. His total of 381 species is more than most birders see in a lifetime and his dramatic story is told in his book *Arrivals and Rivals: a Birding Oddity* (Brambleby Books, 2004). Despite having suffered many white-knuckle journeys and two near-death experiences (one involving hypothermia in the remote island of Foula, Shetland and another, a front-wheel blow-out at 70mph), Riley was ready for the next challenge.

In 2003, he started his life's work – essentially begun in about 1969 – on the butterflies of Great Britain and Ireland. During the course of this project, he gained much inspiration and a sense of discipline from his gruelling experiences and many contacts as a birder. For example, within 24 hours, he drove from Norfolk to Penzance, took a helicopter to St Mary's in the Isles of Scilly, a chartered speedboat to Tresco, a boat back to St Mary's, a helicopter to Penzance and then drove back to Norfolk before his local pub called last orders (23 hours in total). Thus, as a consequence of this marathon effort, photographs are here published of the Isles of Scilly Meadow Brown and the Isles of Scilly Speckled Wood. The stress, after three drives to Scotland during the previous week, cost the author a minor stroke. A stay in Rhum, sheltering against the rain for most of his time there, allowed him to photograph the little known Hebridean subspecies of the Small Heath butterfly, also produced here, but also resulted in him catching tick-borne Lyme Disease. The author has taken photographs of all the British and Irish butterfly subspecies and that, as far as he and the publishers are aware, has never been achieved before.

Adrian Riley now offers services running bird- and 'bug'-watching tours. His latest fancy are dragonflies and damselflies and he knows a thing or two about these too! (Visit *www.enterprise-io.co.uk* for more details).

† Riley, A.M. (1999). The Macrolepidoptera of the Rothamsted Estate, Harpenden, Hertfordshire. *Entomologist's Rec. & J. Var.* **3**: 71-94

Swallowtail

Contents

Foreword	13
Preface	15
Acknowledgements	17
Introduction	19
How to use this book	22
Basic habitat types	29
Systematic checklist of species, subspecies and common forms	38
British and Irish butterflies	43
The Skippers (Hesperiidae)	43
The Swallowtails and Apollos (Papilionidae)	67
The Whites and Yellows (Pieridae)	75
The Hairstreaks (Lycaenidae, subfamily Theclinae)	113
The Coppers (Lycaenidae, subfamily Lycaeninae)	131
The Blues (Lycaenidae, subfamily Polyommatinae)	139
The Metalmarks (Lycaenidae, subfamily Riodininae)	183
The White Admirals (Nymphalidae, subfamily Limenitinae)	187
The Emperors (Nymphalidae, subfamily Apaturinae)	191
The Vanessids (Nymphalidae, subfamily Nymphalinae)	197
The Fritillaries (Nymphalidae, subfamily Argynninae)	217
The Browns (Nymphalidae, subfamily Satyrinae)	255
The Monarchs (Nymphalidae, subfamily Danainae)	315
Appendix I. Alphabetical list of foodplants	319
Appendix II. Useful contacts	324
Appendix III. Table of flight periods (phenological table)	325
Appendix IV. Index of butterflies found within each geographical region	329
Appendix V. Vice-counties of Britain and Ireland	331
References and further reading	333
General index	339

Vanessids and Browns on Hemp Agrimony

Foreword

In Britain and Ireland we are fortunate in having a great wealth of books on our butterflies to choose from, many with their own particular attractions, thus making it necessary to find much space on the bookshelf. Readers of Adrian Riley's previous works will be aware that birds, insects and other natural wonders have been an important source of inspiration in his life. Prior to reading the manuscript for this volume, I personally could not have conceived of a vacant niche for yet another butterfly book. However, there is absolutely no doubt in these pages that he has indeed – to quote his favourite TV show *Star Trek* – 'boldly gone where no one has gone before'.

I was brought up in Dorset with its wealth of diverse habitats, perhaps the English county most likely to spark an interest in butterflies. There was nothing I enjoyed more than cycling off into the 'back of beyond' and discovering for myself the best haunts. Nets and killing jars were then part of the scene, and the thrill of the chase was undeniable. Even so, I never did discover the whereabouts of certain species such as the Marsh Fritillary (perhaps a good thing bearing in mind where some of them would have ended up!). Times have changed. The camera has largely replaced the net, but the excitement is undiminished. There is no longer such a thriving market for set specimens and the need for secrecy over sites has all but evaporated, except for those of the most endangered species. Indeed, in order to generate the increased interest in our butterflies necessary to provide the social and political pressure for their conservation, people must be able to find and admire them. The charity 'Butterfly Conservation' (born in Dorset in my youth thanks to the far-sightedness of Robert Goodden) has been instrumental in making this possible, and branch members will be well aware of prime sites in their region. Yet never before has one book made the search for all of the species so easy. As well as the detailed information on locations, the field tips provided with the description of each butterfly are invaluable in maximising the chance of a sighting, correct identification and a photograph.

Having said that, in one way, Adrian has made the search more difficult. Until now, we seemingly had only around 60 taxa to interest us. The other unique aspect of this book is that we are presented with an authoritative account of *all* the clearly distinguishable species, subspecies and common forms and where to find them, thus providing an opportunity to track down over 100 taxa.

Adrian Riley is a perfectionist, and he is surely also a driven man. I cannot think of anybody else who could have achieved what he has here. Countless days of patient research, drawing heavily on his experience as a scientist at the world-renowned Rothamsted Research in Hertfordshire, have gone into the collection of the information for this book. Many of those days will have resulted in frustration, fewer in elation. As a result of his efforts, the balance for

Foreword

the rest of us has shifted towards elation and I plan to waste no time in making the acquaintance of some of those species which, when I was a child, were worth more points in the *I-Spy* book than I could then have dreamed of. Many readers will do the same and, as a result, the future of these vital and magnificent components of the ecosystem will hopefully be more secure.

**Richard Harrington, Ph.D.,
Harpenden,
July 2007**

Preface

After birds, butterflies are probably the most popular – and therefore most studied – group of animals in the British Isles. As there are only 59 species that breed here, seeing them all is a relatively easy task and spending time in the wild places where some of the more specialized species live gives enormous pleasure and excitement. The stubborn Small Mountain Ringlet battling against the spectacular Highlands of Scotland, the exotic Swallowtail amongst the swaying reedbeds of the Norfolk Broads and 'His Majesty' the Purple Emperor on his lofty throne of Oak in the early morning freshness of an English woodland are just three examples of the joy that these creatures and their surroundings can bring. The 'innocence' and delicacy of butterflies have inspired poets, songwriters and painters throughout the generations. Their beauty gladdens all but the weariest of hearts.

Apart from their obvious beauty they also form an extremely important group of animals. They pollinate our garden flowers, crops and wildflowers in the countryside and they and their larvae constitute a vital part of the diet of insect-eating birds and mammals. They are in fact an essential piece of the huge jigsaw puzzle of our ecological systems. Because they are insects, some species can reproduce in large numbers and some like the Small Copper, may have as many as three generations per year. This provides them with the means to react quickly to changes in their environment. Sometimes they benefit from such changes and are able to expand their distributions by colonizing new sites. On other occasions, the changes may be detrimental and they are forced to retreat in terms of habitat occupation and range – sometimes, as in the case of the Large Copper, to the point of extinction. Of course, when one species suffers this fate then others associated with that particular habitat are also greatly at risk. If the environmental changes are caused by Man (and often they are) then we have a scientific and moral obligation to reassess our behaviour and the way it affects the world that we share with our fellow creatures. Ultimately, *Homo sapiens* will benefit from such awareness and action, as a fragmented ecosystem is an unhealthy, and potentially dangerous, place for any species to try to survive – perhaps even mankind.

Until the 1970s, collecting butterflies was a popular hobby and in earlier times, especially the late 19th and early 20th centuries, was encouraged as a worthwhile scientific pastime. It helped young people to understand the natural world and how its inhabitants were ordered in a cohesive way (see Salmon, 2000). I suspect it was also deemed to be a diversion from boredom and mischief during the long summer school holidays when butterflies are, collectively, at their most abundant. Whatever the motives, they worked for me. My first aimless wanderings into the local fields and woodlands with a child's plastic fishing net and an empty jam jar led to a

Preface

fascination with insects that has since filled my life with intrigue and wonderment – to say nothing of providing a long and highly rewarding scientific career.

Today the net and the killing jar are largely things of the past. The advent of digital photography and its subsequent technological evolution means that these fragile creatures no longer need to be killed and collected, save occasionally for scientific purposes such as demographic studies. It is now within everyone's scope, both financially and in terms of technical expertise, to pursue our quarry with a camera and capture in digital images the beauty of living butterflies. The added stealth and patience needed to obtain close-up photographs simply adds to the excitement and sense of achievement. To emphasise these remarks I should perhaps point out that at the onset of the present project I had never owned a camera. However, over the following four years I was able to photograph all of the species, subspecies and common forms of butterfly resident in Britain and Ireland and present the results in this book. If my basic digital camera, fumbling fingers and creaking old knees can accomplish this, then so can anyone's. During the course of the work I was able to solve many problems that were left unanswered by previous authors. Most importantly though, I discovered many more questions that will keep my mind occupied for years to come. This is how scientific enquiry works: for every answer there is another question. The really important thing about it, though, is that lepidoptery is also great fun.

Adrian M. Riley

Acknowledgements

My association with Butterfly Conservation goes back to the late 1980s when Mike Williams, the then Regional Officer for the West Midlands, secured part funding for my book on the Lepidoptera of Shropshire (Riley, 1991). During the four years' field work for the present project I once again found myself in great debt to the organization. I am particularly grateful to Mark Parsons, a long-standing entomological colleague, who has supplied me with several useful contacts and has always generously given his time whenever I was in need of information. I also thank Richard Fox for relieving me of the task of distributing to Regional Recorders all of the 2,000 or so records contributed to the organization over the course of the project. I hereby acknowledge the tremendous help given by the many Butterfly Conservation's Regional Recorders and thank them all, along with their colleagues working independently for the organization, for their sterling support. Without hard-earned local expertise, publication of this book would have been impossible and I hope that, reading between the lines, those who kindly helped me will see their names shining brightly with my gratitude.

The photographs of most of the resident species, subspecies and forms were taken by myself, but some, particularly of the scarce immigrants and vagrants, were obtained from other sources. For these I am pleased to thank the following: Kevin Earp, Richard Harrington, Rob Laughton, C. 'Will' Cook, Simon Coombes, Steve Doyle, Alex McLennan, Gillian McLennan, Rebecca Nesbit, Wilf Powell, Gary Thoburn, Robert Thompson and Ian Woiwod. Of my former colleagues at Rothamsted Research, besides those already mentioned, I additionally most sincerely thank Phil Gould, Jason Chapman and Ian Denholm for their enthusiastic support.

Of the many who supplied me with information and were often the recipients of desperate phone calls from the field, I thank the following for their special help: Martin Anthoney, Mike Banham, David Barbour, Andy Barker, Peter Boardman, Pat Bonham, Roger Bristow, David Brown, Richard Buckland, Nick Cook, Gordon Craine, Gary Curtis, Peter Davey, Peter Duncan, Michael Easterbrook, Ron Elliott, Debbie Evans, Alan Ferguson, Ian Ferguson, Lin Gander, Roger Gaunt, Andrew Graham, John Halliday, Russel Hobson, John Hope, Andrew King, Jessie MacKay, Roy McCormick, Jimmy McKellar, Alex McLennan, Richard Mearns, Peter Moore, Bob Palmer, Alex Parker, Rob Parker, Graham Parris, Rob Petley-Jones, Barry Prater, Jim Reid, Ian Scott, Bernard Skinner, Rob Smith, Richard Southwell, Simon Spencer, Chris Stamp, Barry Stewart, Julie Stoneman, Richard Sutcliffe, Roger Sutton, Gary Thoburn, Brenda Thompsett, Martin Townsend, John Wacher, Alan Wagstaff, Jill Warwick, Christine Welsh, Terence Whitaker, Robert Whitehead, David

Acknowledgements

Whittaker, Mike Williams, Pat Woodruff and Mark Young.

Special thanks are also extended to my wonderful contacts in Ireland. The coverage of this book would have been far less extensive without the expertise of Kenneth Bond, Trevor Boyd, Maurice Hughes and Kenny Murphy.

The cooperation of the local Wildlife Trusts, the Countryside Council for Wales, The Dublin Naturalists' Field Club, Natural England, The Forestry Commission, The National Trust and Scottish Natural Heritage is gratefully appreciated.

I also thank Julie Harvey at the Natural History Museum, London, Val McAtear at The Royal Entomological Society and Sabine Gaal-Haszler at the Naturhistorische Museum Wien, Austria, for their help with providing scientific references, thank the Biological Records Centre for the permission to use the vice-counties and 100km square maps and thank also Mr. Martin George for allowing me to reproduce the photograph of his 'Swallowtail garden' at Strumpshaw Fen.

Last but not least, I am most grateful to Brambleby Books for all the help and advice I received with the production of this book, including both technical and scientific matters, and especially thank Nicola and Hugh Loxdale and Alison Miller for their careful editing of the text and Tanya Warren for design and layout.

Introduction

Monitoring the number and diversity of butterflies provides an excellent means of monitoring the environment as a whole for the following reasons:
- The ability of butterflies to reproduce in large numbers usually means there are many individuals on the wing at any given site or time. This provides a valid population sample from which to make comparative statistical analyses.
- Like many other insects, butterflies reproduce quickly and their reactions to environmental changes are therefore more immediately noticeable than those of, for example, large mammals.
- Their large size relative to many other invertebrates usually makes them easy to find and count accurately.
- Compared with most other insects their conspicuous and diagnostic wing patterns make their identification relatively straightforward.
- Being a small group of animals, with comparatively few species, it is possible to monitor the status of all of those species throughout the British Isles and therefore assess changes in geographical distribution.
- Collectively, they occupy a wide range of habitats which allows monitoring of the health of many different types of ecosystems. Each species has its own particular adult flight period and adjustments of these over time can be compared with changes in overall climatic conditions, i.e. phenological changes.
- Because butterflies are so popular amongst amateur entomologists, there is potentially a large number of available volunteer recorders. However, recorders and other enthusiasts must know what to look for and how to find it.

The purpose of this book is to enable anyone interested in butterflies, especially beginners, to find and identify all of the species, subspecies and common forms, or 'taxa', found in Great Britain and Ireland. Here, for the first time, are included:
- photographs of living specimens of all the recognized taxa;
- comprehensive details, including Ordnance Survey grid references, of prime sites within each of nine geographical regions where they can be found throughout the British Isles;
- field tips explaining how to find particular species of butterfly on visiting a site;
- concise notes outlining all of the comparative features for correct identification.

There are 59 species of butterfly that breed in Britain and Ireland. Added to these are 12 occasional immigrant species that sometimes do so but, in most cases, their occurrence is unpredictable and often they are absent for many years in succession. For some of these species there is no record of their having successfully bred here. Four formerly resident species are now considered extinct (Large Chequered Skipper, Black-veined White, Large Copper and Mazarine Blue), although serious attempts have been made to re-introduce

Introduction

the Large Copper. One species, the Geranium Bronze, has inadvertently been introduced. Yet, at the moment, its establishment as a breeding resident seems unlikely as our climate and the requirements of the species' life-cycle appear to be incompatible. The status of two further species (Arran Brown and Apollo) is at present uncertain. Apart from the extinct residents, this therefore gives a total of 74 species that possibly could be seen in the British Isles.

Amongst the 59 breeding species there are two well-known forms (Hutchinson's Comma and the Greenish Silver-washed Fritillary) that are distinctly different in appearance from the usual forms. A further form (Helice Clouded Yellow) occurs regularly during years when the typical Clouded Yellow arrives in large numbers from mainland Europe. However, there is a large group of geographical 'races' and subspecies that are resident here and recognition of these forms a pivotal part of this work.

A subspecies might be described as being only one evolutionary step away from becoming a species in its own right. Within the British and Irish butterflies, each is geographically isolated from other subspecies and is distinct in appearance. Over time, as its appearance, structure and behaviour evolve in response to the selective pressures unique to its particular local environment, this genetic isolation may ultimately lead to an inability to breed further with individuals from other populations. When this happens a new species is 'born'. In the British Isles there are no fewer than 31 subspecies. One of these (Hebridean Small Heath) is known only from a single Scottish Island and many of the others (such as those found in the Burren district of western Ireland) are restricted to extremely sensitive habitats. Because they live in such isolated outposts, often on the edge of the species' geographical range, they are extremely sensitive and vulnerable to changes in their environment. If their populations are not monitored, those interested in their welfare may be left unaware of impending problems – not only for the animal itself but also for the ecosystem in which it, and other specialized organisms, lives.

Conserving the genetic variation expressed by these isolated subspecies maintains the butterfly's ability to further adapt, thereby helping us to understand how selective processes at a regional level contribute towards the evolution of new species. For the species as a whole, genetic diversity is essential to safeguard its capacity to persist and thrive in an ever-changing world by creating strong and adaptable populations.

Science aside, subspecies are fascinating to the casual observer. Someone who lives near the open heathlands of the New Forest in South Hampshire, and is familiar with the Silver-studded Blue that lives there, will doubtless be delighted and intrigued to see how its tiny relative, the Western Silver-studded Blue, survives on the wind-swept rocky outcrops of the

Introduction

Great Ormes Head in Caernarvonshire. Anyone who has seen a fragile Wood White struggling against the merest breeze in an English woodland would surely marvel at its robust counterpart, the Irish Wood White, as it battles for survival on the exposed limestone pavement of the Burren in western Ireland. The colours and markings of some of the subspecies are also very different from those of the 'typical' form. For example, the Burren Dingy Skipper can be so 'black and white' in appearance that it looks more like a Grizzled Skipper than its English cousin the Dingy Skipper.

Much of the previous literature has ignored the subspecies of British and Irish butterflies and many enthusiasts are not even aware of their existence. Clearly this is an unsatisfactory situation and one of the main aims of this book is to raise public awareness of their presence and current distributions. To this end, each has been treated in the text in the same detailed way as the species themselves and each has, for the first time, been given an English name as an alternative to what many beginners consider to be off-putting and cumbersome Latin titles. It must be stressed that subspecific status has not been granted by the present author but conforms to the latest authoritative review of the British and Irish Lepidoptera published by J. D. Bradley (2000).

The photographs shown in this book of all the species, subspecies and common forms of British and Irish butterflies, complemented as they are by extensive site guides, identification notes and detailed field tips, constitute – I hope – the most complete guide yet available to the 108 butterfly taxa found in these islands.

How to use this book

As stated in the Introduction, each species, subspecies and common form is treated in the text with equal status and, for ease of reference, the individual accounts are divided into standard sections. The contents of each section are explained below so that the reader can maximize their usefulness.

Literature references
Reference is sometimes made to the work of previous authors and, in such cases, the name of the author and the date of publication are stated in the text (e.g. Emmet & Heath, 1989). The reader is then directed to the References section where the complete title and the publisher's details can be found.

Subspecies type locality and authority
The 'type' is the actual specimen on which the first published description for a new species, subspecies or form (taxon) is based. The 'type locality' is the geographical location at which that specimen was discovered. The 'subspecies type locality' is therefore the place where the first specimen of a newly described subspecies was found. A formal published description will then have followed and it is to that description that all future identifications of the subspecies must conform. A so-called 'nominate' subspecies is indicated by the repetition of the specific name. The person first describing a new taxon is known as the 'authority'. The name of the authority is given in this section and the literature reference with the authoritative description cited in the reference section. Hence the subspecific and form designations as presented throughout this work are not those of the author but follow the official published taxonomic descriptions.

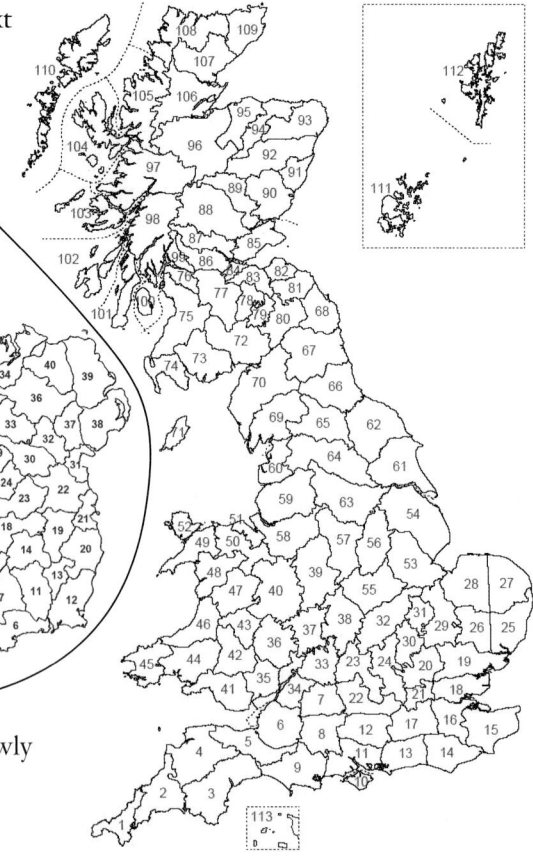

Fig. 1 Vice-counties of the British Isles.
See appendix V.

How to use this book

General distribution and status

General distribution

The general distribution of each of the butterflies is based on its presence, absence and abundance within the Watsonian vice-counties of England, Scotland and Wales and the Praeger vice-counties of Ireland (Fig. 1). These divisions were originally established by the botanists H. C. Watson and R. L. Praeger in 1852 and 1901, respectively, and have since been used in many biological disciplines. The advantage of this system is that the vice-county boundaries, unlike those of their administrative counterparts, do not change according to political needs – thus giving consistency over time. In the sections dealing with regional prime sites more detail is given concerning the abundance within the relevant vice-counties.

Status

A short summary is first given explaining whether the butterfly is a resident or an immigrant. These two basic categories are further divided as follows.

- **Resident** – remains in the British Isles throughout the year and survives the winter in at least one stage of its life-cycle i.e. egg, larva, pupa or adult butterfly.
- **Breeding immigrant** – arrives during the spring or summer, completes at least one full life-cycle and is able to survive the winter, thus supplementing the resident populations.
- **Summer visitor** – arrives during the spring or early summer and completes at least one full life-cycle. However, the resulting adult butterflies are rarely capable of surviving the winter and, in some cases, most individuals migrate south in the autumn to mainland Europe or Africa.
- **Scarce immigrant** – occurs irregularly but with occasional years of relative plenty. It rarely, if ever, completes a full life-cycle in the British Isles.
- **Vagrant** – occurs extremely rarely and with little or no evidence of attempted breeding.
- **Extinct resident** – a former resident that is now considered extinct in the British Isles.
- **Re-introduced resident** – an extinct resident that has successfully been re-introduced using stock from mainland Europe.
- **Introduction** – introduced either inadvertently or without official consent (see Section 14 of the Wildlife and Countryside Act 1981), having not previously occurred naturally in the British Isles.
- **Uncertain** – historical records suggest former or possible resident but not recorded for many years. Subsequent reports suggest vagrant or introduction.

Legal status

Where the butterfly is subject to legal protection under Schedule 5 of the Wildlife and Countryside Act 1981 (as amended) or the Wildlife (Northern Ireland) Order 1985, its status is summarized as follows.

- **Protected from sale**. It is illegal without licence to sell dead specimens

How to use this book

or wild-caught livestock originating from Great Britain (GB) and/or Northern Ireland (NI).
- **Fully protected**. It is illegal to harm, remove or kill any stage of the life-cycle of individuals found in Great Britain (GB) and/or Northern Ireland (NI).

At the present time there is no legislation protecting butterflies in The Republic of Ireland, the Isle of Man or the Channel Isles.

Distribution of records

For the vagrants and some of the scarce immigrants a detailed list of the vice-counties in which they have been recorded has been included. This may be helpful in suggesting the most likely regions where they might be seen again. For example, the recent bias of records for the Monarch in South Devon, East and West Cornwall and the Isles of Scilly strongly indicates that attention should be directed towards south-west England during appropriate periods and weather conditions.

Flight period

The flight period is the time of the year when the adult butterflies are on the wing. Each species and subspecies has its own particular flight period but this often varies according to geographical location. For example, populations of the Dark Green Fritillary in northern Scotland may emerge as adults up to three weeks later than those in the south of England, and high altitude populations of the Large Heath usually fly later than those from lowland localities. Such phenological factors should always be considered if one is visiting a new region and the 'optimum' periods for observation or times of 'peak emergence' given in the text are adjusted accordingly. The optimum period in which to see the butterfly is estimated as one week either side of the date of peak emergence. For example, a species flying between mid-May and mid-June would best be sought during the last week of May and the first week of June. Even so, the overall weather conditions can also influence the timing of the flight period and, during an unusually warm or cold spring for example, emergence may be advanced or delayed, respectively. Consequently, beginning in late winter, one should make frequent checks for unseasonable weather throughout the British Isles. Most species produce between one and three broods of adults each year. However, during very warm seasons, an extra generation may sometimes occur and where it has been recorded regularly for a particular species it is discussed in this section of the text. Appendix III gives the flight periods in tabulated form.

Larval foodplants

A major aim of this book is to enable anyone interested in butterflies to actually find the adult stages. The immature stages (egg, larva and pupa) are therefore not discussed in detail here. Those wishing to learn more about them can find concise accounts in Asher *et al.* (2001), more detailed descriptions in Emmet & Heath

How to use this book

(1989) and excellent photographs of the larvae in Porter (1997). However, the larvae of each species feed on specific plants and an ability to identify these can be extremely helpful as the adult butterflies will inevitably be found close in their vicinity. For example Common Cowwheat, the larval foodplant of the Heath Fritillary, blooms during the butterfly's flight period. It often grows in dense 'carpets', its distinctive yellow flowers being conspicuous from some distance, and being able to identify this plant will often lead one directly to the butterfly. It is therefore advisable to purchase well-illustrated botanical field guides. The following are recommended: Blamey, Fitter & Fitter (2003) (flowers); Fitter, Fitter & Farrer (1987) (grasses, sedges, rushes and ferns) and Mitchell & Wilkinson (1989) (trees). In this guidebook only the most commonly utilised foodplants are listed in the text and their Latin names can be found in Appendix I.

Habitat requirements

Many species are restricted to particular habitats such as, for example, chalk grassland. Some, such as the Large Blue, further require those grasslands to be grazed by sheep or rabbits to produce a very short sward. Identifying the correct habitat and recognizing the way in which it has been managed is therefore essential for finding many species. In this section the favoured habitat for each species is described along with any specific environmental features that should be looked for. Photographs illustrating the basic habitat types are sometimes shown in the species accounts or are referred to in the 'Basic habitat types' section (p. 29).

Identification characters, variation and similar species

The average wingspan is calculated as twice the measurement from the centre of the thorax to the tip of one of the forewings. This measurement conforms to the standard set by Emmet & Heath (1989) and avoids the problems caused by individual variation in resting postures.

The markings on a butterfly's wings often vary from the typical form, sometimes to a dramatic degree. Most such variants occur only very rarely and these are known as 'aberrations'. Some can occur frequently within populations (e.g. the form *taras* of the Grizzled Skipper) and are known as 'forms'. These are described in the text under the relevant species. So scarce and spectacular are some of these aberrations and forms that some enthusiasts devote much of their time in their pursuit. Most of the recent popular literature has tended to avoid this large and specialized subject but excellent illustrations and descriptions can be found in Howarth (1973), Russwurm (1978) and Harmer (1999). Three forms (Helice Clouded Yellow, Hutchinson's Comma and the Greenish Silver-washed Fritillary) are so popular with butterfly-watchers that they have been treated as separate taxa within the species accounts.

Where there are potential identification

How to use this book

problems caused by confusion with similar species, tabulated comparative notes are provided.

Field tips

Once directed to a known site for a particular species, a degree of 'field craft' is needed to actually find the butterfly. This section gives the reader tips on the most favourable weather conditions and time of day during which to observe and photograph the insects in question. Helpful notes on the butterfly's behaviour, preferred nectar sources and favoured topographical features within its habitat are also provided.

Regional prime sites

For the purpose of this book, the British Isles have been divided into nine geographical regions: Scotland, northern England, central England, eastern England, south-east England, south-west England, Wales, eastern Ireland and western Ireland. Within each of these regions a general overview of distribution and a selection of 'prime sites' is provided where each species, subspecies or form is known to occur. Each site is given the name by which it is popularly known along with a six-figure Ordnance Survey grid reference. In some cases the grid reference refers to an access point, such as a car park, followed by a written description of where to find the butterflies and in others it directs one to the exact location to be searched. Whilst the author has made every attempt to ensure that information about the locations and details of how to access them are up-to-date, the author and publishers cannot be held responsible for any changes to access, or failure to see, the relevant butterfly at a site. On visiting a site, the following points must be observed:

1. Access to some sites is by permit only. Where this is the case it is stressed in the text and a permit must be obtained before visiting.
2. Where there is a ban on carrying butterfly nets this rule must be observed. The author hereby discourages collecting at any of the sites mentioned in this book. It should certainly not take place without prior permission on nature reserves or land owned or managed by the National Trust, the Forestry Commission, the Royal Society for the Protection of Birds, the Wildlife Trusts, Butterfly Conservation or any other official organization, manager or land-owner.
3. Care should always be taken not to trample vegetation as this will damage the habitat. Always stay on the paths and wait for the butterflies to come to you.
4. Some of the sites are potentially dangerous. Where obvious hazards are present these are discussed in the text and all advice given should be heeded. Whichever sites are visited, neither the author nor the publishers can accept responsibility for injury, damage to personal possessions or loss of life or limb.
5. Always abide by the rules of the Countryside Code. Full details are

How to use this book

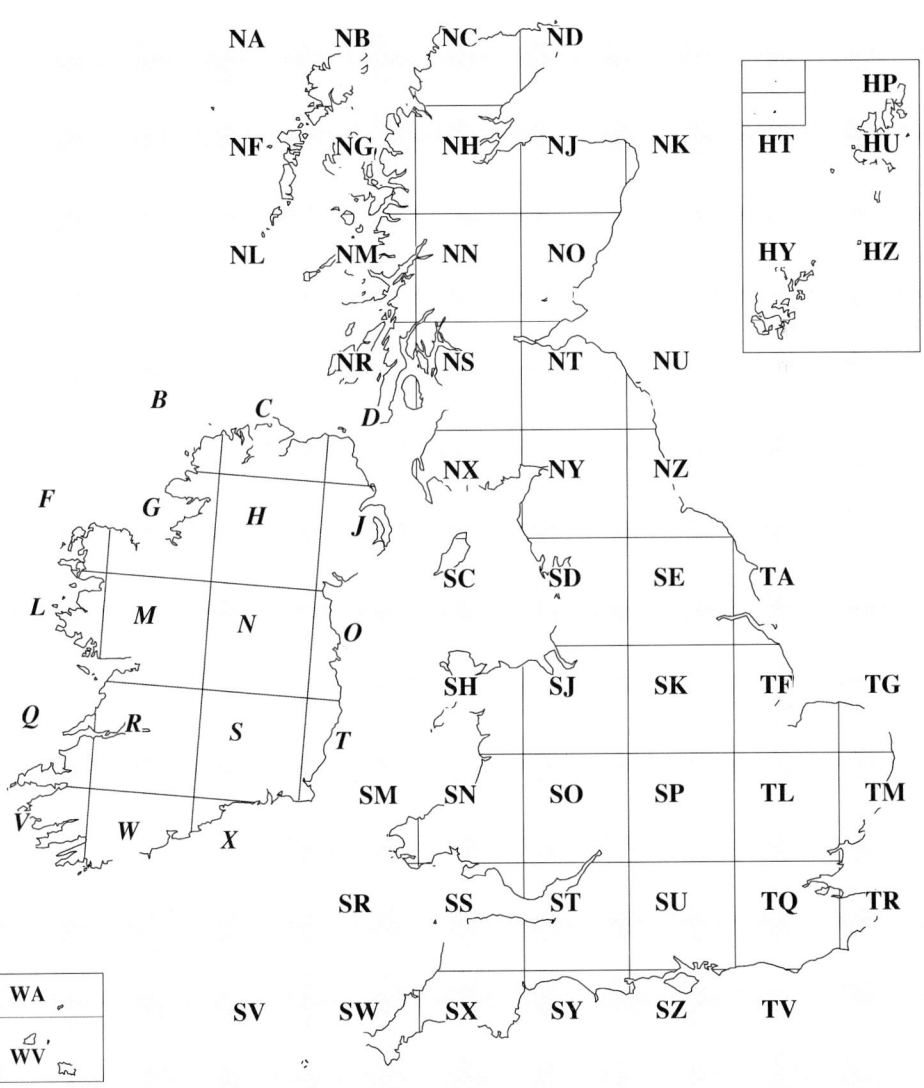

Fig. 2 100km squares of Britain and Ireland

How to use this book

available from Natural England at www.countrysideaccess.gov.uk . The basic guidelines are:
- always plan ahead and check for access restrictions;
- follow signs; leave gates and property as you find them;
- do not harm plants or animals;
- take litter home;
- keep dogs under close control;
- show consideration towards other users of the countryside;
- do not light fires;
- always adhere to local byelaws.

Appendix IV gives a regional index of all the species, subspecies and forms for which prime sites are detailed in the main section. This provides the visitor to any of the geographical regions a convenient reference to the taxa found there along with page numbers for the appropriate text entries.

Recording butterflies

Records of butterflies seen should be sent to Butterfly Conservation. The 'Butterflies for the New Millennium' section of their website (www.butterfly-conservation.org) has standard recording forms that can be downloaded. There is also a list of contact details for each of the official regional recorders. For those without access to the internet a recording information pack can be obtained by writing to Butterfly Conservation at Manor Yard, East Lulworth, Wareham, Dorset, BH20 5QP, UK. Whenever records are submitted it is important to include the following information:
- the name of the county and site (or the name of the nearest place marked on the relevant Ordnance Survey map) where the record was made;
- the correct six-figure Ordnance Survey grid reference;
- the type of habitat in which the sighting was made;
- the date on which the record was made;
- the number of individuals of each species seen (an estimate can be made for large numbers);
- the recorder's name, address and contact telephone number.

Basic habitat types

Fig. 3 Woodland tracks in Scotland (Glasdrum Wood, West Inverness-shire). Ideal habitat for the Chequered Skipper, Northern Small Pearl-bordered Fritillary and Scotch Argus.

Fig. 4 Lowland peat bog (Whixall Moss, Shropshire). The habitat type of the Southern and Northern Large Heath. Note the characteristic patches of white Cottongrass flower-heads.

Basic habitat types

Fig. 5 Rough grassland and scrub (Craigavon Lakes, Co. Down). Many common butterflies are found in such places. Typical species are the Small and Essex Skipper, Green-veined White, Common Blue, Small Tortoiseshell, Meadow Brown and Ringlet. This particular site holds a strong colony of Réal's Wood White.

Fig. 6 Coastal sand dunes (Holkham, West Norfolk). In such places one might expect to see the Dark Green Fritillary, Grayling and Brown Argus.

Basic habitat types

Fig. 7 Grazed chalk downland (Collard Hill, South Somerset). Typical habitat for the Silver-spotted Skipper, Chalkhill Blue and Adonis Blue. At this site one can see the reintroduced Large Blue.

Fig. 8 Chalk downland with scrub (Whipsnade Downs, Bedfordshire). A thriving colony of Duke of Burgundy lives at this site. Also present are the Dingy Skipper, Grizzled Skipper, Brimstone, Green Hairstreak, Small Blue, Brown Argus and Marbled White.

Basic habitat types

Fig. 9 Abandoned quarries (Great Orme, Caernarvonshire). This is the home of the Western Silver-studded Blue and the Great Orme Grayling. In similar habitats elsewhere one might expect to find the Southern Silver-studded Blue and Castle Eden Argus.

Fig. 10 Limestone pavement (The Burren, Co. Clare). This spectacular site holds the Burren Dingy Skipper, Irish Wood White, Irish Small Copper, Irish Common Blue, Burren Grayling, Irish Meadow Brown and Scottish Dark Green Fritillary. In the hedgerows along the outskirts of the Burren the Irish Brimstone and Brown Hairstreak can be seen.

Basic habitat types

Fig. 11 Fenland (Strumpshaw Fen, East Norfolk). The magnificent British Swallowtail can be seen flying over the reedbeds and visiting flowers along the margins. Such fenland was once the habitat of the now extinct Large Copper.

Fig. 12 Mature woodland rides (Bentley Woods, South Wiltshire). The Small Pearl-bordered Fritillary, Pearl-bordered Fritillary, Silver-washed Fritillary, Duke of Burgundy and White Admiral may be seen visiting flowers in rideside openings or 'scallops' such as this. Purple Emperors may also come to ground along the ride itself to take minerals from stones used to make the track. Purple Hairstreaks fly around the canopies of the taller oak and ash trees and, in similar localities, Wood Whites are found amongst the rideside vegetation.

Basic habitat types

Fig. 13 Light woodland clearings (Hadleigh Great Wood, South Essex). The home to south-east English colonies of the Heath Fritillary.

Fig. 14 Coastal undercliffs (Hordle Cliffs, South Hampshire). The fragile habitat of the Glanville Fritillary. Similar places in South Devon, such as Branscombe Cliffs, hold colonies of the Wood White and, in eastern Ireland, Réal's Wood White can be seen on similar undercliffs near Rosslare harbour in Co. Wexford.

Basic habitat types

Fig. 15 Ancient hedgerows (Bernwood Meadows, Buckinghamshire). Such scarce habitat is home to the Brown and Black Hairstreaks.

Fig. 16 Heathland (Chobham Common, Surrey). Typical habitat of the Silver-studded Blue. Graylings can also be seen along the sandy tracks that traverse such heaths.

Basic habitat types

Fig. 17 Rocky coastal grasslands (Port O' Warren, Kirkcudbrightshire). In such places are found the Northern Brown Argus, Hebridean Meadow Brown, Scottish Grayling and, in north-western Scotland, the Scottish Dark Green Fritillary and Atlantic Grayling.

Fig. 18 Grassland, scrub and bracken mosaic (Marsland Valley, North Devon). Such habitat is home to the High Brown Fritillary, Dark Green Fritillary, Small Pearl-bordered Fritillary and Pearl-bordered Fritillary. Populations of the Heath Fritillary are seen in similar localities in south-west England.

Basic habitat types

Fig. 19 Damp meadows (Lydlinch Common, Dorset). This is one of the preferred habitats of the Marsh Fritillary. The Brimstone and Green-veined White abound in such localities.

Fig. 20 Mountains and wet moorland (Creag Meagaidh, West Inverness-shire). Scottish and English Small Mountain Ringlets live on the high ground in such areas. At this particular site, they are seen flying in wet areas along with the Scottish Large Heath. On similar sites at lower elevation, the Small Pearl-bordered Fritillary might also be seen.

Systematic checklist of species, subspecies and common forms

The nomenclature follows that of the most recent checklist of British and Irish butterflies (Bradley, 2000). Most of the subspecies and forms have not previously been given English names and this has been done here purely for the purpose of this book. They have no scientific standing and should not be used in future publications without reference to their accompanying official Latin names.

1. **Chequered Skipper**
   Carterocephalus palaemon (Pallas)
2. **Large Chequered Skipper**
   Heteropterus morpheus (Pallas)
3. **Small Skipper**
   Thymelicus sylvestris (Poda)
4. **Essex Skipper**
   Thymelicus lineola (Ochsenheimer)
5. **Lulworth Skipper**
   Thymelicus acteon (Rottemburg)
6. **Silver-spotted Skipper**
   Hesperia comma (Linnaeus)
7. **Large Skipper**
   Ochlodes faunus (Turati)
8. **Dingy Skipper**
   Erynnis tages ssp. *tages* (Linnaeus)
9. **Burren Dingy Skipper**
   Erynnis tages ssp. *baynesi* Huggins
10. **Grizzled Skipper**
    Pyrgus malvae (Linnaeus)
11. **Apollo**
    Parnassius apollo (Linnaeus)
12. **British Swallowtail**
    Papilio machaon Linnaeus ssp. *britannicus* Seitz
13. **Continental Swallowtail**
    Papilio machaon ssp. *gorganus* Fruhstorfer
14. **Scarce Swallowtail**
    Iphiclides podalirius (Linnaeus)
15. **Wood White**
    Leptidea sinapis ssp. *sinapis* (Linnaeus)
16. **Irish Wood White**
    Leptidea sinapis ssp. *juvernica* Williams
17. **Réal's Wood White**
    Leptidea reali Reissinger
18. **Pale Clouded Yellow**
    Colias hyale (Linnaeus)
19. **Berger's Clouded Yellow**
    Colias alfacariensis Berger
20. **Clouded Yellow**
    Colias croceus (Geoffroy)
21. **Helice Clouded Yellow**
    Colias croceus form *helice* Hübner
22. **Brimstone**
    Gonepteryx rhamni ssp. *rhamni* (Linnaeus)
23. **Irish Brimstone**
    Gonepteryx rhamni ssp. *gravesi* Huggins
24. **Black-veined White**
    Aporia crataegi (Linnaeus)
25. **Large White**
    Pieris brassicae (Linnaeus)

Systematic checklist of species, subspecies and common forms

26. **Small White**
    Pieris rapae (Linnaeus)

27. **British Green-veined White**
    Pieris napi (Linnaeus) ssp. *sabellicae* (Stephens)

28. **Irish Green-veined White**
    Pieris napi ssp. *britannica* Müller & Kautz

29. **Scottish Green-veined White**
    Pieris napi ssp. *thomsoni* Warren

30. **Bath White**
    Pontia daplidice (Linnaeus)

31. **British Orange-tip**
    Anthocharis cardamines (Linnaeus) ssp. *britannica* (Verity)

32. **Irish Orange-tip**
    Anthocharis cardamines ssp. *hibernica* (Williams)

33. **Green Hairstreak**
    Callophrys rubi (Linnaeus)

34. **Brown Hairstreak**
    Thecla betulae (Linnaeus)

35. **Purple Hairstreak**
    Neozephyrus quercus (Linnaeus)

36. **White-letter Hairstreak**
    Satyrium w-album (Knoch)

37. **Black Hairstreak**
    Satyrium pruni (Linnaeus)

38. **Small Copper**
    Lycaena phlaeas (Linnaeus) ssp. *eleus* (Fabricius)

39. **Irish Small Copper**
    Lycaena phlaeas ssp. *hibernica* Goodson

40. **Large Copper**
    Lycaena dispar (Haworth)

41. **Long-tailed Blue**
    Lampides boeticus (Linnaeus)

42. **Geranium Bronze**
    Cacyreus marshalli Butler

43. **Small Blue**
    Cupido minimus (Fuessly)

44. **Short-tailed Blue**
    Everes argiades (Pallas)

45. **Silver-studded Blue**
    Plebejus argus ssp. *argus* (Linnaeus)

46. **Southern Silver-studded Blue**
    Plebejus argus ssp. *cretaceus* Tutt

47. **Northern Silver-studded Blue**
    Plebejus argus ssp. *masseyi* Tutt

48. **Western Silver-studded Blue**
    Plebejus argus ssp. *caernensis* Thompson

49. **Brown Argus**
    Aricia agestis ([Denis & Schiffermüller])

50. **Northern Brown Argus**
    Aricia artaxerxes ssp. *artaxerxes* (Fabricius)

51. **Castle Eden Argus**
    Aricia artaxerxes ssp. *salmacis* (Stephens)

52. **Common Blue**
    Polyommatus icarus ssp. *icarus* (Rottemburg)

53. **Irish Common Blue**
    Polyommatus icarus ssp. *mariscolore* (Kane)

54. **Chalkhill Blue**
    Lysandra coridon (Poda)

55. **Adonis Blue**
    Lysandra bellargus (Rottemburg)

Systematic checklist of species, subspecies and common forms

56. **Mazarine Blue**
    Cyaniris semiargus (Rottemburg)

57. **Holly Blue**
    Celastrina argiolus (Linnaeus) ssp. *britanna* (Verity)

58. **Large Blue**
    Maculinea arion ssp. *arion* (Linnaeus)

59. **Duke of Burgundy**
    Hamearis lucina (Linnaeus)

60. **White Admiral**
    Limenitis camilla (Linnaeus)

61. **Purple Emperor**
    Apatura iris (Linnaeus)

62. **Red Admiral**
    Vanessa atalanta (Linnaeus)

63. **Painted Lady**
    Vanessa cardui (Linnaeus)

64. **American Painted Lady**
    Vanessa virginiensis (Drury)

65. **Small Tortoiseshell**
    Aglais urticae (Linnaeus)

66. **Large Tortoiseshell**
    Aglais (=*Nymphalis*) *polychloros* (Linnaeus)

67. **Camberwell Beauty**
    Aglais (=*Nymphalis*) *antiopa* (Linnaeus)

68. **Peacock**
    Inachis io (Linnaeus)

69. **Comma**
    Polygonia c-album (Linnaeus)

70. **Hutchinson's Comma**
    Polygonia c-album form *hutchinsoni* Robson

71. **European Map**
    Araschnia levana (Linnaeus)

72. **Small Pearl-bordered Fritillary**
    Boloria selene ssp. *selene* ([Denis & Schiffermüller])

73. **Northern Small Pearl-bordered Fritillary** *Boloria selene* ssp. *insularum* (Harrison)

74. **Pearl-bordered Fritillary**
    Boloria euphrosyne (Linnaeus)

75. **Queen of Spain Fritillary**
    Issoria lathonia (Linnaeus)

76. **High Brown Fritillary**
    Argynnis adippe ([Denis & Schiffermüller]) ssp. *vulgoadippe* Verity

77. **Dark Green Fritillary**
    Argynnis aglaja ssp. *aglaja* (Linnaeus)

78. **Scottish Dark Green Fritillary**
    Argynnis aglaja ssp. *scotica* Watkins

79. **Silver-washed Fritillary**
    Argynnis paphia (Linnaeus)

80. **Greenish Silver-washed Fritillary** *Argynnis paphia* form *valesina* Esper

81. **Marsh Fritillary**
    Euphydryas aurinia (Rottemburg)

82. **Glanville Fritillary**
    Melitaea cinxia (Linnaeus)

83. **Heath Fritillary**
    Melitaea athalia (Rottemburg)

84. **Speckled Wood**
    Pararge aegeria (Linnaeus) ssp. *tircis* (Godart)

Systematic checklist of species, subspecies and common forms

85. **Scottish Speckled Wood**
    Pararge aegeria ssp. *oblita* Harrison
86. **Isles of Scilly Speckled Wood**
    Pararge aegeria ssp. *insula* Howarth
87. **Wall**
    Lasiommata megera (Linnaeus)
88. **English Small Mountain Ringlet**
    Erebia epiphron (Knoch) ssp. *mnemon* (Haworth)
89. **Scottish Small Mountain Ringlet**
    Erebia epiphron ssp. *scotica* Cooke
90. **Irish Small Mountain Ringlet**
    Erebia epiphron ssp. *aetheria* (Esper)
91. **Scotch Argus**
    Erebia aethiops ssp. *aethiops* (Esper)
92. **Western Scotch Argus**
    Erebia aethiops ssp. *caledonia* Verity
93. **Arran Brown**
    Erebia ligea (Linnaeus)
94. **Marbled White**
    Melanargia galathea (Linnaeus) ssp. *serena* Verity
95. **Grayling**
    Hipparchia semele ssp. *semele* (Linnaeus)
96. **Great Orme Grayling**
    Hipparchia semele ssp. *thyone* (Thompson)
97. **Scottish Grayling**
    Hipparchia semele ssp. *scota* (Verity)
98. **Atlantic Grayling**
    Hipparchia semele ssp. *atlantica* (Harrison)
99. **Burren Grayling**
    Hipparchia semele ssp. *clarensis* de Lattin
100. **Irish Grayling**
    Hipparchia semele ssp. *hibernica* Howarth
101. **Gatekeeper (Hedge Brown)**
    Pyronia tithonus (Linnaeus) ssp. *britanniae* (Verity)
102. **British Meadow Brown**
    Maniola jurtina (Linnaeus) ssp. *insularis* Thomson
103. **Irish Meadow Brown**
    Maniola jurtina ssp. *iernes* Graves
104. **Isles of Scilly Meadow Brown**
    Maniola jurtina ssp. *cassiteridum* Graves
105. **Hebridean Meadow Brown**
    Maniola jurtina ssp. *splendida* White
106. **Small Heath**
    Coenonympha pamphilus ssp. *pamphilus* (Linnaeus)
107. **Hebridean Small Heath**
    Coenonympha pamphilus ssp. *rhoumensis* Harrison
108. **Southern Large Heath**
    Coenonympha tullia (Müller) ssp. *davus* (Fabricius)
109. **Northern Large Heath**
    Coenonympha tullia ssp. *polydama* (Haworth)
110. **Scottish Large Heath**
    Coenonympha tullia ssp. *scotica* Staudinger
111. **Ringlet**
    Aphantopus hyperantus (Linnaeus)
112. **Monarch**
    (Milkweed) *Danaus plexippus* (Linnaeus)

Skippers

British and Irish Butterflies
The Skippers
(Hesperiidae)

Chequered Skipper
***Carterocephalus palaemon* (Pallas)**

General distribution and status
Resident; protected from sale (GB). This species has had a remarkable recent history in the British Isles. It was recognized as being in severe decline in England by the beginning of the 20th century and by 1972, was on the point of extinction. Its last footholds were in north-eastern parts of Northamptonshire but by 1976, it became extinct as an English species. However, in 1939 the butterfly was discovered at Loch Lochy in West Inverness-shire (Thomson, 1980) and was subsequently found to be locally common in the area. This was a remarkable finding considering the distance between the new locality and the only known (then) extant and endangered colonies in England. In fact, E. B. Ford, the great butterfly expert of the time, wrote in his famous book *Butterflies* (Ford, 1945) that the discovery of this species in Scotland was '...one of the most extraordinary events in British entomology in recent years.' I doubt that such a discovery will ever occur again but the precedent should inspire us all. Today the Chequered Skipper is confined to a small area of western Scotland centred on Fort William, West Inverness-shire. In England, attempts are being made at reintroduction but success has been limited and the whereabouts of the sites should remain unpublished for the time being.

Flight period
Single brooded between the third week of May and the end of June. However, vagaries of the British climate can delay emergence by a week or so and it has been seen regularly as late as early July. The first two weeks in June are optimal for seeing the butterfly. The males emerge some two weeks before the females.

Larval foodplants
In Scotland the principal foodplant is Purple Moor-grass, though False Brome (the former foodplant in England) and, as in mainland Europe, other species of grass are also used.

Habitat requirements
It is often stated (e.g. Asher *et al.*, 2001) that the Chequered Skipper inhabits open grassland in Scotland but this is not always the case. In the area around Spean Bridge it can also be seen along minor roads that pass through woodland where it favours small glades or 'scallops' along the road's edge. It can also be found along the artificial tracks formed where vegetation has been cut below power lines

Chequered Skipper

Fig. 21 Chequered Skipper upperside.
Glasdrum Wood, West Inverness-shire

Fig. 22 Chequered Skipper underside.
Glasdrum Wood, West Inverness-shire

such as those at Glasdrum Wood (Fig. 3). In areas where it is known to occur, the butterfly should be sought in and around damp woodlands. Small, sheltered and sunny openings along woodland tracks and damp grassland on the edges of woodlands where Purple Moor-grass dominates are favoured haunts.

Identification characters, variation and similar species
Average wingspan 30mm; this species is unlike any other found within its geographical range. Variation is more or less restricted to the depth of colour of the pale upperside markings. These fade with age and in older individuals can appear pale cream.

Field tips
The males defend their territories with vigorous flying during sunny periods but often rest conspicuously on grass stems and flower heads when the sun is not shining. At these times they are easy to approach and photograph, particularly when the sun first breaks through the clouds. Days of bright sunshine will undoubtedly provide the best opportunities for seeing the butterflies but those of periodic sun are best for finding them settled with their wings open. During early morning, at around 8 till 9am, they are relatively sluggish and at this time of day often feed from the flowers of thistles and bluebell as they take on fuel for the day's activities. This is when photographing the species is at its easiest, especially the elusive undersides, as later in the day they usually rest with their wings held open.

Regional prime sites
Scotland. For many years it has been traditional for butterfly-watchers to visit the area around Spean Bridge and Fort William to see this species. There are potentially many new localities within this general area where Chequered

Skippers could be found as it is a fairly common species in the appropriate habitats. On approaching **Spean Bridge** from the west along the A82 take the small and inconspicuous minor road on the right next to the Spean Bridge Hotel. Go through the small housing estate and bear left until the road passes over a railway bridge. There is a small parking space immediately on the right (OS grid ref. NN 227 815). Carry on by foot east along the minor road and check the small recesses in the woods on either side. **Allt Mhuic** at Loch Arkaig is a recently-opened reserve that is managed jointly by Butterfly Conservation and the Forestry Commission, Scotland. It is situated approximately 20 miles north of Fort William and six miles west of Clunes at NN 121 912. Here sightings of the Chequered Skipper can be more or less guaranteed in good weather during the first two weeks of June. The path around the reserve is marked clearly and leaflets are obtainable on site. The Chequered Skipper favours the south-facing slopes and clearings. Further to the west, on the Ardnamurchan peninsula, the reserve at **Ariundle Forest** has areas managed specifically for this species and here it can be seen in good numbers along the main track leading from the car park at NM 829 634. **Glasdrum Forest**, on the shores of Loch Creran, has been mentioned as a prime site for the Chequered Skipper by Hill & Twist (1998). The species is indeed common here but is mostly seen off the reserve's marked trails and potentially damaging visits to this sensitive habitat are discouraged when more easily accessible sites such as those at Spean Bridge and Allt Mhuic are available. Visitors to this area should instead try the public car park and forest track on the east side of the loch at **Eas na Circe** (NM 005 443). Small numbers of the insect can usually be seen there.

Other Regions. Absent.

Large Chequered Skipper
Heteropterus morpheus **(Pallas)**

Status
Extinct resident; introduction. First recorded in 1946 at a locality near Bouley Bay in Jersey, Channel Isles. Its origin is attributed to importation with large amounts of hay from France during the German occupation of the islands from 1940 to 1945. Hay was then an important commodity as the scarcity of petrol resulted in a great increase in the use of horses. There were at one time three colonies at the original site but two quickly became extinct. Numbers reached a peak during the 1960s with some 50 individuals seen in one visit (Asher *et al*., 2001). After 1985, the species went into decline with only a few recorded annually, including some years when

Large Chequered Skipper / Small Skipper

Fig. 23 Large Chequered Skipper upperside. France (W. Powell)

Fig. 24 Large Chequered Skipper underside. France (W. Powell)

none was seen. The last Large Chequered Skipper was reported in the British Isles in 1996 and it is now presumed extinct.

Flight period
In Jersey the species flew from mid-July to mid-August in a single brood.

Foodplants
The only recorded foodplant in Jersey was Purple Moor-grass. In mainland Europe a variety of other grasses are used.

Habitat requirements
In Jersey, it inhabited the north-facing slope of a flush area on the edge of a bog adjacent to woodland. In mainland Europe (for example in north-western France) it occupies damp grassland in similar situations and in woodland clearings. The weak flight of this species requires the habitat to be sheltered from excessive wind.

Small Skipper
Thymelicus sylvestris (Poda)

General distribution and status
Resident. Widespread and common south-east of a line running approximately between Westmorland in the west and North Northumberland in the east. It is absent from the Isle of Man and the Channel Isles. Its recent discovery in Cumberland and more frequent sightings in north-eastern England suggest that the species is extending its range northwards.

Flight period
Single brooded from the last week in June to the first week in August with a

Small Skipper

peak during the second and third weeks of July. At northern sites, individuals are occasionally seen until the end of August.

Larval foodplants
Almost exclusively Yorkshire Fog. Other grasses have been recorded only rarely.

Habitat requirements
Any area of rough grassland where the foodplant is allowed to grow until it flowers. These can be uncut meadows, field edges, roadside verges, hedgerows or woodland rides (Fig. 5). Egg-laying females appear to locate the host plant by visual recognition of its flower-heads as all other species of grass are ignored during oviposition flights. Grassland that is cut regularly, where the development of flower-heads is prevented, is therefore not suitable for the species.

Identification characters, variation and similar species
Average wingspan 30mm; significant variation is rare. This species is very similar to the Essex and Lulworth Skippers, particularly the former. Both Small and Essex Skippers are orange-fulvous in colour and, at a distance or on the wing, appear identical. However, examination of the underside of the antennae reveals that the tips are black in Essex Skipper, contrasting markedly with the ground colour (Fig. 28). In the Small Skipper the tips are brown and not conspicuously different to the rest of the antennae (Fig. 27). Males of these species have a line of black androconial or 'scent' scales on each forewing. In the Small Skipper, this line reaches from the thorax to approximately half way along the wing and has a distinct kink midway along its length. In the Essex Skipper the line is shorter, finer and straight. Only specimens at rest, feeding or in captivity can be easily identified. Good quality close-focusing binoculars are a great help in the field as they prevent disturbance from too close an approach.

Fig. 25 Small Skipper male. Fakenham, West Norfolk

Fig. 26 Small Skipper female. Thetford Forest, West Suffolk

Small Skipper

Fig. 27 Small Skipper antennae. Syderstone, West Norfolk

Fig. 28 Essex Skipper antennae. Holkham, West Norfolk

Another similar species is the Lulworth Skipper which is restricted in its distribution to the coastal hinterland of Dorset. Both sexes are generally darker and more olive-toned than Small Skippers. The females have a distinctive and conspicuous crescent of bright fulvous spots towards the apex of the forewing which precludes confusion with the Small Skipper. However, the males can be difficult to separate on the wing and it is wise to wait until the insect has settled for close examination. The overall dark appearance is usually diagnostic and, even in specimens that are quite orange, a weakly expressed replica of the aforementioned crescent of spots can usually be seen.

Field tips

A visit to any uncut roadside verge or field where the foodplant grows during the middle of July is likely to prove successful. Areas containing the favoured nectar plants, such as thistles, knapweeds, trefoils and vetches, should be sought. During the early morning, the butterflies can be found readily on flower-heads where they congregate to warm up and feed. At this time of the day, they are both conspicuous and sluggish and can be examined and photographed. Later in the morning, males defend territories actively from chosen perches and will chase other butterflies that stray too close. The females are less active and may be observed during their egg-laying flights. During these they fly quite slowly but with very rapid wingbeats until they locate a flowering stem of Yorkshire Fog. The butterfly will then land and walk rapidly backwards, down the stem until, with the tip of her abdomen, she locates the top of the leaf sheath inside which she lays a linear batch of eggs. As afternoon approaches, both sexes feed avidly and can again be approached easily. However, the males will still investigate anything that appears to be

Small Skipper / Essex Skipper

a female Small Skipper, including individuals of other species.

Regional prime sites
Scotland. Absent.

Northern England. Widespread and common almost to the Scottish borders in the east and to Westmorland in the west. The northernmost site in the west is at **Smardale Gill**, Westmorland, at NY 740 082, where it was discovered in 2004. In the east, it is present northwards to the border with Scotland.

Central, eastern, south-east and south-west England. Widespread and common.

Wales. Widespread and common throughout with the exception of Anglesey and the adjacent mainland where it is scarce or absent.

Ireland. Absent.

Essex Skipper
Thymelicus lineola **(Ochsenheimer)**

General distribution and status
Resident. Widespread and common south-east of a line approximately between Dorset in the west and North Lincolnshire in the east, including the Channel Isles. There have been recent records from East Cornwall but their authenticity has not been verified and some may be the result of an unauthorized introduction (Asher *et al.*, 2001). There has been a remarkable northward and westward expansion of the species' range in recent years.

Flight period
Single brooded from early July to late

Fig. 29 Essex Skipper male. Fakenham, West Norfolk

Fig. 30 Essex Skipper female. Syderstone, West Norfolk

Essex Skipper

August, emerging approximately a week later than the Small Skipper. The optimum time to see this species is during the last week of July and the first week of August.

Larval foodplants
Eggs are usually laid in the leaf-sheaths of either Cock's-foot or Creeping Soft-grass. Yorkshire Fog, the foodplant of its close relative the Small Skipper, is apparently not used.

Habitat requirements
Similar to those of the Small Skipper. The two species can often be found together on uncut rough grassland in meadows, woodland rides and along roadside verges and field margins (Fig. 5).

Identification characters, variation and similar species
Average wingspan 28mm; easily confused with the Small and Lulworth Skippers and the diagnostic features are discussed under the former of these two (p. 46).

Field tips
The habitat preferences and behaviour of this species are very similar to those of the Small Skipper and both may be common at any suitable site. Male Essex Skippers appear to be more active than those of the Small Skipper, tending to seek females by patrolling in preference to the defence of territories by perching and chasing. However, Essex Skippers will sometimes adopt the latter strategy. The female egg-laying flight is also similar but Yorkshire Fog appears to be actively avoided, thus strengthening the belief that the host-plant is located by sight or, perhaps, odour. Cock's-foot and Creeping Soft-grass have the tighter leaf-sheaths required for oviposition but the 'wrong' species is never tested and rejected. The correct grass seems always to be chosen before landing.

With practice the black underside of the antennal tip can easily be seen using good quality, close-focusing binoculars when the butterfly is at rest or feeding.

Regional prime sites
Scotland. Absent.

Northern England. Very scarce and restricted to the extreme south of the region. It has recently been recorded from the **Spurn Peninsula**, South-east Yorkshire (explore south from the car park at TA 416 155) and the RSPB reserve at **Old Moor**, South-west Yorkshire (SE 422 022).

Central England. Widespread and common in the south-eastern half of the region. A site on the northern limit of its range is **Cooper's Mill Meadow** in the Wyre Forest, Shropshire (SO 758 768).

Eastern England and south-east England. Widespread and common.

South-west England. Widespread and common in the far east of the region approximating to the western county boundaries of North Somerset, South Wiltshire and South Hampshire. In the south of the region, its known range extends into Dorset as far west as the area around **Powerstock Common** (access from SY 547 974) in the south and, in North Somerset, **Severn Beach** (ST 543 840), **Shapwick Heath** (ST 424 412) and **Sand Point** (access from ST 330 659) in the north. Further west in the region, the species was introduced at a reserve near **Polscoe**, East Cornwall (SX 115 605), in 1993 but has not been seen there since 1995. In 1998, several specimens were discovered at **Gwithian Towans**, West Cornwall (SW 579 413), but none has been recorded subsequently (Wacher *et al.*, 2003).

Wales and Ireland. Absent.

It must be stressed here that this species is undergoing a rapid expansion in its known range and the observer should be aware of this when working outside the areas cited.

Lulworth Skipper
Thymelicus acteon (Rottemburg)

General distribution and status
Resident; protected from sale (GB). Restricted to the county of Dorset where it is mainly coastal with colonies extending only around 10km inland. Its range is centred on Lulworth and extends approximately between Weymouth and the Isle of Purbeck. There are a few records from Devon and Cornwall but these probably do not represent extant colonies. Some are thought to be the result of escaped or introduced individuals. It is

Fig. 31 Lulworth Skipper male. Portland, Dorset

Fig. 32 Lulworth Skipper female. Portland, Dorset

Lulworth Skipper

absent from the Channel Isles.

Flight period
Single brooded from the last week of June to the third week of September. The optimum time for seeing the species is during the first three weeks of August.

Larval foodplants
Exclusively Tor-grass.

Habitat requirements
Lulworth Skippers require rough grassland that contains patches of tall Tor-grass with a minimum sward height of around 10cm. Inland it is found occasionally on roadside verges where chalk or limestone has been used as ballast for road construction, but its usual habitat is on calcareous coastal grassland where south-facing slopes are often preferred.

Identification characters, variation and similar species
Average wingspan 26mm; in flight, this species can easily be confused with Essex and Small Skippers. At rest or when feeding, the dark overall colour is usually indicative of the Lulworth Skipper and the females have a distinctive crescent of golden spots on the outer third of each forewing. Some males may lack the usual dark olive tinge but usually display a weak representation of this crescent. It is unwise to attempt identification of flying individuals.

Field tips
Lulworth Skippers will usually only fly in sunshine. They favour areas that are sheltered from the wind, often on south facing aspects. The purple flowers of Rest-harrow are particularly favoured nectar sources. Locating patches of this plant and waiting patiently is the best strategy for close observation and photography. Unlike the Essex and Small Skippers this species can be difficult to locate early in the morning or during dull weather, however warm the air may feel. Once the sun breaks through one can often be surprised by the appearance of dozens of butterflies where none was apparently in residence. Some colonies can be huge, numbering tens of thousands of individuals. Thomas (1983) estimated that one at Lulworth was around a million strong.

Regional prime sites
Scotland, northern, central, eastern and south-eastern England. Absent.

South-west England. Restricted to the county of Dorset. The coastal grassland around **Lulworth Cove** (SY 826 800) has traditionally been the centre of attention for finding this species and very large populations are still present there. A walk along the cliff tops in this general area will almost certainly result in success as, in habitats supporting mature Tor-grass, this species can be abundant and easy to find. A visit to **Ballard Down** is certainly recommended (from just north of the lay-by at SZ 022 808 walk east along the south-facing slope). The members of staff at the bird observatory at **Portland** are very helpful and will inform the visitor of the best sites to visit on a daily basis in that area. A regular haunt of the species there is the grass bank behind the Pulpit Inn public house (SY 677 718) where, on sunny days, dozens of individuals can be seen.

Wales and Ireland. Absent.

Silver-spotted Skipper
Hesperia comma (Linnaeus)

General distribution and status

Resident; protected from sale (GB). This is an extremely localized species which is restricted to close-grazed chalk downland in the south-eastern corner of England as far west as Dorset. Formerly it could be found at several limestone grassland sites to South Somerset in the west and northwards to isolated localities as far as Westmorland in the west and North-east Yorkshire in the east. A decline in its range occurred through most of the twentieth century as the grazing of stock lessened and rabbit numbers plummeted after the introduction of myxomatosis. However, this trend seems to have slowed and there even appears to be evidence of a slight re-expansion in recent years. This is probably due to a recovery in rabbit numbers and the results of conservation efforts to clear scrub and restore grazing regimes on what was formerly suitable grassland. It is absent from the Channel Isles (Thomas *et al*., 1986).

Flight period

Single brooded from late July to early September with the best chance of seeing the butterfly during the second and third weeks of August.

Fig. 33 Silver-spotted Skipper upperside.
Martin Down, South Hampshire

Fig. 34 Silver-spotted Skipper underside.
Martin Down, South Hampshire

Silver-spotted Skipper

Larval foodplants
Sheep's Fescue is the sole foodplant.

Habitat requirements
The Silver-spotted Skipper has very specific needs and only inhabits well-grazed chalk grassland (Fig. 7). South-facing slopes are usually preferred. For egg-laying, the females require areas where the turf is sparse and the foodplant grows on, or adjacent to, patches of bare earth. Crumbling slopes, animal tracks and rabbit scrapes often provide these relatively warm microhabitats. For detailed accounts of the ecological requirements of this species the reader is referred to Thomas & Jones (1993) and Warren *et al.* (1999).

Identification characters, variation and similar species
Average wingspan 32mm; the undersides of both fore- and hindwings are adorned with the characteristic striking silver-white spots which give this species its name. The uppersides of both sexes are superficially similar to those of the Large Skipper but are much darker and lack the orange tones of that species. Towards the tips of the forewings on the upperside of the Silver-spotted Skipper there is a group of whitish spots that is not present in the Large Skipper. It would be unusual to see the two flying together, though areas of taller grass adjacent to close-cropped downland may provide such an opportunity. However, this is made even less likely by the fact that Large Skippers usually fly earlier in the year from late May to early August. Any still flying at the end of this period are likely to appear very worn by comparison with the then freshly emerged Silver-spotted Skippers.

Field tips
South-facing slopes are often preferred but are not prerequisite. Areas with bare patches of earth amongst sparse turf in hot sheltered locations such as that shown in Fig. 35 should be sought. This species does not usually fly in temperatures below about 20°C or in overcast conditions. Individuals found early in the day often vibrate their wings very rapidly, in a moth-like manner, whilst attempting to generate body heat. This makes sharply-focussed photographs very difficult to obtain at that time. Later in the day they are very active, the males perching and chasing potential mates with great speed at low level over the turf. When so doing, they are extremely difficult to follow by eye as they are able to change direction with remarkable rapidity. Even so, they frequently settle to feed from flowers such as those of Small Scabious and Dwarf Thistle or to bask in sunny sheltered spots. They are then usually very approachable. Days with periodic sunshine can provide the best opportunities to see the butterflies closely as they often remain at the spot where they land when the sun goes in. At such times they usually rest in the open with their wings held in characteristic and photogenic skipper fashion and are reluctant to fly again until the sun reappears.

Silver-spotted Skipper

Fig. 35 Heavily grazed chalk grassland with exposed patches of earth at Martin Down, South Hampshire

Regional prime sites
Scotland, northern, central and eastern England. Absent.

South-east England. This species can be seen in good numbers at **Lydden Down**, East Kent (TR277 453) and at **Box Hill** (TQ 182 523) and **Headley Heath** (TQ 196 535) in Surrey. There is ample car parking at, and easy access to, each of these sites and the butterflies can be found readily on the south-facing chalk slopes. In the west of the region, the species is very common at **Aston Rowant** in Oxfordshire (SU 730 970). In the south-west there is a strong colony at **Broughton Down**, South Hampshire (SU 291 328).

South-west England. On the border with south-east England, **Martin Down**, South Hampshire, is a large area of grassland where good numbers of the species can be seen in the heavily grazed areas around Hanham Hill (Fig. 35). The easiest access is from the car park at the west end of Sillens Lane, Martin Village (SU 058 192). The broken chalk slopes inhabited by Silver-spotted Skippers can be seen about 1km to the south of the car park. Natural England provides very informative leaflets on site which include a detailed map of the area. Some 20km to the west, near Fontmell Magna in Dorset, are the steep chalk slopes of **Fontmell Down**. Park at ST 888 185 in the lay-by opposite a small airfield on the minor road going east from the A350. The entrance to the reserve is opposite here on the west side of the main road. It must be stressed that these hills are very steep indeed and working their slopes would be difficult for those with walking disabilities.

Wales and Ireland. Absent.

Large Skipper
Ochlodes faunus (Turati)

General distribution and status
Resident. Widespread and common throughout mainland Britain as far north as North Northumberland in the east and Ayrshire in the west. There is some evidence of a northward expansion of the species' range in north-eastern England (Asher *et al.*, 2001). It is absent from Ireland and the Isle of Man, and in the Channel Isles is restricted to Jersey where it is widespread and common.

Flight period
Single brooded, usually from late May to early August, with a peak during the first two weeks of July.

Larval foodplants
Cock's-foot grass is the main foodplant with occasional records of Purple Moor-grass and False Brome. Other species are used only rarely.

Habitat requirements
Most often encountered on rough grassland where the foodplants are allowed to grow to maturity. Sheltered situations are favoured such as those found in woodland rides and clearings, field edges, roadside verges, hedgerows and large gardens. The males require sunlit shrubs up to about 1.5m tall on which to perch whilst watching for passing females.

Identification characters, variation and similar species
Average wingspan 34mm. This species is larger, darker and more heavily built than the Small, Essex or Lulworth Skippers with which it can sometimes be seen. The bold markings of both sexes make confusion with these unlikely. There is a superficial resemblance to the Silver-spotted Skipper, though confusion is again unlikely, and the reader is referred to the identification section dealing with that species (p. 53).

Field tips
During the early part of the day, males can be found basking openly and females

Fig. 36 Large Skipper male. Glapthorn Cow Pasture, Northamptonshire

Fig. 37 Large Skipper female. Farley Mount, South Hampshire

Large Skipper / Dingy Skipper

Fig. 38 Large Skipper underside. Thetford Forest, West Suffolk

less conspicuously, near their roosting sites amongst grasses and low shrubs. During dull weather, they will remain in these areas to continue basking and to feed from the flowers of brambles and thistles. As the morning progresses or the sun begins to shine, males will either patrol in search of females or employ a perching strategy. A perching male selects a particular sunlit leaf from which to dart out and investigate passing potential mates. If these sorties are unsuccessful he will almost inevitably return to the same leaf. Locating these favourite perches and sitting unobtrusively near them is without doubt an excellent way of obtaining close views and photographs. Females are far less active and therefore less often seen except when basking first thing in the morning or when feeding. Searching thistle or bramble flowers is the most likely route to success.

Regional prime sites
Scotland. Restricted to the extreme south-west where it can be seen in good numbers at **Wood of Cree**, Wigtownshire. Park at NX 382 709 and explore the track to the south-east.

Northern England. Recent range expansion in the north-east, where it is found north to the Scottish border, suggests that it is only a matter of time before the species crosses into south-eastern Scotland.

Central, eastern, south-east and south-west England and Wales. Widespread and common.

Ireland. Absent.

Dingy Skipper
Erynnis tages subspecies *tages* (Linnaeus)

General distribution and status
Resident; fully protected (NI). Widely distributed in central and southern England. Very localized in the east and the north and mainly coastal in Scotland (though it is absent from all of the islands) and Wales. Of widely scattered distribution in Ireland where it is most frequently found in the north-west. Throughout its range it is locally common but numbers have declined in recent years. In the limestone areas of County Clare and parts

Dingy Skipper

of South-east Galway it is widespread and common and is represented by the Burren Dingy Skipper (p. 61). It is absent from the Channel Isles.

Flight period
Usually single brooded, flying from the end of April to the end of June, with a peak during the third and fourth weeks of May. At sites in northern Scotland the flight period is delayed by some two weeks, and the optimum time to see the butterfly is during the first two weeks of June. There is a partial second emergence, mainly in southern England, during late July and August.

Larval foodplants
Common Bird's-foot Trefoil is used throughout the species' range. Greater Bird's-foot Trefoil is also used in damp meadows and Horseshoe Vetch is often chosen on chalk grassland.

Habitat requirements
A wide range of habitats is suitable for this species. On the coast, it can be found on dunes and undercliffs and inland it inhabits grassland, woodland rides, disused railways, roadside verges, limestone pavement and heathland (Figs 5, 8, 10, 13 and 14). Sheltered areas, where the foodplant grows adjacent to bare patches of ground, are preferred. Tall plants and grass stems, amongst which the butterflies can roost, are also required.

Identification characters, variation and similar species
Average wingspan 30mm. Variation is more or less restricted to general lightening or darkening of the ground colour. In appearance the Dingy Skipper is unlike any other butterfly found in the British Isles. However, it is often confused in the field with the Burnet Companion moth (*Euclidia glyphica* (Linnaeus): Noctuidae) (Fig. 41) which is similar in appearance, behaviour and habitat preference. The two can often be seen flying together. With practice they can be separated on the wing, as the

Fig. 39 Dingy Skipper upperside. Foulden Common, West Norfolk

Fig. 40 Dingy Skipper underside. Foulden Common, West Norfolk

Dingy Skipper

Burnet Companion is slightly larger and the pale orange of the hindwings can usually be seen. Once settled, this feature is even more noticeable but it can be difficult to see on a hot day when the moths are easily put to flight. The use of good quality, close-focusing binoculars is recommended to avoid this problem. If the forewing only is in view, look for the smooth neatly-defined dark bars present in the Burnet Companion. These appear more chequered and less precise in the Dingy Skipper.

Field tips
The Dingy Skipper spends much of its time engaged in rapid low-level flight interspersed with short periods of basking on low vegetation or, more usually, on bare ground or stones. It rarely visits flowers. When in flight, it can be very difficult to follow, often seeming to disappear completely. The best opportunities for photography are during the early part of the day when the flight is slower and easier to follow and the periods of basking are longer. During dull weather and at night, the butterflies roost with their wings wrapped around dead flower-heads and the inflorescences of grasses. At this time, they are extremely well camouflaged but can be found with patience and practice.

Regional prime sites
Scotland. Absent from much of the country but in the north-east it is fairly plentiful at **Nairn Dunes**, East Inverness-shire (NH 895 575) and at **Lein of Garmouth**, Moray, (NJ 333 657). In the south-west the species has disappeared from most of its former sites but can still be seen at **Port O' Warren**, Kirkcudbrightshire (from NX 880 535 explore the cliff-top footpath to the south-west).

Northern England. Localized in the west but frequent around Morecambe Bay. Here it can be seen readily at **Arnside Knott**, Westmorland (SD 450 775). In the east, it is more widespread and can be seen in good numbers in North-east Yorkshire at **Ellerburn Bank** (SE 853 848) and **Deepdale** (SE 911 910). In Durham, the butterfly is quite common in many of the abandoned limestone quarries such as that at **Bishop Middleham** (NZ 332 326). In the south-west of the region, it can be found reliably at **Lathkill Dale**, South-west Yorkshire (park in the village of Over Haddon (SK 203 664) and follow the paths south and then west along the dale), the disused limestone quarry at **Llanymynech**, Shropshire (SJ 266 221),

Fig. 41 Burnet Companion moth. Foulden Common, West Norfolk

Dingy Skipper

the abandoned ironstone quarry at **Twywell Hills**, Northamptonshire (explore the Whitestones area north of the car park at SP 945 775) and at **Monk Wood**, Worcestershire (park at SO 804 607 and follow the marked trails).

Central England. The overall distribution is somewhat patchy but the species is locally fairly common.

Eastern England. Very localized and absent from most of the region. Small numbers can be seen at **Narborough** disused railway line, West Norfolk (park at TF 750 118 and follow the track south-east) and, in the same county, larger numbers can be found at **Foulden Common** (park at TL 765 999 and explore the common to the south-west). In North Lincolnshire the butterfly can reliably be found at Little Scrub's Meadow, part of the **Chambers Farm Wood** complex, at TF 145 744. The visitor centre here supplies excellent local information.

South-east England. Locally common in suitable habitats throughout the region. Favoured sites include the chalk downland and grasslands at **Whipsnade Downs** in Bedfordshire (SP 999 185), **Lydden Down**, East Kent (TR 277 453), **Pitt Down** (SU 418 293), South Hampshire and **Stony Green Hill**, Buckinghamshire (park at SU 866 991 and explore the west-facing slopes to the north).

South-west England. Absent or very scarce on the higher moorlands of North and South Devon and West and East Cornwall but widespread and fairly common on the border of south-east England on the extensive grassland at **Martin Down** in South Hampshire (park at SU 037 200 and explore the tracks and the earthworks to the south-east), at **Buckland Wood** (ST 185 175) and **Ubley Warren** (ST 505 556) in South Somerset and **Penhale Sands** in West Cornwall (park at SW 767 587 and search the edges of the dunes area to the south near SW 767 570).

Wales. Very scarce or absent from most western and central areas, though strong colonies can be found in northern and southern localities. These include **Loggerheads Country Park**, Denbighshire (SJ 197 625) where directions to the 'Butterfly' or 'Top' glade should be sought at the visitor centre and, in the south, on the grasslands at **Welsh Moor**, Glamorgan (SS 520 927).

Western Ireland. Found at only a few widely scattered localities outside the Burren district of Co's Clare and Southeast Galway where the species is represented by the Burren Dingy Skipper (p. 61). Recommended sites are at **Murvagh**, West Donegal (G 895 731) and **Aughinish Island**, Limerick (R 290 527).

Eastern Ireland. Very localized but can be seen reliably at **Skerries Station**, Dublin (O 246 599) and at **Finnamore Lakes** in the Boora Peatlands Park, Offaly (N 209 208).

Burren Dingy Skipper
Erynnis tages subspecies *baynesi* Huggins

Subspecies type locality and authority
Specimens from the Burren in Co. Clare, Ireland, were first described as a subspecies by Huggins (1956a).

General distribution and status
Resident; almost wholly restricted to the Burren in Clare, where it is very common, though there are occasional records from the neighbouring county of South-east Galway.

Flight period
As for the Dingy Skipper (p. 57).

Larval foodplants
The apparent absence of Horseshoe Vetch in Ireland and the preference of Greater Bird's-foot Trefoil for damp localities suggest strongly that the sole foodplant of the Burren Dingy Skipper in the Burren district is Common Bird's-foot Trefoil.

Habitat requirements
The Burren Dingy Skipper is restricted to the open limestone pavement that is characteristic of its native area (Fig. 10). Here Common Bird's-foot Trefoil grows in fissures in the bare limestone, thus providing the ideal microhabitat for both egg-laying and basking. It prefers areas adjacent to scrub and taller plants amongst which the adults can shelter and roost.

Fig. 42 Burren Dingy Skipper. Boston, Co. Clare (G. McLennan)

Burren Dingy Skipper / Grizzled Skipper

Identification characters, variation and similar species
Average wingspan 30mm; variation is usually restricted to the degree of conspicuousness of the pale markings. The Burren Dingy Skipper differs from the typical subspecies in having a much darker, brownish-black ground colour with the light markings very pale and, in some individuals, almost white. The row of whitish spots along the outer edges of both forewings and hindwings are particularly conspicuous. These strongly contrasting markings create a very striking overall appearance that cannot be seen throughout the rest of the species' range.

Field tips
The best way to see the Burren Dingy Skipper is to find an area of grassland adjacent to scrub where bare patches of limestone and some taller plants are present. In such places there are often large patches of Common Bird's-foot Trefoil and it is here that the butterflies abound. A short wait will reveal them flying rapidly over the grass between their basking stations on the bare rock.

Regional prime sites
Western Ireland. It is widespread and common throughout the Burren. A suggested site for the first-time visitor is amongst the Hazel scrub on either side of the R480 road that runs south from **Ballyvaughan**. The area around **Caherconnell** (R 240 970) is a good example.

Other regions. Absent.

Grizzled Skipper
Pyrgus malvae (Linnaeus)

General distribution and status
Resident. Widely distributed but localized in England south of a line approximately between West Gloucestershire in the west and North Lincolnshire in the east. Further north, there is a colony in Shropshire but probably no naturally established colonies elsewhere. Very localized in Wales and absent from Scotland, Ireland, the Isle of Man and the Channel Isles.

Flight period
Usually late April to late June with a peak during the last two weeks of May. However, individuals have been recorded as early as mid-March (Asher *et al.*, 2001) and are frequently seen into August. The reason for these late sightings may be protracted emergence from the first generation, overlapping with a partial second brood (Emmet & Heath, 1989).

Larval foodplants
Several plants of the family Rosaceae, the most frequent being Wild Strawberry. Agrimony and Creeping Cinquefoil are also used commonly.

Grizzled Skipper

Fig. 43 Grizzled Skipper upperside.
Foulden Common, West Norfolk

Fig. 44 Grizzled Skipper underside.
Foulden Common, West Norfolk

Habitat requirements
This skipper is found only in sheltered warm localities with short flower-rich turf and adjacent taller vegetation or scrub (Fig. 8). These requirements are met in wide woodland rides, sheltered valleys on calcareous grassland, disused industrial sites and railways, coastal dunes and, occasionally, heathland.

Identification characters, variation and similar species
Average wingspan 26mm. On rare occasions the black of the upperside is replaced with brown. A form which occurs fairly frequently at some sites has the white spots of the forewings confluent, thus forming large conspicuous blotches. This form is known as *taras* Bergstrasser. The striking black and white chequered pattern of this species is unlike that of any other butterfly found in the British Isles. However, confusion can arise for the unpractised eye between the Grizzled Skipper and the Mother Shipton moth (*Callistege mi* (Clerck): Noctuidae) (Fig. 45). They are superficially similar and fly at the same time in the same type of habitat. A blur of black and white wings can catch out the unwary but, once the insect has settled, it is clear that the moth is larger than the butterfly, with a wingspan of approximately 32mm, and it lacks its very clearly defined chequered markings, particularly on the forewings.

Field tips
Provided the ambient temperature is warm enough, the Grizzled Skipper will fly right through the day until the last rays of the sun in the evening. It is a very active species that spends most of its time flying rapidly from flower to flower, preferring those of buttercups, Bugle and bird's-foot trefoils. It takes frequent breaks to bask on rocks or bare ground and the males occupy territorial perches from which they inspect any approaching butterfly. The best way to see the species is to find an area of short grass adjacent

Grizzled Skipper

to taller vegetation. There needs to be one of the foodplants present and a profusion of nectar plants amongst bare ground and short turf. If the butterflies are there they should be seen after a short wait. Alternatively, one might try searching grass or flower heads during the early morning for individuals still at roost with their wings held erect over their backs. This certainly provides the best chance for photographing the underside as, during the rest of the day usually, only the upperside is visible.

Regional prime sites
Scotland. Absent.

Northern England. A few individuals are occasionally seen at one locality in this region but they are believed to originate from an unauthorized introduction. In any event, the species is in decline there and it would be inappropriate to give details of the site.

Central England. Widespread in the south-eastern half of the region with isolated colonies elsewhere. In Shropshire, there is a well-known site at **Llanymynech**, on the border with Wales (SJ 266 221). Also in Shropshire it can be seen in the **Wyre Forest**, in the area known as 'The Pipeline', just north-east of the Earnwood Copse car park at SO 744 783. In the south-east, there are strong colonies in the area around the disused quarries at **Twywell Hills** in Northamptonshire (explore the Whitestones area north of the car park at SP 945 775).

Eastern England. Restricted mainly to the west of the region on the border with central England, though there are outlying colonies at **Narborough** disused railway line (park at TF 750 118 and follow track south-east), **Foulden Common** (park at TL 765 999 and search the common to the south-west) and **Wretton Cut-off Channel** (TL 685 993) in West Norfolk. In North Lincolnshire, the species is frequent in **Chambers Farm Wood** at Little Scrub's Meadow (TF 145 744). At this last location is a visitor centre where local information can be obtained.

South-east England. Widespread but localized. On the border with eastern England this species is quite common in the sheltered downland valleys at the southern end of **Whipsnade Downs**, Bedfordshire (SP 999 085). In East Kent, it can be seen on the coastal shingle at **Dungeness** (from TR 089 169 explore the shingle ridges to the

Fig. 45 Mother Shipton moth. Bentley Woods, South Wiltshire

Grizzled Skipper

north and north-west) and in West Kent it is common at **Trosley Country Park** (TQ 633 611). In the **New Forest**, South Hampshire (SU 20/30) it is widespread and found in small numbers along many of the broader rides and clearings. It is also common in South Hampshire at **Pitt Down** (SU 418 293).

South-west England. Locally frequent in the east with a sparser distribution in the west. In the north of the region, the butterfly can be seen at the RSPB reserve at **Nagshead**, West Gloucestershire (follow the forest trails from the visitor centre at SO 606 085). Further south, on the border with south-east England, it is found in good numbers on the chalk grasslands of **Martin Down**, South Hampshire. Here it is particularly common along Bockerley Dyke and the earthworks south of the car park at SU 036 200. Then, travelling west, visits are recommended to **Ubley Warren** (ST 505 556) and **Stoke Camp** (park at ST 486 513 and walk east for 300m to the reserve entrance at ST 489 512), North Somerset, **Haldon Woods**, South Devon (SX 882 847) and **Penhale Sands**, West Cornwall (dunes south of the parking area at SW 767 587 to approximately SW 765 570). At this last site, a significant number of individuals belong to the spectacular form *taras* Bergstrasser described earlier (p. 63).

Wales. Restricted to the north and the south of the country. In the north, it can be seen at **Loggerheads Country Park**, Denbighshire (follow the marked trails from the information centre at SJ 197 625) and, in the south, there is a good chance of success at **Pembrey Country Park**, Carmarthenshire (SS 405 005).

Western and eastern Ireland. Absent.

Swallowtail

The Swallowtails and Apollos
(Papilionidae)

Apollo
Parnassius apollo (Linnaeus)

Status

Uncertain; introduction; possible extinct resident; probable vagrant. Some records are probably attributable to the accidental importation of immature stages on horticultural stock. There has been speculation about the possibility of the species formerly being resident in Scotland. In mainland Europe, it is found in most of the major mountain ranges from Spain in the west and as far north as southern Fennoscandia.

Distribution of records

During the 19th century, there were over 20 records for Scotland, mainly from the Isle of Lewis and the Highlands. There is little chance of misidentifying this striking butterfly, but the origin of the specimens is unknown and has been the subject of much debate. Morley & Chalmers-Hunt (1959) suggest they may have resulted from attempted introductions. Outside Scotland, the records can be summarized as follows: East Cornwall (date unknown but probably 19th century), East Kent (1847 or 1848, 1889 (two individuals), 1955 and 1986), South Essex (1847 or 1848), Isle of Wight (1865), North Somerset (date unknown but probably 19th century), North Wiltshire (1920), East Suffolk (1928) and Middlesex (1957). Of these dates, four coincided

Fig. 46 Apollo. Switzerland (R. Harrington)

with large immigrations that included several specimens of the Camberwell Beauty and a form of the Scarce Silver Y moth (*Syngrapha interrogationis* (Linnaeus): Noctuidae) that was believed to have originated from the western slopes of the Alps (Emmet & Heath, 1989). This corroborative evidence supports the assumption that the Apollo is a genuine, if very scarce, immigrant to the British Isles.

Flight period

All of the accurately dated records for Britain occurred during August and September. Abroad, the species usually flies during July and August.

Larval foodplants

The early stages have never been found in Britain. On the Continent, the foodplants are various species of stonecrop.

Apollo / British Swallowtail

Habitat requirements
In mainland Europe, the Apollo is usually seen on subalpine mountain passes and meadows. There is little detailed information relating to the preferred localities of specimens recorded in Britain.

Identification characters and similar species
Average wingspan 80mm; the female is slightly larger than the male. The large size and conspicuous markings make this species unlike any of the well-documented butterflies occurring in the British Isles.

British Swallowtail
Papilio machaon Linnaeus subspecies *britannicus* Seitz

Subspecies type locality and authority
Specimens from Norfolk, England, were first described as a subspecies by Seitz (1907); no specific locality is given. The nominate subspecies is widespread in continental Europe but does not occur in the British Isles.

General distribution and status
Resident; fully protected (GB). This endemic subspecies of the Swallowtail is restricted to the Norfolk Broads in eastern England where it is not uncommon in certain favoured localities.

Flight period
Usually from late May to mid-July with a peak during the second and third weeks of June. In most years there is a partial second emergence during August.

Larval foodplants
Adults of the first generation will usually only lay their eggs on Milk Parsley. Those of the partial second generation will also use Angelica. Larvae have occasionally been found on cultivated carrot in gardens adjacent to its fenland habitats (Emmet & Heath, 1989)

Habitat requirements
The British Swallowtail is found only in open fens and marshes where there is an abundant growth of Milk Parsley. The preferred habitats are usually dominated by sedges or reeds and have on their edges a rich mixture of herbaceous plants and shrubs on which the adults can search for nectar (Fig. 11). The favoured nectar sources are Ragged Robin, brambles and thistles.

Identification characters, variation and similar species
Average wingspan 85mm; the female is significantly larger than the male. The large size and spectacular markings of the Swallowtail make it unmistakable. Differences between the British and Continental Swallowtail are discussed under the latter subspecies (p. 70).

British Swallowtail

Field tips

The Swallowtail spends much of its time gliding over reed beds in search of mates, Milk Parsley or nectar sources. When doing so it often remains tantalizingly out of range for viewing unless binoculars are used. In many ways, looking for Swallowtails can then be akin to birdwatching. This elusive behaviour is particularly evident in the heat of the afternoon. However, in all of their favoured localities there are sure to be spots where they come close to the margins of the wetlands in order to feed or to lay eggs. The observer should therefore look for clumps of Ragged Robin, brambles, thistles or the larval foodplant near paths through, or alongside, the fens and wait for the appropriate visitor. Several people working in tandem at some few-metre intervals along the paths can improve the efficiency of this exercise, provided they remain within collective sight or sound of each other. The adults will sometimes wander further afield in search of nectar and will then visit nearby flowery meadows and even gardens. Individual flowers are often chosen repeatedly and, if these can be found, good opportunities for close observation and photography should follow as the butterflies become so engrossed with feeding that human intruders are ignored. Nine am to late

Fig. British Swallowtail. Strumpshaw Fen, East Norfolk

morning is the best time to try as Swallowtails 'fuel-up' for the day's activities.

Regional prime sites
Eastern England. Restricted to the east of the region where it is confined to the Broadlands of East Norfolk. By far the easiest site to see Swallowtails at close quarters is at RSPB **Strumpshaw Fen**. From the south-east end of the village of Brundall take the Strumpshaw Road south-east for *c*.1.5km and then the acute right turn along Low Road for approximately 1km to the reserve car park at TG 341 067. From here one should go back onto the road on foot and turn immediately left onto Tinkers Lane, then continue for about 100m past the cottages and enter the reserve by crossing the railway line to the left. The butterflies often visit bramble flowers near the reserve entrance. It is important that all visitors to the reserve check in at the visitor centre on arrival. One of the cottages on the edge of the reserve keeps a well-stocked herbaceous border that is often visited by Swallowtails. There is a sign inviting butterfly-watchers to walk around the garden in their pursuit (p. 352). Clearly this very generous attitude must be treated with the respect it deserves and one must never walk *on* the flower beds.

An alternative site is the southern end of **Hickling Broad**. Park near the church at Potter Heigham (TG 420 199) and take the path north across a field and through a small wood on to the Weavers' Way trail. The butterflies can be seen either east or west from here where they sometimes come close to the path to visit the flowers of Ragged Robin.

Other regions. Absent.

Continental Swallowtail
Papilio machaon Linnaeus subspecies *gorganus* Fruhstorfer

Status
Scarce immigrant; introduction. Although specimens of the British Swallowtail are very occasionally recorded outside its usual home of the Norfolk Broads, these individuals are thought to result from accidental transportation of the pupae in harvested thatching reeds. The British subspecies is not considered to be migratory. However, the Continental Swallowtail is a known migrant throughout mainland Europe and specimens are recorded almost annually in the British Isles. During the early to mid-19th century and early to mid-20th century, the Continental Swallowtail formed small established colonies at several localities along the south coast of England between Dorset and East Kent. In the Channel Isles, it is recorded regularly and, although larvae have been found occasionally, it is not considered to be a permanent

Continental Swallowtail

Fig. 48 Continental Swallowtail. Switzerland (R. Harrington)

resident. The subspecies is widespread throughout Europe.

Distribution of records

Outside of the south-eastern vice-counties of England and the Channel Isles, the Continental Swallowtail is recorded only rarely. The majority of sightings come from south-east of a line between South Devon in the west and West Norfolk in the east, with the larger numbers recorded along the south and east coasts between Dorset and East Suffolk. It should be noted that this species is often bred in captivity by enthusiasts and is released regularly as adult butterflies.

Flight period

From late April to early September in two broods, peaking in mid-May and early August. Unlike the British Swallowtail, which has only a partial second generation, the Continental Swallowtail is recorded in much larger numbers later in the year. Emmet & Heath (1989) suggested that this second brood may be a mixture of immigrants and genuine British-bred individuals.

Larval foodplants

Larvae discovered in England have most often been found on cultivated carrot. In mainland Europe the favoured

Continental Swallowtail / Scarce Swallowtail

foodplant is Fennel.

Habitat requirements
Unlike the British Swallowtail, this subspecies is not restricted to fenland. Most sightings occur near the coast where it appears to favour cliff tops, downs and flowery meadows near the sea. It is often seen visiting garden flowers such as buddleia and lavender.

Identification characters, variation and similar species
Average wingspan 90mm; the female is significantly larger than the male. Very similar to the British Swallowtail but differs in its slightly larger size and overall paler appearance. The dark markings, especially in the female, are finer and less extensive with correspondingly larger areas of pale yellow. The blue spots on the hindwings are usually brighter and more conspicuous. The main difference, however, lies in the shape of the dark band that runs down the submargin of the outer edge of the forewings. In the British Swallowtail this band is broader at the base than at the apex of the wing, thus forming an elongated wedge, whereas in the continental subspecies the band is of an even width throughout. Although this feature is slightly less obvious on the upperside of some female British Swallowtails, it is clear when their undersides are examined.

Field tips
As with all vagrant species, its incidence is erratic and unpredictable. Possibly the best chance of finding a Continental Swallowtail would be to search the cliff tops and coastal downs of south-eastern Kent during an extended period of warm weather during early August when the winds are light southerly or south-easterly.

Scarce Swallowtail
Iphiclides podalirius (Linnaeus)

Status
Vagrant; introduction. The Scarce Swallowtail is an extremely rare immigrant with some records almost certainly attributable to accidental importation and release or escape from captivity. The species is popular with butterfly breeders. It is widespread in mainland Europe south of a line approximately between Belgium in the west and Poland in the east. Migrant individuals have been recorded as far north as southern Scandinavia.

Distribution of records
At least four adults and several larvae were recorded between 1822 and 1828 at Netley, Shropshire. There has been much debate regarding the origin of these specimens (see Allen, 1980) but it is likely that they resulted from captive-bred stock. Since the first documented capture of a 'British' specimen in Bedfordshire in

Scarce Swallowtail

1803 there have been single records from East Kent (1858 (a larva) and 1903), South Devon (1895), North Devon (1901), West Gloucestershire (1963), Herefordshire (1984) and South Essex (1987). There are two records from the Channel Isles (1893 and 1931).

Flight period
Specimens have been recorded in Britain during each month from May to August. In continental Europe, the species has two generations peaking during late May and late August.

Larval foodplants
Larvae in Shropshire were said to have been found on Bullace. Blackthorn and other cultivated fruit trees are used elsewhere in Europe.

Habitat requirements
Abroad, the species is usually found in scrubland and flowery meadows and is often seen in and around orchards.

Identification characters and similar species
Average wingspan 80mm; the female is slightly larger than the male. The large size, striking markings and long 'tails' make the Scarce Swallowtail unmistakable.

Fig. 49 Scarce Swallowtail. Italy (R. Laughton)

Orange-tip

The Whites and Yellows
(Pieridae)

Wood White
Leptidea sinapis subspecies *sinapis* (Linnaeus)

General distribution and status
Resident; protected from sale (GB). Widely scattered but highly localized distribution over southern and central England with outlying colonies in the north and east which probably result from unauthorized introduction. There are a few known colonies in Wales. In Ireland it is apparently restricted to the Burren limestone district of Co's Clare and South-east Galway where it is represented by the Irish Wood White (p. 78). It is absent from the Isle of Man and the Channel Isles.

Flight period
Over much of its range, including Ireland, this species is single brooded and flies from late May to the end of July. The optimum time to see it is

Fig. 50 Wood White. Salcey Forest, Northamptonshire

Wood White

during the last two weeks of June. However, during warm seasons at many southern localities, the Wood White is double brooded and flies from early May to the end of June (with a peak during the last week of May and the first week of June) and from mid-July to the end of August, peaking during the first two weeks of August. The males emerge at least one week before the females.

Larval foodplants
Mainly Meadow Vetchling, Bitter Vetchling and Common Bird's-foot Trefoil. Greater Bird's-foot Trefoil and Tufted Vetch are used occasionally.

Habitat requirements
The Wood White is usually associated with wide woodland rides and clearings where it breeds amongst scrub and rideside vegetation (Fig. 12). It also inhabits scrub and grassland along coastal undercliffs (Fig. 14), disused railway lines and, occasionally, overgrown field margins. It prefers partly shaded localities where the larval foodplants flower above the level of the surrounding vegetation. Heavily shaded woods where rides or coppicing have not been maintained are not suitable for this species. In Ireland, far more open habitats are used and these are discussed under the section dealing with the Irish Wood White (p. 78).

Identification characters, variation and similar species
Average wingspan 40mm. The large rectangular dark spot on the forewing is easily viewable in flight and will separate this species from all but one of the other whites (Réal's Wood White, p. 80). When feeding or at rest, this feature is less obvious as the Wood White always settles with its wings closed. However, it can still be seen on the underside as a greenish representation. Its long forewings, dusky hindwings with a long clear whitish patch extending from the body to the centre of the wing and overall delicate appearance are also diagnostic. Its flight is remarkably weak and with practice can be identified at some distance as being different to that of any Small or Green-veined Whites which may be present. In the female, the dark spot on the forewing is paler than that of the male and, in individuals of the second generation, this spot is usually darker and more intense in both sexes. Major variation is otherwise uncommon, though specimens where the forewing spot is pale brown instead of black are seen occasionally. This form is known as *brunneomaculata* Stauder.

The recently discovered Réal's Wood White (p. 80) is identical in appearance and the two species cannot be separated without dissection and examination of the genitalia. However, Réal's Wood White is presently known to occur only in Ireland and therefore any English or Welsh specimens can reasonably be assigned to Wood White. In Ireland, Réal's Wood White does not appear to be present in the Burren, to which the Irish Wood White is restricted, and there seems to be no overlap in the distribution of the two species in that

Wood White

country (Hughes, pers. comm.). Therefore, as a general rule, any wood whites seen in the Burren can reasonably be identified as the Irish Wood White. It must be stressed that the distribution in Ireland of the two species is imperfectly known and all of the observations made there should be treated accordingly.

Field tips

The males of this species are very active and their feeble, yet somehow determined, flight can easily be seen as they patrol woodland rides and scrub. They can often be found congregating at muddy puddles and animal excreta from which they drink, presumably to obtain minerals. At such times excellent opportunities to photograph the butterflies present themselves and a recommended tactic is to find such a puddle on a hot day and wait for the Wood Whites to arrive. Both sexes also feed from the flowers of various vetches and can often be seen with their head and thorax partly buried in the flower as they attempt to take nectar. When at rest, or feeding, the wings are always held closed with only the underside visible. The females are less active and the best method of finding them is to gently search patches of the foodplant where they can usually be found laying eggs. They often seem to appear from nowhere, and vanish just as mysteriously, so continuous searches of the plants are needed. Several males flying together over a particular spot usually signals the presence of a female in the vegetation below.

Regional prime sites
Scotland. Absent.

Northern England. There is only one colony in this region and it is thought to be the result of an unauthorized introduction. The species is only occasionally seen there and it is considered inappropriate to publish details of the locality.

Central England. In the east of the region, the Wood White can be seen in good numbers at **Salcey Forest**, Northamptonshire (from the car park at SP 810 509 follow the main ride south). In the west, it is found at **Monk Wood**, Worcestershire (from SO 804 607 follow the marked trails and search the broader rides and clearings) and along the small stream just north-east of **Coldwell Copse** in Shropshire's Wyre Forest (SO 751 795). The form *brunneomaculata* Stauder has been recorded from Salcey Forest.

Eastern England. There is a well-known colony that is probably the result of an unauthorized introduction at **Chamber's Farm Wood**, North Lincolnshire. Small numbers of the butterfly can be found at Little Scrubs Meadow (TF 145 744). There is a visitor centre on site where local information can be obtained.

South-east England. Usually seen frequently along the broader woodland rides at **Oaken Wood**, Surrey (SU 995 338) and, in small numbers, at

Wood White / Irish Wood White

Whitecross Green Wood, Oxfordshire (along the ride running south-west of the car park at SP 600 150). Visitors to the latter site should be very careful not to trample the rideside vegetation as this will damage the breeding areas of the butterfly. Patience will provide ample photographic opportunities from the path itself.

South-west England. In South Devon, the species can be found in different habitats to those mentioned above. At **Haldon Woods** (SX 882 847) it should be sought in the conifer plantations where scrub has been cleared beneath power lines, though the species appears to be at a very low ebb at this site. Along the coast between Sidmouth (South Devon) and Lyme Regis (Dorset) fairly large colonies inhabit the grassy undercliffs. Suggested sites here are at **Dunscombe Cliffs**, near Sidmouth (SY 157 878) and, a little further east, at **Branscombe Cliffs** (park at SY 206 881 and search the undercliffs to the west). Further north, it may still be present in small numbers at **Dunsdon** National Nature Reserve in North Devon (SS 295 078) and at **Staple Common**, South Somerset (park at about ST 266 157, take the track south-west to the timber stacking area and search the small ride and scrubland immediately to the north).

Wales. There are few known colonies and the species is regarded as being endangered in this region. It is therefore not appropriate to publish site details here.

Western Ireland. Restricted to the Burren district of Co's Clare and South-east Galway where it is represented by the Irish Wood White (see below).

Eastern Ireland. All examined samples of Irish *Leptidea* species so far suggest that the Wood White is absent from this region where its place is taken by Réal's Wood White (p. 80).

Irish Wood White
Leptidea sinapis subspecies *juvernica* Williams

Subspecies type locality and authority
Specimens from Kildare, Ireland, were first described as a subspecies by Williams (1946).

General distribution and status
Resident. Restricted to the limestone district of the Burren in Clare and South-east Galway, western Ireland. Here it is widespread and can sometimes be the commonest butterfly on the wing.

Irish Wood White

Flight period
Single brooded, flying from late May to the end of July, the optimum time being during the last two weeks of June. The males emerge at least one week before the females. Baynes (1964) states that the subspecies is double brooded but this probably refers to occasional, rather than usual, circumstances.

Larval foodplants
The profusion of Common Bird's-foot Trefoil on the Burren and the relative scarcity of other possibilities suggest that this is the main foodplant of the Irish Wood White. Further research is needed on this subject.

Habitat requirements
As mentioned earlier, the Irish Wood White is found only on the limestone pavement of the Burren. Here it can be seen along lanes and hedgerows as well as in the open, flower-rich habitats so typical of the district. In these more exposed situations, the butterfly favours sites that afford shelter such as large sunny openings amongst the Hazel thickets that dominate parts of the north and north-east of the area (Fig. 10).

Identification characters, variation and similar species
Average wingspan 40mm. This subspecies can easily be distinguished

Fig. 51 Irish Wood White. Boston, Co. Clare

Irish Wood White / Réal's Wood White

from the Wood White by the distinctive greenish-yellow ground colour of the hindwing undersides. The flight of the Irish Wood White is much stronger than its British counterpart and resembles more that of the Small or Green-veined White. For this reason, care should be taken with distant flight identification. The Irish Wood White and Réal's Wood White are identical in appearance and cannot be separated without microscopic examination of the genitalia. However, although the distributions of the two species are presently only imperfectly known, it appears that Réal's Wood White does not occur in the Burren. Therefore any *Leptidea* specimens seen there can reasonably be assigned to the Irish Wood White.

Field tips
Searches of warm sheltered areas where there is protection from the wind should be successful throughout the Burren. The males in particular are very active and the females are more so than those of the Wood White. Males on the wing before the females have emerged are extremely restless and difficult to photograph as they seem rarely to settle. Later in the flight period, both sexes can easily be approached as they feed from various flowers, although the wings are always held closed.

Regional prime sites.
Western Ireland. It is common and widespread throughout the Burren and may be expected in most of the lower sheltered areas. The R480 road, running south from **Ballyvaughan** (starting at M 225 065), and the minor roads to the west of **Boston** (e.g. R 350 975) cut through perfect habitat for this butterfly and it is these areas that are recommended for the first-time visitor.

Other regions. Absent.

Réal's Wood White
Leptidea reali Reissinger

General distribution and status
Resident. Réal's Wood White was described from specimens collected in the French Pyrenees as a new species to science as recently as 1988. It was originally given the name of *Leptidea lorkovicii* Réal but this was later changed to *L. reali* and the findings were published in 1993 (Lorkovic, 1993). Subsequent examination of specimens from Ireland revealed the presence of Réal's Wood White there and its discovery as a new species for the British Isles was published in 2001 (Nelson *et al.*, 2001). These, and other recent studies, have failed to confirm the presence of the species elsewhere in the British Isles. It is now thought to be present throughout Ireland with the exception of the Burren limestone district

Réal's Wood White

of Clare and South-east Galway, as aforementioned. Here its place appears to be taken by the Irish Wood White. Where Réal's Wood White occurs it is usually common.

Flight period
Usually late May to early July in a single generation peaking during the second and third weeks of June. The males are on the wing several days before the females. In years when there is very warm weather during the spring the flight period may be slightly advanced and an occasional second emergence then takes place during late July and August.

Larval foodplants
Meadow Vetchling and possibly Common Bird's-foot Trefoil and Tufted Vetch as both of the latter are common at most sites where the butterfly is found.

Habitat requirements
The main habitat types favoured in Ireland appear to be mixed scrub/grassland mosaics (Fig. 5), roadside verges, broad woodland tracks and edges (e.g. Fig. 13), disused railway lines and coastal undercliffs (Fig. 14) such as those at Rosslare harbour in Wexford.

Identification characters, variation and similar species
Average wingspan 40mm. This species is identical in appearance to the Irish Wood White and can only be separated by dissection and examination of the genitalia. Specimens from mainland Europe are identical to the typical

Fig. 52 Réal's Wood White. Rosslare, Wexford

subspecies of the Wood White and, should Réal's Wood White be discovered in England, this is again likely to be the case. As with both subspecies of Wood White, the large dark rectangular spot on the forewings precludes confusion with other white butterflies. There is little recorded significant variation.

Field tips
The males are very active and conspicuous as they fly just above the herbage level during warm bright weather. Females tend to spend more time amongst vegetation that contains the foodplants but can be found with careful searching even in dull weather. In

Réal's Wood White / Pale Clouded Yellow

flight it is indistinguishable from the Irish Wood White and can also be confused with Small or Green-veined Whites. Care should therefore be taken when identifying flying individuals. In hot weather the butterflies will visit muddy puddles and animal excreta from which presumably they obtain minerals. At this time they are very tolerant of disturbance and excellent photographic opportunities become available. When at rest or feeding the wings are always held closed.

Regional prime sites
Western Ireland. In south-east Galway it can be seen at **Ballydoogan Bog** (M 677 179) and, further south, it is present at **Ballyhoura** in North Cork (R 657 113).

Eastern Ireland. Réal's Wood White is common along the rail causeway that bisects **Craigavon Lakes** in Co. Down. Park at J 060 580 and follow the course of the railway south-west between the lakes. The butterflies are most common at the southern side of the south lake where they inhabit mixed scrub and grassland. The species can be seen in the woodland habitat of the **Raven National Nature Reserve** in Wexford. Park at the official car park at T 110 250 and search the broader tracks and clearings along the marked trail south through the woods. At **Rosslare Harbour**, Wexford, it can be seen in good numbers on the adjacent undercliffs. There is a small car park on the left of the exit from the ferry terminal at T 145 130. From here search for the butterflies along the footpath to the south-east.

Other regions. Absent.

Pale Clouded Yellow
Colias hyale (Linnaeus)

Status
Scarce immigrant. Until 1950 the Pale Clouded Yellow was a frequent and sometimes common visitor to Britain. The highest annual total was some 2,200 recorded in 1900. Through the latter half of the 1940s annual numbers still reached in excess of 850, but since that time recorded sightings have declined to the point where it is now regarded as a very scarce immigrant that is absent in most years. Abroad it is found from Spain and France eastwards to Romania and north to Estonia and southern Scandinavia where it occurs occasionally as a migrant.

Distribution of records
The great majority of sightings come from the south and south-east coastal counties of England with the highest concentrations of records in East Sussex, East and West Kent and South Essex. Problems in separating the species from

Pale Clouded Yellow

Berger's Clouded Yellow (p. 85) and confusion with the *helice* form of the Clouded Yellow (p. 88) make accurate interpretation of the records difficult. However, confirmed identifications indicate that, outside the south of England, the Pale Clouded Yellow has been recorded in small numbers in most of the English counties north to Westmorland in the west and North-east Yorkshire in the east. In Wales, there are records (mainly of singletons) from Glamorgan, Carmarthenshire, Montgomeryshire, Merionethshire, Denbighshire and Caernarvonshire. In Ireland, there are several records from the southern coastal counties from West Cork in the west to Wexford in the east. There is no confirmed record for Scotland. Very few have been seen in the Channel Isles since 1950.

Flight period

Individuals of the first generation arrive in Britain during May and June and their offspring have produced large 'home-bred' second generations in August and September. It appears unable to survive the British winter.

Larval foodplants

The usual foodplants are clovers and Lucerne, although other leguminous plants are sometimes used.

Fig. 53 Pale Clouded Yellow. France (S. Coombes)

Pale Clouded Yellow

Habitat requirements

On the Continent, the Pale Clouded Yellow can be seen in a variety of habitats including flower-rich meadows and fields cultivated with its foodplants. Individuals arriving in Britain tend actively to seek fields containing the foodplant and once these have been located the butterflies rarely go elsewhere.

Identification characters, variation and similar species

Average wingspan 48mm. In the female, the pale yellow of the male upperside and that of the forewing underside is replaced with white. This species cannot be separated confidently in the field from Berger's Clouded Yellow. Even close inspection of set specimens often necessitates microscopic examination of the genitalia which are figured in detail by Emmet & Heath (1989). The following features of the Pale Clouded Yellow compared with those of Berger's Clouded Yellow may be useful but no single characteristic is conclusive and in all there is some degree of overlap.

1. General. Outer edges of forewing straighter and less convex, giving a more angular appearance.
2. Forewing upperside with yellow of male paler and less rich in tone; dark scaling at base more extensive and fan- rather than wedge-shaped; discal spot more elongate and less rounded.
3. Hindwing upperside with more extensive dark markings in outer margin, sometimes almost absent in Berger's Clouded Yellow; discal spot less conspicuously orange; dark scaling at base more extensive.
4. Hindwing underside with yellow less bright and 'pure' in tone due to more extensive dark suffusion.

Form *helice* of the Clouded Yellow (p. 88) is similar to the females of both of the above species but the black outer band of the forewing upperside is much broader and of more even width. The yellow areas of the underside are also distinctly tinged greenish in colour. Reasonable views of a resting or feeding individual should allow successful identification of this form.

The larvae are very different in appearance and are figured by Porter (1997).

Field tips

When searching for this species, efforts should be concentrated in and around fields containing clovers or Lucerne. Pale *Colias* species encountered in such places are more likely to be this species, as Berger's Clouded Yellow tends to be found in the vicinity of Horseshoe Vetch growing on chalk grassland. The males, particularly, are rapid fliers and are difficult to photograph. Pale Clouded Yellows almost always rest and feed with their wings closed and only the underside on view.

Berger's Clouded Yellow
Colias alfacariensis **Berger**

Status
Scarce immigrant. This is the rarest of the clouded yellow species that visits the British Isles. Apart from a period of relative abundance in the 1940s, records are few and far between. Confusion with the Pale Clouded Yellow has certainly led to a degree of under-recording but there is no doubt that Berger's Clouded Yellow is indeed a very scarce immigrant. Abroad, the species is resident throughout southern Europe north to a line approximately between Belgium in the west and Poland in the east.

Distribution of records
Berger's Clouded Yellow was described as a new species to the British Isles in 1948 (Berger, 1948). Until that time all records of 'pale' clouded yellows were attributed to the previous species. Subsequent examination of collection specimens has revealed that, prior to 1940, there were approximately 49 records from the southern counties of England, the great majority of which (35) originated from West and East Kent. Other records come from West and East Sussex, South Hampshire and the Isle of Wight, Dorset, North Somerset and East Cornwall. During the 1940s, the species was relatively common with as many as 80 recorded in East Kent during 1948 and 1949. It was again seen in most of the counties listed above and there were also two records from South Wiltshire. Between 1950 and 1990, the only

Fig. 54 Berger's Clouded Yellow. Switzerland (R. Harrington)

Berger's Clouded Yellow / Clouded Yellow

confirmed record came from Polruan, East Cornwall, on 6th August 1960. At least one was identified in 1990 from near Princes Risborough, Buckinghamshire on 14th August and three other individuals from West Kent and East Sussex were probably of this species. In September 1991, four pupae and 31 adults were found at Portland, Dorset. A further two were recorded that year from Honiton, South Devon. There has been no confirmed record since 1991, although there is a report of an egg-laying female in Dorset in 1996. There appears to be no record for the Channel Isles.

Flight period
May/June and August/September in two generations. In southern Europe there is occasionally a third emergence in October.

Larval foodplants
Horseshoe Vetch. In mainland Europe, Crown Vetch is also used and this species has become established in some non-calcareous habitats in Britain.

Habitat requirements
Berger's Clouded Yellow has almost invariably been found in Britain on calcareous coastal grassland and cliff-tops where the larval foodplant is present. In mainland Europe it also inhabits rough rocky ground and hillsides.

Identification characters, variation and similar species
In the female, the pale yellow of the upperside and that of the forewing underside is replaced with white. The present species and the Pale Clouded Yellow are extremely difficult to separate and there are also similarities with the *helice* form of the Clouded Yellow. The reader is referred to the section on the Pale Clouded Yellow for details (p. 82).

Field tips
The chances of finding a Berger's Clouded Yellow are remote indeed. The best option would be to concentrate on the calcareous coastal downs and cliffs of south-east England during the flight period of the second, and usually larger, brood in August and September. Sites on which Adonis and Chalkhill Blues are found may be worth attention as these are precisely the habitats preferred by Berger's Clouded Yellow (Fig. 7).

Clouded Yellow
Colias croceus (Geoffroy)

Status
Summer visitor; possible resident. This strongly migratory species is an annual visitor to the British Isles but the numbers recorded each year vary to an extraordinary degree. There has been no confirmed successful attempt to overwinter and it therefore seems unlikely

Clouded Yellow

Fig. 55 Clouded Yellow. Martin Down, South Wiltshire

at the moment that the Clouded Yellow will be able to establish itself as a resident species. However, there is circumstantial evidence of overwintering in recent years in South Hampshire and the Isle of Wight. In most years transient breeding colonies lasting for two, or even three, generations are established in the southernmost counties of England. Abroad, the species is very common in northern Africa and southern Europe northwards to France, central Germany and Poland. Records from further north are attributable to migrants.

Distribution of records

Although usually scarce in Scotland, the north-western half of Ireland and north-west England, the Clouded Yellow has been recorded regularly elsewhere in the British Isles. In southern counties of England, it can be expected annually but totals vary greatly from year to year. Occasionally there are years when the numbers arriving in Britain reach invasive proportions. These are usually referred to as 'Clouded Yellow Years' and, once one has been experienced, the abundance of the butterflies cannot be forgotten. The most notable in the last hundred years occurred in 1913, 1928, 1937, throughout most of the 1940s (with a peak of approximately 36,000 individuals recorded in 1947), 1983, 1992, 1994 and 1996. In 1983, it was seen in almost all the vice-counties of England and Wales. Just as there are years of great plenty, there are sometimes extremely poor years. For example in 1963, only seven were recorded nationwide.

Flight period

In northern Africa and southern Europe the Clouded Yellow is continuously brooded. In the British Isles, the first arrivals are usually seen in May or June with further, sometimes large-scale, immigrations between July and September. These are often greatly supplemented by local breeding in southern counties and, in favourable years, the species continues to be seen into October.

Larval foodplants

Clovers and Lucerne are the usual foodplants but other leguminous species, such as Common Bird's-foot Trefoil, are also used occasionally.

Habitat requirements

This species might be expected in many habitat types where there is an abundance of nectar sources. In southern England, there seems to be a distinct preference for calcareous downland and cliff-tops. Fields

Clouded Yellow / Helice Clouded Yellow

of cultivated clover are visited commonly.

Identification characters, variation and similar species

Average wingspan 57mm. The rich golden ground colour, accompanied by the striking broad black borders to the wings, make the typical form of this butterfly unmistakable. The female differs from the male in having the black wing borders of the upperside broken with large golden spots. In the form *helice* Hübner, the golden yellow of the upperside and that of the forewing underside is replaced with white (see Helice Clouded Yellow, below).

Field tips

Even in years of large arrivals, the greatest concentrations of Clouded Yellows occur on the south coast of England and it is here where the best chance of seeing the species lies. Flower-rich calcareous downs, grasslands and cliff-tops are perhaps the best areas in which to concentrate, though one should always be on the lookout for clover fields as this is where the females will often go to lay their eggs. The males, particularly, are very active and powerful fliers and can be difficult to approach and photograph. They regularly stop to feed from flowers but their visits are usually brief and therefore a great deal of perseverance is needed for success. The Clouded Yellow almost always feeds and rests with its wings closed.

Helice Clouded Yellow
Colias croceus form *helice* Hübner

Status.
Form of summer visitor; possible resident. Though neither a species nor subspecies in its own right, this form of the female Clouded Yellow is so distinctive in appearance and of such regular occurrence that it deserves special mention. About ten per cent of females are of this form in which the usual golden yellow of the upperside and that of the forewing underside is replaced by white. In flight it can cause great confusion for the unwary – especially as it can then appear similar to the much scarcer Pale and Berger's Clouded Yellows (see Pale Clouded Yellow p. 82).

As the annual numbers of Clouded Yellow vary greatly from year to year so

Fig. 56 Helice Clouded Yellow. Portland, Dorset

therefore, does the frequency of *helice* individuals. When the species is present in large numbers this white form should be sought in and around fields where clover (the larval foodplant) is being grown, as it is here that the butterflies will lay their eggs.

Brimstone
Gonepteryx rhamni subspecies *rhamni* (Linnaeus)

General distribution and status

Resident; fully protected (NI). Widely distributed and common throughout England south of a line approximately between Cheshire in the west and South-east Yorkshire in the east. Elsewhere in northern England, it is very scarce outside the Morecambe Bay area of West Lancashire and Westmorland and probably only occurs in most places as a vagrant. In the Isle of Man in 1986, an attempt was made to introduce the species but the paucity of subsequent records suggests that this was unsuccessful. However, there have been occasional recent sightings in the island of presumably vagrant individuals. As a resident species it is absent from Scotland, although there are occasional records, again probably of vagrants. A large-scale introduction scheme began in 1986, mainly in the Edinburgh district, and it seems this has also been unsuccessful. In Wales, it is found mainly in the south with scattered colonies elsewhere. In Ireland, where it is represented by the Irish Brimstone (p. 91), its strongholds are in central and western areas. Elsewhere, records of its occurrence are widely scattered and usually unpredictable. An introduction

Fig. 57 Brimstone male. Narborough, West Norfolk

Fig. 58 Brimstone female. Thetford Forest, West Suffolk

Brimstone

using English stock was made in Tipperary in 1894. This was successful, and interbreeding almost certainly took place between the two subspecies. It is widespread in the Channel Isles.

Flight period
The Brimstone hibernates as an adult butterfly and is usually one of the first species to be seen on the wing in late February and March. It continues to fly until late June and early July, the second generation appearing in late July and August before entering into hibernation in the autumn. It is therefore possible to see a Brimstone during any month of the year but the optimum months are April, May and August.

Larval foodplants
On calcareous sites the butterflies lay their eggs on Buckthorn and, in other habitats, on Alder Buckthorn. Various cultivated buckthorns will be accepted in captivity and the successful introduction in Ireland was made using *Rhamnus alaternus* and *R. alpina* (see p. 92).

Habitat requirements
The Brimstone is highly nomadic and can often be seen wandering far from its breeding grounds. Many of the records from outside the normal geographical range of the species, such as those from Scotland, are almost certainly attributable to such individuals. It is usually associated with calcareous scrubland (Fig. 8), meadows and hedgerows or damp wood-land (Fig. 19), heaths and fenland on acidic soils.

Identification characters, variation and similar species
Average wingspan 67mm. The large sulphur-coloured males are unmistakable. The greenish-white females can be mistaken for a male Large White at a distance but they lack the conspicuous black wing tips of that species. Variation is very rare, though irregular brownish spots are sometimes present on the wings. These are thought to result from exposure to chemicals or dampness (Emmet & Heath, 1989) and appear to be more common in post-hibernation individuals.

Field tips
This harbinger of spring is a delight to see on a bright March day but getting close to one is a difficult task. The males emerge from hibernation before the females and are then extremely restless as they patrol the scrubland or woodland clearings, inspecting any pale object that resembles a potential mate. The reason for this intensive behaviour is the fact that pairing does not take place during the previous summer, when the adults are freshly hatched, but is delayed until after the winter. After mating during early spring, activity becomes less frenetic as the females settle down to egg-laying and the males to feeding. At this time, and during late summer, they are easier to approach and photograph. Through August and September, both sexes spend much of their time feeding as they build up their reserves for the oncoming winter. They show a distinct preference

Brimstone / Irish Brimstone

for purple or lilac-coloured flowers such as thistles, buddleia or knapweeds and one should simply find these and await the arrival of the butterflies.

Regional prime sites
Scotland. Absent as a resident species with only occasional records of presumed vagrants.

Northern England. Mainly restricted to the south-west and south-east of the region. In the former it is fairly common at **Arnside Knott**, Westmorland (SD 450 775) and, in the south-east, a reliable site towards its northerly limit is at **Staveley Lagoon**, Mid-west Yorkshire (access from SE 365 635). Here the butterflies are most often seen along the wooded approach track from the north-east side of Staveley village and in the clearings to the west of the lagoon.

Central, eastern, south-east and south-west England. Widespread and common.

Wales. Absent from much of the higher ground. In the north, it is very localized but is seen regularly in the more sheltered parts of the **Great Orme**, Caernarvonshire (e.g. the nature trail at SH 781 835). In the south, it is widely distributed in Glamorgan and can be found at the nature reserves at **Oxwich** (SS 502 865) and **Kenfig** (SS 802 810).

Western and eastern Ireland. Very localized in distribution and represented by the Irish Brimstone (see below).

Irish Brimstone
Gonepteryx rhamni subspecies *gravesi* Huggins

Subspecies type locality and authority
Specimens from Kildare, Ireland, were first described as a subspecies by Huggins (1956b), although no specific locality is given.

General distribution and status
Resident; fully protected (NI). The strongholds of the Irish Brimstone lie in a small area centred on the borders of West Galway and West and East Mayo and along a band through central Ireland approximately from Clare in the west to Kildare in the east. Elsewhere in Ireland there are scattered records which, in some instances, indicate the presence of colonies but many are probably of vagrant individuals. Within its limited range it is usually fairly common. Specimens of the British subspecies were introduced into Tipperary in 1894. This was successful and the offspring are known to have intermingled with the Irish Brimstone.

Flight period
Adults are on the wing for a year from late July to the following July in a single

Irish Brimstone

brood. They hibernate over the winter months, emerging in late February and March. The peak flight times are during April, May and August with the freshest specimens found during the latter period before they enter hibernation.

Larval foodplants
Buckthorn growing on calcareous sites such as the limestone district of the Burren and the very similar-looking Alder Buckthorn in hedgerows and damp woodland edges are the usual foodplants. The introduction in Tipperary was established on the cultivated buckthorns *Rhamnus alaternus* and *R. alpina*.

Habitat requirements
Calcareous scrubland (Fig. 8 and 10) and hedgerows and damp woodland edges.

Identification characters, variation and similar species
Average wingspan 67mm. The Irish Brimstone differs from the typical subspecies in the following ways:

1. Male upperside of fore- and hindwings less yellow.
2. Male hindwing upperside tinged greenish.
3. Male forewing underside with central area tinged greenish white.
4. Female forewing upperside with yellowish borders.
5. Female hindwing upperside tinged yellow.

These features make the sexes appear far more similar to each other than those of the typical subspecies and they can sometimes be difficult to distinguish on the wing. It should not be confused with any other species likely to be encountered in Ireland.

Field tips
Like the typical subspecies, the Irish Brimstone is highly nomadic and is likely to be encountered anywhere within its known range. Late summer offers the best photographic opportunities, as individuals flying then are likely to be in

Fig. 59 Irish Brimstone male. Lough George, Co. Clare

Fig. 60 Irish Brimstone female. Lough Bunny, Co. Clare

good condition and preoccupied with feeding rather than searching for mates or egg-laying sites.

Regional prime sites
Western Ireland. The Burren district of Clare and South-east Galway is by far the best locality to see the Irish Brimstone but, even here, it can be difficult to locate. Suggested sites are the hedgerows along the minor road to the east of **Mullagh More**, Clare, at approximately R 345 955 and the wet meadows at the southern tip of **Lough George**, Clare (just west of the car park at R 375 924).

Away from the Burren it can be seen at **Hurney's Point** in West Galway (M 255 310) and at **Dromore Wood**, Clare (R 365 870).

Eastern Ireland. The distribution here is extremely patchy but the butterfly can be seen regularly in the north at **Craigavon Lakes**, Down (park at J 060 580 and search the causeway between the lakes) and, further south, in Kildare at **Boherbawn Lower** (N 662 022) and **Lullymore** (N 695 626).

Other regions. Absent.

Black-veined White
Aporia crataegi (Linnaeus)

Status
Extinct resident. In 1634, the Black-veined White was one of the first butterflies to be described as a British insect (Mouffett, 1634). Until the mid-1800s it was regarded as being locally abundant and was recorded from over 30 counties in England, as far north as North Lincolnshire, and south Wales. So common was it at some localities that certain collectors of the day would see how many individuals could be caught with a single stroke of their net; four or five at a time were recorded. It could be found roosting by the hundred near Leominster in Herefordshire and its abundance in gardens made it a potential pest of fruit trees. However, during this period many of the smaller colonies were already being lost. By the beginning of the latter half of the 19th century, it was reduced to strongholds in the New Forest, South Hampshire, East Kent and parts of the Welsh borders, and by the end of the century it is clear that the species was in great decline. By the early 1920s, the butterfly hung on only at localities in Worcestershire and East Kent. 1925 is believed to be the year that the Black-veined White ceased to be a resident British butterfly. For an excellent detailed review of the species' fortunes the reader is referred to Pratt (1983).

Flight period
Single brooded from late June to the end of July.

Black-veined White / Large White

Fig. 61 Black-veined White. Switzerland (R. Harrington)

Foodplants
In Britain, Hawthorn and Blackthorn were the main foodplants but cultivated fruit trees were also occasionally used.

Habitat requirements
The Black-veined White was found on scrubland and along woodland edges, hedgerows and in orchards. In mainland Europe, it is usually seen in warm flower-rich meadows.

Large White
Pieris brassicae (Linnaeus)

General distribution and status
Resident; breeding immigrant. Until the 1950s this was an extremely abundant species but its numbers then fell significantly following increased use of agricultural pesticides and the introduction from mainland Europe (presumably on migrating adult

Large White

butterflies) of granulosis virus (Asher *et al.*, 2001). Even so, the Large White is still very common and can be seen throughout the British Isles in most habitat types except at very high altitudes. Its preference for laying eggs on cultivated *Brassica* plants makes it a familiar agricultural and garden pest and has earned it the popular name of 'Cabbage White'. Numbers are sometimes boosted during the summer by the arrival of immigrants from the Continent.

Flight period
There are usually two generations peaking in May and late July/early August. The second emergence is always much larger than the first. In warm summers, a third brood can sometimes be seen during late September and early October.

Larval foodplants
In urban or agricultural situations there is a strong preference for cultivated *Brassica* species such as cabbage, Brussels sprout and oilseed rape. In gardens, eggs are also often laid on ornamental Nasturtium. In more natural habitats, Wild Mignonette, Wild Cabbage and Sea Kale are the more commonly chosen plants.

Habitat requirements
Apart from the highest of mountain areas, the Large White can be seen in almost any habitat type. It is a very familiar visitor to gardens and is often common on agricultural land, especially where oilseed rape is grown.

Identification characters, variation and similar species
Average wingspan 60mm; the female is slightly larger than the male. Variation is rare and is usually limited to size. The spring generation differs from that of the summer in having the black tips to the forewings more or less suffused with pale grey. In fact, in the early part of the 19th century, this was even considered to be a separate species ('The Great White Butterfly' of Stephens, 1829). Individuals of the occasional third generation are often

Fig. 62 Large White male upperside.
Holkham, West Norfolk

Fig. 63 Large White female upperside.
Kelling, East Norfolk

Large White / Small White

smaller than average. The large size and striking black and white markings of the female should preclude confusion with any other species. The plainer male may be mistaken at distance for a female Brimstone on the wing but the black tips to the forewings of the present species easily separate the two. Small males are similar to those of the Small White but they have much blacker wing-tips and lack the black spot at the centre of the forewing upperside. The male undersides are also similar to the Small White but the Large White has two large and conspicuous black spots in the centre of each forewing.

Field tips
During the major part of the day, the butterflies are very active but often land either to lay eggs or to feed from various flowers; they are a familiar sight at garden buddleias. In such circumstances they usually have their wings closed but until approximately 9am they can often be very lethargic, usually basking with their wings at least partly open, and this is the best time to obtain photographs.

Regional prime sites
Scotland. Widespread and common apart from the Highlands and the north-west.

Northern England. Widespread and common apart from on the higher ground of the Lake District of Westmorland and Cumberland.

Wales. Widespread and common apart from on the higher ground of Radnorshire, Montgomeryshire and Merionethshire.

Other regions. Widespread and common throughout.

Fig. 64 Large White underside. Sculthorpe, West Norfolk

Small White
Pieris rapae (Linnaeus)

General distribution and status
Resident; breeding immigrant. This species is widespread throughout Britain, Ireland and the Channel Isles but is absent from the Isles of Orkney and Shetland. It is very common in most places, though less so in the Highlands and the north-west of Scotland. It is scarce in the Outer Hebrides. This is a highly migratory species and numbers are

Small White

usually greatly boosted each summer by the arrival of immigrants.

Flight period
There are usually two generations peaking in late May and late July. Individuals of the first brood can be seen as early as the beginning of April. The second generation is usually significantly more numerous. There is an occasional third emergence during August and September.

Larval foodplants
The Small White has a distinct preference for cultivated *Brassica* species, most notably cabbage, oilseed rape, Brussels sprout and ornamental Nasturtium. Consequently it is regarded as a serious pest of gardens, allotments and farms. Various wild cruciferous plants are also used including Wild Cabbage, Charlock, Garlic Mustard and Wild Mignonette.

Habitat requirements
Found commonly in most habitat types but especially on wastelands, gardens and allotments containing cabbages or sprouts and fields where oilseed rape is grown.

Identification characters, variation and similar species
Average wingspan 46mm. The female differs from the male in having two dark spots on the forewing upperside rather than one. Females of the spring generation are also usually tinged with cream. In the early part of the 19th century, this was even considered to be a separate species – Mr Howard's White Butterfly (Stephens, 1829). Individuals of the third generation are often smaller than average. The Small White lacks the striking black wing-tips of the Large White, small specimens of which might otherwise appear similar. In flight, the present species can easily be confused with the Green-veined White and identification at distance on the wing should not be attempted. However, closer views reveal the characteristic dark wing-veins, particularly conspicuous on the

Fig. 65 Small White male upperside.
Sculthorpe, West Norfolk

Fig. 66 Small White female upperside.
Narborough, West Norfolk

Small White / Green-veined White

underside, that are always present in the Green-veined White.

Field tips
As a very familiar visitor to gardens there should be little difficulty in finding the Small White. It feeds commonly on Buddleia and other garden flowers and seems to prefer purple and white blossoms. As with the Large White, it is lethargic early in the morning and this is therefore the best time to obtain photographs as the butterflies bask open-winged to absorb warmth.

Fig. 67 Small White underside. Sculthorpe, West Norfolk

Regional prime sites
Scotland. Widespread and common with the exception of the Highlands, the north-west and the Western Isles where it is scarce, and, as aforementioned, it is absent from Shetland and Orkney.

Northern England and Wales. Widespread and very common apart from at high altitude.

Other regions. Widespread and very common.

The Green-veined White Group
Pieris napi (Linnaeus)

Introductory notes
There are three subspecies of the Green-veined White: one found in Ireland, one in parts of Scotland and northern England and the other throughout the rest of Britain. Although the three vary in appearance, their taxonomy depends largely on the presence and type of certain specialized 'scent' scales (known as androconial scales) found on the surface of the male butterfly's wings. These scales produce the pheromones with which the sexes communicate during courtship and their structure is specific to a particular species. They are not visible to the naked eye and require examination through a microscope. In some cases, such as in the Green-veined White, the presence of different types of scent scales can also be used to distinguish subspecies. In the British subspecies, which is found throughout England, Wales and parts of Scotland, there is only one type of scale present. However, there are at least four on the wings of the Irish and Scottish subspecies, of which none is present in the

Green-veined White / British Green-Veined White

British subspecies. For further discussion on this complex subject the reader is referred to Warren (1968), Thomson (1980) and Emmet & Heath (1989). The question as to whether or not the Scottish form should warrant subspecific status has caused much debate as it is not known whether or not it and the British subspecies are separated in some way that precludes interbreeding. This genetic separation is a vital prerequisite for such status. The Irish subspecies satisfies this requirement due to its geographical isolation. Clearly more research is needed on this subject and, for the purpose of this book, the presently accepted systematic classification is adhered to and all three subspecies are therefore here included.

British Green-Veined White
Pieris napi subspecies *sabellicae* (Stephens)

Subspecies type locality and authority
Specimens from London and Ripley (it is assumed in Surrey), England, were first described as a distinct form by Stephens (1827). The form was first given subspecific status by Verity in 1916. The nominate subspecies is widespread in continental Europe but does not occur in the British Isles.

General distribution and status
Resident; possible breeding immigrant. This subspecies is endemic to Britain and is found commonly throughout England, Wales and parts of Scotland. In Scotland, the relative distributions of this and the Scottish Green-veined White (p. 103) are imperfectly known at present. It appears to be absent from Ireland where the species is represented by the Irish Green-veined White (p. 101). Although fairly

Fig. 68 British Green-veined White male upperside. Fakenham, West Norfolk

Fig. 69 British Green-veined White female upperside. Fakenham, West Norfolk

British Green-Veined White

mobile, the Green-veined White is not a renowned migrant. At the present time it is not clear which subspecies occupies the Channel Isles and the Isle of Man.

Flight period
In parts of northern England, at altitudes greater than about 250m, and on high ground in parts of Scotland, the Green-veined White forms small discrete colonies that have only one generation per year flying during June and July. Elsewhere there are usually two broods, the first on the wing from late April to late June (peaking in late May), and the second from late June to late August (peaking in late July/early August). During warm summers, there may be a third emergence in September and early October. As there can be an overlap between each of these generations, it is possible to see the species in each month from April to October.

Larval foodplants
The single-generation populations of northern England and parts of Scotland appear to be restricted to Cuckooflower. This plant is also used elsewhere along with a wide variety of crucifers including Garlic Mustard, Hedge Mustard, Watercress, Wild Cabbage and several others. Ornamental Nasturtium is used commonly in gardens.

Habitat requirements
At higher altitudes, the butterfly is found almost exclusively in wet meadows, bogs, wet moorland and along the edges of streams or flushes. Elsewhere it may be expected in most habitat types but is commonest in damp localities such as damp meadows (Fig. 19), ditches, the margins of lakes and rivers, woodland rides (Fig. 12) and hedgerows.

Identification characters, variation and similar species
Average wingspan 45mm. It is most similar to the Small White and to females of the Orange-tip and can easily be confused with either species on the wing. Close views reveal the dark green streaks (actually a mixture of yellow and black scales) along the wing veins, particularly evident on the underside, that are so characteristic of the Green-veined White. The summer generation is far more heavily marked than specimens seen in the spring. This is particularly evident with regard to the dark spots on the upperside as they are much blacker and more striking in summer individuals. The female differs from the male in having two dark spots on the forewing upperside whereas the male has only one. In the spring generation this spotting is often absent or faint. Variation is extensive. Cream-tinted individuals are not uncommon in the summer generation and these are referred to as form *flava* Kane. In Ireland, and very rarely elsewhere, this type of variation can reach its extreme in form *sulphurea* Schöyen where all of the white is replaced with lemon yellow. The extent of the dark markings may vary a great deal and the darkest individuals, where the inner half of the forewing is heavily suffused with black, are known as form *fasciata* Kautz.

British and Irish Green-veined White

Fig. 70 British Green-veined White underside. Holkham, West Norfolk

Field tips
The Green-veined White is such a widespread and common species that finding it should present few problems. It is a familiar visitor to gardens where it regularly feeds at cultivated flowers. It also regularly lays its eggs on ornamental Nasturtiums and can then sometimes be regarded as a pest. On high ground, it is often the only species evident on the wing. During spring, the butterflies tend to congregate in their favoured habitats as the foodplants that grow there are used not only for egg-laying but also as a source of nectar. The flowering period of most of the species concerned is usually over by the time of the butterfly's second generation and alternative food sources are then sought including knapweeds, bramble, thistles and mints. Where the latter grows in large patches in damp meadows many dozens of Green-veined Whites can often be seen during August.

Regional prime sites
Scotland. Probably represented throughout most of the country by the Scottish Green-veined White (p. 103). It is absent from the Shetland Isles.

Northern England. The relative distributions of this and the Scottish Green-veined White (p. 103) are at present unknown.

Western and eastern Ireland. Represented by the Irish Green-veined White (see below).

Other regions. Widespread and very common.

Irish Green-veined White
Pieris napi subspecies *britannica* Müller & Kautz

Subspecies type locality and authority
Specimens from Ireland were first described as a subspecies by Müller & Kautz (1939), although no specific locality is given.

General distribution and status
Resident. Restricted to Ireland where it is common throughout.

Flight period
There are usually two generations

Irish Green-veined White

Fig. 71 Irish Green-veined White male upperside. Lough George, Co. Clare

Fig. 72 Irish Green-veined White female upperside. Lough George, Co. Clare

between late April and late August, peaking in late May and late July/early August. Rarely is there a third emergence during September.

Larval foodplants and habitat requirements
As for the British Green-veined White (p. 99).

Identification characters, variation and similar species
Apart from microscopic examination of the scent scales as discussed earlier (p. 98), the Irish Green-veined White differs from the British Green-veined White in the following ways:

1. Upperside ground colour often more heavily suffused with black scales, thereby creating an overall darker appearance. This is particularly noticeable in females.
2. Upperside with dark markings usually blacker and more extensive.
3. Hindwing underside with 'green' veins much darker and more striking.
4. There is far less difference in appearance between the spring and summer generations.
5. There is a higher incidence of cream-tinted individuals.

Possible confusion with other species is discussed under the British Green-veined White (p. 99).

Fig. 73 Irish Green-veined White underside. Lough George, Co. Clare

Irish and Scottish Green-veined White

Field tips and regional prime sites
Western and eastern Ireland. The Irish Green-veined White is widespread and common throughout Ireland. It is often the commonest species on the wing in damp meadows during spring.

Other regions. Absent.

Scottish Green-veined White
Pieris napi subspecies *thomsoni* Warren

Subspecies type locality and authority
Specimens from Sheriffmuir in West Perthshire, Scotland, were first described as a separate subspecies by Warren (1968).

General distribution and status
Resident. The only documented attempt to ascertain the distribution of this subspecies was published by Thomson (1970) and from his detailed survey of scent scale types (see Notes on the Green-veined White, p. 98) and his distribution map we can summarize its known distribution as follows: The main concentration of records comes from a belt of locations reaching approximately from the counties of Argyll Main in the north-west to Fifeshire and East Lothian in the south-east with occasional scattered records from slightly further south-east. Its presence has been confirmed throughout the Isle of Arran and there is one further stronghold in the Thurso district of Caithness. There are then a few widely scattered records from elsewhere in Scotland, the furthest north being from Orphir in the Orkney Islands. In England, there are several records from Durham, North-east Yorkshire and Westmorland. In Thomson's later work

Fig. 74 Scottish Green-veined White male upperside. Loch Creran, West Inverness-shire

Fig. 75 Scottish Green-veined White female upperside. Loch Creran, West Inverness-shire

Scottish Green-veined White

(1980) he surmises that it is found throughout Scotland. A great deal more research is required to ascertain the true distribution of this subspecies relative to that of the British Green-veined White.

Flight period
In some localities at high altitude, and at the northern extreme of the species' range in Orkney, the Scottish Green-veined White is usually single brooded, flying in June and July. Elsewhere it can be seen at any time between late April and late September in two generations, peaking in late May and late July/early August. There may be an occasional third emergence in September, although this is very unusual.

Larval foodplants and habitat requirements
As for the British Green-veined White (p. 99).

Identification characters
Apart from the differences in the scent scales already described (see p. 98), this subspecies differs from the British Green-veined White in the following respects, particularly in the female:

1. Hindwing underside deeper and brighter yellow, sometimes even tinged with orange.
2. Upperside with dark markings more extensive and more heavily suffused with black. This suffusion often extends to the spaces between the veins.
3. There is a much higher incidence of cream- or yellowish-tinged individuals.

Fig. 76 Scottish Green-veined White underside. Loch Creran, West Inverness-shire

In general appearance this and the Irish subspecies are very similar but the latter usually lacks the brighter yellow of the hindwing underside and the upperside markings are more heavily suffused with black.

Field tips
As for the British Green-veined White (p. 99).

Regional prime sites
Scotland. To see the Scottish Green-veined White, a trip to Scotland is advisable as the distribution in northern England is not clearly understood at the present time. In the north, it is known to occur in Caithness around **Scrabster** and **Thurso** (ND 110 680). Further south, in West Inverness-shire, it is plentiful at **Glasdrum Wood** (NM 998 453) and **Eas na Circe** (NM 005 443). It is known to be widespread in **West** and southern **Mid-Perthshire**, **Fifeshire** and **Stirlingshire** and

Scottish Green-veined White / Bath White

throughout the **Isle of Arran** in the Clyde Isles. Further research will undoubtedly find it to be far more widespread than is suggested here.

Northern England. Distribution unclear at present.

Other regions. Absent.

Bath White
Pontia daplidice (Linnaeus)

Status
Scarce immigrant. The Bath White is a very scarce visitor to the British Isles and in most years it is not recorded. There have been occasional times of relative abundance but these are few and far between. In mainland Europe, it is a common resident in the Mediterranean region and as far north approximately as northern France in the west to Poland in the east. It is noted as a migrant from further north into Fennoscandia.

Distribution of records
The great majority of records come from the southern counties of England as far north as East Gloucestershire in the west and South Essex in the east. There are old records, mainly of singletons, from East Norfolk, East Suffolk, Leicestershire, Warwickshire, Northamptonshire and Shropshire in England, Pembrokeshire in Wales and South Kerry in Ireland. It was common in the Channel Isles in 1945 but appears not to have been recorded there since. From 1850 to 1939, there are about 40, mainly single, records apart from in 1872 when some 35 were seen, and 1906 when upwards of 200 were reported at Durdle Door in Dorset. Between 1944 and 1950, it was seen every year with a remarkable influx in 1945 when there were approximately 700 records, the majority in East and West Cornwall and the Channel Isles. Since 1950, there have been perhaps 15 reports, though some of these cannot be substantiated. The most recent confirmed sighting is from Levin Down, West Sussex, in 2000. In recent decades (apart from 1945) most records come from East and West Kent and South Hampshire.

Flight period
Abroad, the Bath White flies between late February and October in two or

Fig. 77 Bath White. Spain (R. Nesbit)

three broods. In Britain, most sightings have been between July and October, but in 1946 (following the invasion of the previous year) four individuals were seen during April and May, suggesting that successful overwintering had taken place.

Larval foodplants
In Britain, eggs have been found on Wild Mignonette, Hedge Mustard and Sea Radish.

Habitat requirements and field tips
This highly mobile butterfly may be seen in many habitat types but during the invasion of 1945 most were found along cliff tops and fields containing clovers and Lucerne. Abroad, it is often seen on roadside verges and waste ground.

Identification characters, variation and similar species
Average wingspan 50mm. The striking black and white markings on the upperside, particularly of the female, and the moss-green and white pattern on the underside preclude confusion with any other species apart from the female Orange-tip. The Bath White differs from that species in the following ways:

1. Forewing upperside with the black and white markings at the tip of the forewing more extensive and chequered in pattern; the black spot in the centre of the wing is much larger.
2. Female hindwing upperside with conspicuous black and white chequered pattern in outer third of wing.
3. Forewing underside with three conspicuous black spots, the foremost of which meets the leading edge of the wing; the green and white markings at the tip of the wing form a large and conspicuous chequered pattern.
4. Hindwing underside with the green markings much less dappled and more streaked in appearance; areas of green more extensive.

British Orange-tip
Anthocharis cardamines **(Linnaeus) subspecies** *britannica* **(Verity)**

Subspecies type locality and authority
Specimens from Barnwell Wood and Ashton Wold in Northamptonshire, Chattenden in West Kent and Ashdown Forest in East Sussex, England, were first described as a subspecies by Verity (1908). The nominate subspecies is widespread in mainland Europe but does not occur in the British Isles.

General distribution and status
Resident. This endemic subspecies of the Orange-tip is widespread and generally

British Orange-tip

Fig. 78 British Orange-tip male upperside. Stiffkey, West Norfolk

Fig. 79 British Orange-tip female upperside. Foulden Common, West Norfolk

common throughout England and Wales with the exception of exposed high ground. In Scotland, there has been a dramatic increase in the species' range since the 1940s and in the last 20 years the number of 10km squares in which it has been recorded has more than doubled (Asher *et al.*, 2001). It is still scarce in the far north and north-west and is absent as a resident species in the Outer Hebrides, and the Isles of Orkney and Shetland. It is widespread in the Isle of Man where it is represented by the Irish Orange-tip (p. 110) (Chalmers-Hunt, 1970) and in the Channel Isles it is present in Jersey but there are few records from elsewhere. In Ireland, the species is represented by the Irish Orange-tip (p. 110).

Flight period

There is usually one generation a year. In very warm springs, adults have been seen at the end of March but they usually begin to appear during the third week of April; the males emerge about a week before the females. The flight period usually continues until mid-June, though this varies considerably according to spring temperatures and, in very warm years, it may end as early as the end of May. In England, the optimum time to see the Orange-tip is usually during the last three weeks of May. Adults are occasionally seen in August and September and these probably constitute a partial second emergence. In Scotland, the flight period is from mid-May to early July with a peak during the first two weeks of June.

Larval foodplants

Cuckooflower is the usual chosen foodplant in damp meadows and Garlic Mustard is used in other habitats. Dame's Violet, a common garden escape, is used frequently. A wide variety of other cruciferous plants have been recorded.

British Orange-tip

Habitat requirements
The Orange-tip frequents many types of habitat including roadside verges, hedgerows, woodland edges and their wider rides, damp meadows and gardens.

Identification characters, variation and similar species
Average wingspan 45mm. Many aberrant forms have been recorded but all are very scarce. The large orange spots on the forewings of the male make confusion with other species extremely unlikely, even on the wing, and they can be identified confidently at some distance. It is not wise to attempt flight identification of the females as they can appear similar to Small and Green-veined Whites. However, close views will reveal the characteristic dappled green and white pattern that is evident on the underside of the Orange-tip. A similar pattern is present on the underside of the extremely scarce Bath White and the reader is referred to that species (p. 105) for a description of the diagnostic features.

Field tips
The male Orange-tip is a common and welcome sight in the spring along roadsides and in meadows and gardens. They emerge about a week before the females and, during this time, are very active and difficult to observe at close quarters. During the peak of the flight period the butterflies are far more

Fig. 80 British Orange-tip male underside. Fakenham, West Norfolk

British Orange-tip

approachable particularly during the early, cooler part of the day. The males tend to range widely but the females are more sedentary and spend most of their time in the vicinity of the foodplants where their priority is egg-laying. While so engaged they make short flights in search of suitable host plants and, upon landing, can be examined closely and photographed readily. As the female usually lays only one egg on each plant before flying to the next, the camera should always be ready for action as only a short time will be available at each stop.

Regional prime sites
Scotland. With the exception of the Highlands this species is widespread and common north to a line approximately between West Inverness-shire in the west and East Ross in the east. The rapid expansion of the butterfly's range in Scotland makes identification of the northernmost sites difficult and unreliable. Even so, it is now well established and can be seen easily on the **Black Isle** in East Ross (e.g. in the **Fortrose** area at NH 725 565) in the north-east of its range and at **Allt Mhuic**, West Inverness-shire (NN121 912) in the south-west.

Western and eastern Ireland.
Represented by the Irish Orange-tip (p. 110).

Fig. 81 British Orange-tip female underside. Whipsnade Downs, Bedfordshire

British and Irish Orange-tip

Other regions. Widespread and common throughout with the exception of the mountain tops of Wales and those in the English Lake District of Westmorland and Cumberland.

Irish Orange-tip
Anthocharis cardamines subspecies *hibernica* (Williams)

Subspecies type locality and authority
Specimens from Ireland were first described as a subspecies by Williams (1916), though no specific locality is given.

General distribution and status
Resident. Widespread and common throughout Ireland and, according to Chalmers-Hunt (1970), the Isle of Man.

Flight period
The usual flight period is from the end of April to mid-June with the optimum time to see the subspecies during the last three weeks of May.

Larval foodplants and habitat requirements
As for the British Orange-tip (p. 106).

Identification characters, variation and similar species
Average wingspan 42mm, although this is rather variable. Other forms of variation are very rare. The Irish Orange-tip differs from the British subspecies as follows:

1. Average wingspan slightly smaller.
2. Upperside fringes with the black spots larger.
3. Male forewing underside with the white area between the thorax and the orange patch strongly tinged yellow.

Fig. 82 Irish Orange-tip male upperside.
Lough George, Co. Clare

Fig. 83 Irish Orange-tip female upperside.
Boston, Co. Clare

Irish Orange-tip

Fig. 84 Irish Orange-tip male underside.
Lough George, Co. Clare

Fig. 85 Irish Orange-tip female underside.
Ballydoogan Bog, South-east Galway

4. Female hindwing upperside strongly tinged yellow.
5. Female hindwing underside with green markings usually darker and more intense.

Regional prime sites

Western and eastern Ireland. It is widespread and common throughout Ireland and should be expected in any damp meadows or roadsides.

North-west England (Isle of Man). Chalmers-Hunt (1970) states that the Orange-tip is represented throughout the Isle of Man by this subspecies but more research is needed to clarify the situation there.

Other regions. Absent.

Purple Hairstreak

The Hairstreaks
(Lycaenidae, subfamily Theclinae)

Green Hairstreak
Callophrys rubi (Linnaeus)

General distribution and status
Resident. Localized but widespread in most of the British Isles but absent from the Isle of Man, Outer Hebrides and the Isles of Orkney and Shetland. It is widespread and locally common in the Channel Isles. The Green Hairstreak is usually inconspicuous and therefore probably more common than is presently assumed. Colonies are usually small, but annual numbers vary and, in some years, the species can be abundant at some sites.

Flight period
There is one generation a year, flying between late April and the end of June. The optimum time to see the species in England is during the last two weeks of May and the first week of June. In Scotland, the flight period peaks slightly

Fig. 86 Green Hairstreak. Stiffkey, West Norfolk

Green Hairstreak

later and the last week of May to the second week of June are most reliable.

Larval foodplants
In Scotland, and on moorland elsewhere in the British Isles, the main foodplant is Bilberry, known in northern districts as Blaeberry. On calcareous grassland, Common Rockrose and Common Bird's-foot Trefoil are the most favoured species and Gorse, Broom and Dyer's Greenweed are utilized elsewhere. Other foodplants are used occasionally.

Habitat requirements
The Green Hairstreak can be found on calcareous grassland, heathland, moorland, bogs, disused quarries and railway lines, neglected scrubland, coastal cliffs and, less commonly, woodland rides and clearings (Figs. 8, 13, 14, 16 and 18). In Scotland, it is more or less restricted to moorland dominated by Bilberry and here can be found on sheltered parts of the moors, at woodland edges and in the vicinity of scrub vegetation. Similar habitats are used in much of northern England and Wales and occasionally elsewhere. Whatever the chosen habitat, hawthorn bushes appear to be a favoured component as these are an important source of nectar and also provide shelter and territorial perching places for the males.

Identification characters, variation and similar species
Average wingspan 30mm. The sexes are very similar but the males have a small patch of scent scales on the leading edge of the forewing. When freshly emerged this patch is dark grey but, as the scales are shed after a few days on the wing, it appears yellowish brown and can sometimes be seen during flight. Otherwise it is not generally visible as the wings are always held closed during rest or feeding. Variation is limited to the development of the line of white spots on the underside. In some specimens this may be almost absent, whereas in others it can be very bold and conspicuous. The Green Hairstreak is the only butterfly found in the British Isles that has a green underside and confusion with other species is therefore unlikely.

Field tips
The behaviour of the sexes is very different. Males spend much of their time holding territory, perched waiting for passing females or other males. They actively pursue any butterfly or other flying insect that comes too close and, if another male Green Hairstreak is encountered, a lengthy and frenetic confrontation ensues. During these the original perch is sometimes lost to a third male and so the process continues for the remainder of the day. The most favoured sites for this behaviour are bushes, such as hawthorn, situated at the base of a hill, bank or slope and these are used traditionally year after year. Once such a location has been identified future sightings of the butterfly should be guaranteed. The females are far less conspicuous in their habits and are usually seen flying just above the ground or low vegetation as they search for suitable plants on which to lay their eggs.

Green Hairstreak

They often stop briefly to feed from flowers such as Tormentil or hawkweeds. When so engaged, their colour and erratic flight make them difficult to spot but, on chalk downland, scanning through binoculars from the top of a slope will often bring rewards. Both sexes feed avidly from hawthorn blossoms and it is here that the best photographic opportunities present themselves as a very close approach can be made.

Regional prime sites

Scotland. Absent from the Outer Hebrides and Orkneys and Shetlands but otherwise widespread on moorlands throughout most of the country. It is scarce or very localized in the Highlands and the far north. In East Sutherland, it is common at the RSPB reserve at **Loch Fleet** (park at NH 806 958 and explore the links area to the east). In the west, it can be seen frequently along the marked footpaths at **Allt Mhuic** in West Inverness-shire (visitor centre at NN 121 912) and, in the east, it is present in good numbers at **Tentsmuir Forest**, Fifeshire (park at NO 499 242 and search the area to the north at approximately NO 500 268). It is widespread in the **Glen More Forest Park** of East Inverness-shire and usually common there at **Tulloch Moor** (NH 965 164). In the south-west, it is present at **Feoch Meadows** in Ayrshire (NX 263 816).

Northern England. Found throughout the region with the exception of the extreme south-west, most of the extreme south-east and the highest ground of the Lake District. It is found in good numbers at **Arnside Knott** (SD 453 774) and **Meathop Moss** (SD 447 821), Westmorland (at the latter site it can be abundant) and at **Ellerburn Bank**, North-east Yorkshire (SE 853 848) and **Stock Beck Moor**, Mid-west Yorkshire (SE 194 747). A visit to Ellerburn Bank could be coupled with a search of nearby **Pexton Bank** (SE 852 860) where the species also occurs. Although the Green Hairstreak is absent from most of the south-east of the region, it is plentiful on the **Spurn Peninsula** in South-east Yorkshire (TA 416 155).

Central England. Very scarce and localized in the north-eastern quarter of the region but widespread elsewhere. In the northern part of the **Derbyshire Dales**, it can be seen throughout the area and many suitable moorland habitats may be visited south of the A628 north-east of Glossop (SE 19). In the west, it is common in Shropshire on the moorlands of **The Stiperstones** (track north from SO 365 976) and in the **Wyre Forest** (particularly along the disused railway and the Dowles Brook area to the south-west of the car park at SO 762 777). In the east of the region, it is common at **Twyford Wood** (SK 947 238) and **Twywell Hills** in Northamptonshire (explore the Whitestones area north of the car park at SP 945 775).

Eastern England. Restricted almost entirely to the eastern half of the region. In the north, it is seen in good numbers at **Covenham Reservoir** (TF 339 963)

Green Hairstreak

and **Gibraltar Point** (TF 556 581) in North Lincolnshire. It is widespread and common along the coast of West and East Norfolk where it can be found, for example, amongst hawthorn scrub at **Holme-next-the-Sea** (access from TF 697 439) and **Walsey Hills** (TG 062 441). In West Norfolk, it can be very common at **Leziate Country Park** (TF 675 198). In East Suffolk, the butterfly can be seen reliably at **Walberswick** (TM 493 742) and **Wortham Ling** (TM 088 797) and in North Essex is present at **Fingringhoe Wick** (TM 041 195).

South-east England. On the northern boundary of the region with eastern England, it is seen commonly on the chalk grassland of **Whipsnade Downs** in Bedfordshire (SP 999 085) and, further south, is frequent on many of the extensive sandy heaths of Surrey such as **Chobham Common** (SU 965 653). In the far south-east, it occurs regularly at **Lydden Down** in East Kent (TR 277 453) and, in the south-west, may be expected in small numbers in scrubby areas containing gorse and hawthorn throughout the **New Forest**, South Hampshire (SU 20/30). In North Hampshire, there are strong colonies at **Magdalen Hill Down** (SU 505 292) where some 30 individuals or so may be seen on a single visit in good years… with luck!

South-west England. In the east of the region, the Green Hairstreak can be found at **Prestbury Hill**, East Gloucestershire (park at SO 994 248 and walk south along the minor road to explore the reserve to the west at SO 992 242), **Brown's Folly** (ST 793 660), **Thurlbear Quarry** (south-west from parking at ST 273 211) and **Walton Common** (ST 428 738), North Somerset, and **Ballard Down**, Dorset (from just north of the lay-by at SZ 022 808 walk east along the south-facing slope). Further west, in South Devon, it is found at **Little Breach** about 1km south-east of Nicholashayne (park at ST 109 154 (Purchase Farm); follow the bridleway north from opposite the turning for Woodgate and explore the area around Little Breach Wood). In East Cornwall, a reliable site is at **Penlee Point** (access from SX 436 493) and, in the south-west, it is frequent at **Penhale Sands**, West Cornwall (park at SW 767 587 and search the edges of the dunes to the south at approximately SW 767 570), but be aware that this is Ministry of Defence land and there is no access to some areas).

Wales. Any areas of light scrub or sheltered valleys in the extensive areas of moorlands throughout Wales should be searched for this butterfly as it is widespread here. In the north of the country, it is seen regularly at **Lake Trawsfyndd** in Merionethshire (park at SH 707 346 and take the track south-west to the ruined farmhouse at SH 702 341 and search the area around the old orchard). In the south-west, it can be seen at **Pengwern Common** in Glamorgan (access from SS 531 916) and on the dunes at **Pembrey Country Park**, Carmarthenshire (SS 405 005). In the south-east, it is common near **Pen-ffordgoch Pond** in Monmouthshire (walk south from the car park at SO 255 107 and search the sheltered gullies towards Blaenavon). In central Wales, the species is rather under-recorded but is known to be present along the public footpath on the south side of **Llangrannog** in Cardiganshire (SN 315 542).

Western Ireland. The Green Hairstreak is widespread in the far south-west of the region and can be expected to be seen on most of the Bilberry-dominated moorlands and bogs of South Kerry and West Cork. It is very common on **Cape Clear Island**, West Cork (V 965 215). In the north, it can reliably be seen at **Cashel Bog**, Sligo (G 502 084) and **Lettermore** in East Donegal at G 849 831.

Eastern Ireland. There are widely scattered records from the region but the species is fairly common on the scrubland at **Craigavon Lakes**, Down (park at J 060 580 and search the causeway between the lakes). Further south, it is found in Wicklow at **Oldboley's Wood**, Glencree (O 155 162).

Brown Hairstreak
Thecla betulae (Linnaeus)

General distribution and status

Resident; protected from sale (GB). The strongholds of the Brown Hairstreak are on the clay soils of Surrey, Oxfordshire, Buckinghamshire and West Sussex, the sheltered valleys and woodlands of North and South Devon, South Somerset, Cardiganshire and

Fig. 87 Brown Hairstreak female.
Bernwood Meadows, Buckinghamshire

Fig. 88 Brown Hairstreak underside.
Bernwood Meadows, Buckinghamshire

Brown Hairstreak

Carmarthenshire and the Burren limestone district of Clare and Southeast Galway in Ireland. Outside these areas, colonies are few, often small, and widely scattered. Its northerly limit is reached in North Lincolnshire, although it occurred in the late 19th and early 20th century in Cumberland and Westmorland. It has not been recorded from the Isle of Man or the Channel Isles. The species declined greatly in range and abundance during the 20th century. It is thought that this was due mainly to loss of hedgerows (nearly 60 per cent have been destroyed since the end of the Second World War) and the continued practice of indiscriminate mechanical flailing of hedgerows which can destroy every egg laid thereon.

Flight period
There is one generation a year which flies typically between late July and mid-September, although some individuals may survive until early October. The best time to see the species is during the second and third weeks of August.

Larval foodplants
Blackthorn is the usual foodplant, although Bullace is occasionally used.

Habitat requirements
Hedgerows, woodland edges and scrubland are the favoured habitats where Blackthorn is not intensively managed or trimmed (Fig. 15). The females lay most of their eggs at the junction of one- and two-year-old branches or at the base of a bud or spine and such sites are vulnerable where frequent trimming occurs. Blackthorn thickets and hedgerows that are seemingly under-managed therefore provide the best habitats. The cutting of hedgerows on a sectional three-year rotation basis and reinstatement of the traditional practice of hedge laying have proved successful in areas managed specifically for this species. The focal point of activity in most colonies appears to be woodland edges as, although the females range widely, it is here where certain individual trees known as 'master trees' are found. These, often Ash, are always taller than neighbouring trees and their canopy provides a necessary home for the first ten days of the adult female's life as this is where mating takes place and where she will feed on aphid honeydew until her eggs have matured. It is only then that she leaves the canopy in search of potential egg-laying sites. The males remain at the tops of the trees, also feeding on honeydew, and are only rarely seen at lower levels.

Identification characters, variation and similar species.
Average wingspan 40mm. The male lacks the bright orange patches that are so conspicuous on the upperside of the female forewings. Significant variation is very rare. The orange patches of the female should preclude confusion with other species. In Meadow Browns there is a similar, though far less bright, orange patch but a prominent white-pupilled eye-spot is also present. The golden fuscous ground colour and striking black and white cross-lines on the underside of both

Brown Hairstreak

sexes of the Brown Hairstreak are diagnostic. On the rare occasions that a male is seen flying low it could possibly be confused at a distance with a small dark male Meadow Brown, but closer examination will reveal the brightly coloured underside and the absence of the eye-spot. Further, the flight is typical of the hairstreaks and is far more jinking and less flapping than that of the Meadow Brown.

Field tips

The Brown Hairstreak is notoriously secretive and often difficult to see. Unless one knows the exact locality of a site, the best time to start searching suitable habitats is during the winter, after the Blackthorn bushes have lost their leaves. At this time the conspicuous white eggs can be found. Against the very dark bark of the host plant these are surprisingly easy to locate if one knows where to look. Most are laid at a height of less than two metres and almost always at the junction between one- and two-year-old branches or in the joint between the older branch and a spine or bud insert (Fig. 89). An hour or so of searching should be ample to confirm the presence of the species at the locality, and time spent in this way may save many frustrating hours trying to spot the secretive adults later in the year. Having successfully found a site, it should be visited again during the first three weeks of the following August. The butterflies are inactive at temperatures below about 20°C and so a warm sunny day should be chosen. An hour or so either side of noon is the best time during which to

Fig. 89 Brown Hairstreak egg. Bernwood Meadows, Buckinghamshire

search. The observer should stand far enough back to give as wide an angle of view as possible. The use of binoculars for scanning the hedgerow is not recommended as too small a section of the hedge is then in view at any one time. With luck a female Brown Hairstreak will in time appear but quickly settle on the Blackthorn. Its position should be noted carefully (perhaps now using binoculars) and a swift approach should find the settled butterfly. Here it may stay basking for a few moments with its wings apart but, before long, will crawl crab-like into the bush in search of a place to deposit an egg. A short flight to the next chosen Blackthorn then usually takes place and the process is repeated. Later in the day, or towards the end of the flight period when all the eggs are laid, one may be fortunate enough to find a female feeding from the flowers of thistles, Hemp Agrimony, Common Fleabane or Bramble. Males confine themselves

Brown Hairstreak

almost exclusively to the canopy of the 'master' tree and the only views one might expect of them would be through binoculars or a field telescope. On the extremely scarce occasions when they fly at lower elevation they may be seen visiting those flowers listed above.

Regional prime sites
Scotland and northern England. Absent.

Central England. Extremely localized and restricted to one small area in the south of the region where it can be found at **Grafton Wood**, 1km south-east of the village of Grafton Flyford, Worcestershire, (park near the church at SO 963 557 and walk along the path east for approximately 1km to the wood).

Eastern England. Very localized and restricted to a few sites in North Lincolnshire, most of which have restricted, or no, public access. The best chance of finding the butterfly in this region is at **Chamber's Farm Wood** (park at the visitor centre at TF 149 739 and explore the tracks to the north-east). The most reliable place at this site is at the intersection of paths known as 'Five Ways'. Local information is available at the visitor centre.

South-east England. It is very localized in the north of the region but fairly common at **Bernwood Meadows**, Buckinghamshire (park in the official car park at SP 606 111 and search the hedgerows on the opposite side of the field and the thickets to the south-eastern end of the public footpath). In neighbouring Oxfordshire it can also be seen readily at **Whitecross Green Wood** (SP 600 150). In the south of the region, the species is widespread on the clay soils of Surrey, eastern South Hampshire and West Sussex and occurs in good numbers at **Noar Hill**, North Hampshire (SU 741 320). In Surrey, it can be seen in the River Mole valley, just west of **Horley**, at TQ 268 422.

South-west England. Widespread through the central part of the region and seen in fair numbers at **Lydlinch Common**, Dorset (south-west to **Brickles Wood** from ST 737 137), **Thurlbear Quarry**, South Somerset (south-west of the parking space at ST 273 211), **Witch Lodge**, approximately 5km south-east of Taunton, South Somerset (ST 246 201) and **Preston Down**, Paignton, South Devon (from SX 890 624 search the downland edges to the north-west).

Wales. Widespread in the south-western third of the country and seen reliably at **West Williamston** in Pembrokeshire (SN 028 058) and at the **Welsh Wildlife Centre** in Cardiganshire (SN 183 448).

Western Ireland. More or less restricted to the limestone district of the Burren in Clare and South-east Galway, though there are occasional records from elsewhere. Perhaps the easiest places to see the species are in Clare along the minor roads to the west and south-west of **Boston** where large stands of Blackthorn occur (e.g. R 350 980) and at **Dromore Wood** (R 365 870).

Eastern Ireland. Absent.

Purple Hairstreak
Neozephyrus quercus (Linnaeus)

General distribution and status

Resident; fully protected (NI). Widespread and common throughout southern England and Wales, becoming more locally distributed further north. In Scotland, it is restricted to the south-western corner of the country and to the Central Lowlands. In both areas it is locally fairly common. In Ireland, it is found mainly in the hillside oak woodlands between the counties of Wicklow and South Kerry with small scattered colonies elsewhere. It is absent from the Isle of Man and widespread and common in the larger Channel Isles. The Purple Hairstreak spends most of its time at the tops of Oak and Ash trees and therefore can be difficult to see. This has certainly led to it being under-recorded throughout the British Isles as, where it is known to occur, it is often very common and sometimes abundant.

Flight period

Single brooded, flying between early July and early September in the south and late July to mid-September in the north. The optimum viewing time is during the last week of July and the first week in August in southern localities and the second and third weeks of August in Scotland.

Larval foodplants

Any species of oak is suitable; the most commonly recorded are the native Sessile

Fig. 90a Purple Hairstreak female.
Holkham, West Norfolk

Fig. 90b Purple Hairstreak male.
Northamptonshire (A. McLennan)

Purple Hairstreak

Oak and Pedunculate Oak. Turkey Oak and Evergreen Oak are also frequently used.

Habitat requirements

Typically a denizen of deciduous woodlands where it spends the majority of its time out of view in the canopy (Fig. 12). However, it can also be found in parks and on commons and heaths where smaller clumps of oaks are present and even along hedgerows where a colony may be supported by a single mature tree. The butterflies feed almost exclusively on aphid honeydew and, apart from oaks, frequently visit Ash, elms and Alder in search of this resource.

Identification characters, variation and similar species

Average wingspan 36mm. Variation from the typical form is rare. This species can often be seen flying around the treetops with the White-letter Hairstreak and both feed on honeydew on Ash and elms. The Purple Hairstreak is slightly larger and, particularly in sunshine, has a flashing silver and black appearance, the White-letter Hairstreak being distinctly duller. At rest the silver-grey underside of the present species is very distinctive in comparison with the greyish-brown ground colour of the White-letter Hairstreak. Good quality binoculars are recommended for accurate separation of these two species, although, with practice, this can be accomplished with the naked eye. Occasionally the Purple Hairstreak is seen in the company of the Black Hairstreak, but the smaller size and distinctive golden brown ground colour of the latter should prevent confusion.

Field tips

Following prolonged dry periods, the Purple Hairstreak will sometimes fly at low elevations, seeking honeydew on saplings or bracken fronds. It can also occasionally be seen on the ground where it appears to search for minerals in the manner of the Purple Emperor. Yet these are unusual events and the species will almost always be found flying around the tree canopy. Providing one is observant, it is not difficult to find and the best places to try are where tall oaks and Ash or elms grow together, as here the butterfly has both its host plant and an important nectar source in close proximity. With patience, and a good pair of binoculars or field telescope, success should follow; optical aids are usually needed if the butterflies are to be enjoyed to the full. The peak of activity appears to be on warm evenings between 6.30 and 7.30pm, but this is not habitual and for some reason does not occur every day. When it does, the views can be spectacular with dozens, if not hundreds, of individuals displaying their characteristic jinking and flashing flight.

Regional prime sites

Scotland. In the Central Lowlands, it is seen in Stirlingshire along the edges of **Mugdock Wood** in Mugdock Country Park (e.g. NS 545 764). In West Perthshire, it occurs on the north bank of **Duchray Water**, north-east of Duchray Castle (NN 487 003) and in Argyll Main, it can be found in good numbers at **Eredine** (NM 971 094). In the south-west, it is present in **Mabie Forest** (NX 950 708), Kirkcudbrightshire, and **Wood**

Purple Hairstreak

Fig. 91 Purple Hairstreak underside. Holkham, West Norfolk

of Cree (NX 382 709) in Wigtownshire.

The Purple Hairstreak might be expected in oak woodlands throughout most parts of England and Wales but the following sites are recommended as starting points.

Northern England. **Arnside Knott**, Westmorland (SD 453 774), **Wheldrake Ings**, South-east Yorkshire (access from SE 690 448) and **Goldsborough Great Wood**, Mid-west Yorkshire (SE 398 567).

Central England. **Anderton Nature Park**, Cheshire (SJ 649 753), **Wyre Forest**, Shropshire (SO 767 777), **Salcey Forest**, Northamptonshire (SP 810 509) and **Ufton Fields**, Warwickshire (SP 378 615).

Eastern England. **Chamber's Farm Wood**, North Lincolnshire (TF 145 744), **Gallow Hill** and **Great Hockham**, West Norfolk (TF 910 415, TL 934 923, respectively), **Horsford Woods** and **Hickling Broad**, East Norfolk (TG 192 183, TG 428 221, respectively) and **Brampton Wood**, Cambridgeshire (TL 185 698).

South-east England. **Bernwood Forest**, Buckinghamshire (SP 611 117), **Harpenden Common**, Hertfordshire (TL 138 129), **New Forest**, South Hampshire (e.g. **Pondhead Inclosure** (SU 308 070) or the woodlands around **Standing Hat** (SU 315 037)), **Oaken Wood**, Surrey (SU 993 339), **Ashdown Forest**, East Sussex (TQ 42 32) and **Hamstreet Forest**, East Kent

Purple Hairstreak / White-letter Hairstreak

(TQ 988 346).

South-west England. **Thurlbear Quarry** (south-west of parking at ST 273 211) and **Langford Heath** (north-west of parking at ST 107 226), South Somerset, **Lydlinch Common**, Dorset (ST 737 137), **Yarner Wood**, South Devon (SX 79 79), **Marsland Valley**, North Devon (SS 218 172) and **Godolphin Wood**, West Cornwall (SW 602 321).

Wales. **Lake Vyrnwy**, Montgomeryshire (SJ 016 190), **Ynys-hir**, Cardiganshire (SN 678 963) and **Pontycymer Woodland Park**, Glamorgan (SS 90 90). At **Nicholaston Wood**, Glamorgan (SS 522 881) there are excellent opportunities to see the butterfly at head height as the oak trees here are small, rising up the cliffs from the dunes. In the south-western corner of the country, it is very localized but may be viewed at the **Welsh Wildlife Centre** in Cardiganshire (SN 183 448).

In Ireland, any of the hillside oak woodlands between South Kerry and Wicklow may hold this species, and searches there are certainly worth trying. The following sites are recommended: *Western Ireland*. **St John's Wood**, near Rinnagar, Roscommon (M 998 559) and **Cratloe Wood**, Limerick (R 491 609).

Eastern Ireland. **Glen of the Downs**, Wicklow (O 261 113).

White-letter Hairstreak
Satyrium w-album (Knoch)

General distribution and status
Resident; protected from sale (GB).

Fig. 92 White-letter Hairstreak. Holkham, West Norfolk

Widespread and locally common in England, south of a line approximately between South Lancashire in the west and South Northumberland in the east, and in Wales, east of a line approximately between Denbighshire in the north and Glamorgan in the south. It is absent from the Isle of Man and Ireland. In the Channel Isles, it is present in low numbers in Jersey and there is an old record of its occurrence in Alderney. During the 1970s and 1980s, this species' larval foodplants were hit severely by Dutch Elm disease, and there was great concern over the future of the butterfly, particularly as it was

White-letter Hairstreak

thought at the time that mature flowering elms were required for the early development of the larvae. Further research has revealed that this is not the case, and the species is able to thrive on the leaves of regenerative sucker growth. The secretive nature of this butterfly has undoubtedly led to under-recording; it is probably more common than is often assumed.

Flight period

Single brooded, flying during July and August, though high spring temperatures can advance this by up to two weeks. The optimum time to see the species is during the second and third weeks of July. The males emerge approximately a week before the females, and both can be seen around the breeding trees for about a further week after which they often disperse or are predated.

Larval foodplants

Several species and cultivars of elm are used, including Wych, English and Small-leaved Elm. There appears to be a preference for the first. It is also able to utilize the disease-resistant cultivated form of the Dutch Elm, *Ulmus japonica*, known as 'Sapporo Autumn Gold' (Asher *et al.*, 2001).

Habitat requirements

The White-letter Hairstreak can be found on woodland edges and rides, sheltered hedgerows and around large isolated elms, though the last mentioned are a rare sight in today's English countryside. The favoured sites are where flowering elms occur in and around woodlands.

Identification characters, variation and similar species

Average wingspan 30mm. Variation is very rare. When seen settled, the distinctive well-defined white 'W' on a dull greyish-brown ground colour will easily separate this species from the otherwise similar Black Hairstreak. In the Black Hairstreak the 'W' on the underside of the hindwings is poorly defined, there is a row of black spots along the inner edge of the orange marginal band and the ground colour is a rich golden brown. In flight, the two are sometimes very difficult to separate without the use of binoculars, but the overall golden colour of the Black Hairstreak can be discerned with practice. White-letter and Purple Hairstreaks are often seen flying around the same trees; their identification characters are discussed under the latter species (p. 121).

Field tips

Although flowering elms are no longer thought essential for larval development, the White-letter Hairstreak still appears to show a preference for sites containing such trees. With this in mind, searches for suitable localities should begin during late winter and early spring when the elms are conspicuously in bloom. Their mass of pinkish flowers can easily be seen at some distance and even by casual observation during car journeys (Fig. 93). Once located, these sites should be revisited regularly during the flight period and, with luck, the butterflies will be found performing their distinctive jinking flights around the crowns of the trees. They spend most of their time in the canopy

White-letter Hairstreak

Fig. 93 Flowering elms. Titchwell, West Norfolk

feeding from aphid honeydew, but the males can often be seen in aerial combat silhouetted against the sky. They sometimes feed on the nectar of flowers such as Creeping Thistle, brambles, Wild Privet and Hogweed, and where these plants are present near a known colony they should be inspected regularly. The best parts of the day for watching the butterfly feeding at flowers are during the early morning and late afternoon, although they may do so at any time. Searches at around 9am and 5pm are recommended. When engaged in this feeding activity they are very approachable but, if disturbed, their flight is rapid and erratic and they are easily lost from view. The butterfly always rests with its wings closed.

Regional prime sites

Scotland. Not recorded since 1885 and therefore probably extinct.

Northern England. There appears to have been a northward expansion of the species' range in recent years. Some of this perceived expansion may be due to increased recording effort following the attack of Dutch Elm disease during the 1970s and 1980s when there was concern over the butterfly's future. It is seen regularly at **Roundhay Park** in Leeds, Mid-west Yorkshire (SE 331 377) and at **Potteric Carr** in South-west Yorkshire (park at SE 589 007 and walk south-east to the reserve).

Central England. In the north, it is frequent at **Rivacre Valley**, Cheshire where elms grow near the stream along the B 5132 (SJ 384 778) and at **Mattersey Wood**, Nottinghamshire (park at SK 672 887 and walk northwards to the south-east edge of the wood at SK 669 892). Also in Nottinghamshire it is present at **Bunny Old Wood** (SK 579 283). In the centre of the region, it is widespread in the **Wyre Forest**, Shropshire, and should be looked for in the Dowles Brook area (park at SO 767 777 and follow the rides south). The species can also be found in Shropshire in the woodlands surrounding the **Wrekin** (e.g. the **Limekiln Wood** west of Steeraway Farm at SJ 654 096). Further south, in Warwickshire, it is found at **Ufton Fields** (the official car park at SP 378 615 is only available on Sundays but otherwise the reserve has open access). In Leicestershire, it can be seen at **Willesley Wood** (SK330 141), and in Northamptonshire it is present in good numbers at **Fermyn Wood** (park at SP965 859 and follow the main ride south to the elms at the first cross-track).

White-letter Hairstreak / Black Hairstreak

Eastern England. At **Weelsby Woods**, North Lincolnshire (TA 286 075), the species is present in good numbers; it can also be found near the entrance to **Bourne Woods** in South Lincolnshire at TF 076 201. In West Norfolk, it is seen regularly feeding at Wild Privet blossom near the large birdwatching hide west of Lady Anne's Drive in **Holkham Meals** (TF 891 448) and along the cycleway to **Gallow Hill** (TF 910 415).

South-east England. Localized but widespread and might be expected wherever there is suitable habitat with suckering elms. It can reliably be seen at the north-east end of the RSPB reserve at **Northward Hill** in East Kent (TQ 784 764) and at **Barton Hills**, Bedfordshire (TL 085 303). In Middlesex, it is present at **Horsenden Hill** (TQ 163 845).

South-west England. Absent from the south-west of the region, although found at a few sites in South Devon such as **Bovey Valley Woods** (SX 783 793). In South Wiltshire, it is present in **Bentley Woods** (park at SU 258 292 and follow the main ride west and then north to approximately SU 250 298), in South Somerset it can usually be seen at **Witch Lodge** (ST 246 201), whilst in North Somerset it is frequently seen at **Weston Big Wood**, south-west of Portishead (ST 456 750).

Wales. In Denbighshire, it is found in good numbers at **Rhyd y Gaseg** along the single ride running east-west through the wood (SJ 111 565) and in the open glades of **Loggerheads Country Park** at SJ 197 627. Here the 'Butterfly' or 'Top' Glade appears to be the most favoured area. Further south, in Glamorgan, it can be seen in **Bishop's Wood** (SS 594 877).

Western and eastern Ireland. Absent.

Black Hairstreak
Satyrium pruni (Linnaeus)

General distribution and status
Resident; protected from sale (GB). This is a very localized species which is restricted to English woodlands on the heavy clay soils in a band stretching between Cambridgeshire in the north-east and Oxfordshire in the south-west. It was once very common at a site in Surrey, where it was introduced in 1952, but it has not been recorded there since 1990. In 2004, it was seen at a site in

Fig. 94 Black Hairstreak. Glapthorn Cow Pasture, Northamptonshire

Black Hairstreak

North Lincolnshire but this is thought to have originated from an unauthorized introduction. The butterfly is often very secretive in its habits and this makes accurate estimates of its current status difficult. At the present time, it is thought to be found at as few as 45 localities (Asher *et al.*, 2001) but at some of these it is common. It has never been recorded from the Channel Isles.

Flight period
The Black Hairstreak has a very short flight period between mid-June and early July; the most reliable time to see the butterfly is during the last week of June.

Larval foodplants
The most commonly used plant is Blackthorn, though other *Prunus* species, including Bullace, are utilized occasionally.

Habitat requirements
Dense Blackthorn thickets along sheltered sunny woodland edges, rides and clearings (Fig. 95) and sheltered hedgerows are the favoured localities (Fig. 15). Egg-laying usually takes place in unshaded situations with a south or south-westerly aspect and well-established stands of the foodplant are essential. The species has high habitat fidelity with weak powers of dispersal so that colonies are discrete and hence easy to overlook.

Identification characters, variation and similar species
Average wingspan 36mm. Major variation is rare. Because the butterfly spends most of its time high in the tree canopy, good quality binoculars are recommended for accurate identification. It can sometimes be seen flying with White-letter and Purple Hairstreaks and the relevant taxonomic characters are discussed under those species (p. 124; 121).

Field tips
The Black Hairstreak can be very difficult to find, as the majority of its time is spent high in the tree canopy where it feeds, in rather lazy fashion, on aphid honeydew. When doing so it tends to walk rather than fly but, with patience and a good pair of binoculars, it can be spotted amongst the foliage of Ash or Field Maple. During cool or dull weather, it is particularly inactive and will often remain motionless for long periods. Mating takes place from around noon to about 2pm; this is when the peak of flight activity takes place. Even so, individual sorties are usually brief, fast and erratic. Fortunately, the species has a liking for the nectar of Wild Privet and, to a lesser extent, Dog Rose and when feeding at these flowers it can be approached closely and with confidence. Consequently, the best way to see the Black Hairstreak is to find Privet bushes that are in bloom in a sunny situation close to a Blackthorn thicket and simply wait (Fig. 95). The middle of the day is the best time to visit and excellent opportunities to photograph the underside of the butterfly should present themselves. This species always settles with its wings closed.

Black Hairstreak

Regional prime sites
Central England. The Northamptonshire Wildlife Trust reserve at **Glapthorn Cow Pasture** (TL 006 903) is an excellent site to see this species. Here it regularly visits flowers of Wild Privet that grows commonly at some of the ride intersections (Fig. 95).

Eastern England. Good numbers can be seen at **Brampton Wood** in Cambridgeshire (TL 185 698). In 2004, the species was recorded at **Chamber's Farm Wood**, North Lincolnshire (TF 149 739). This was almost certainly the result of an unauthorized introduction but, whilst not condoning such action, it will be interesting to monitor the butterfly's future there.

South-east England. In Buckinghamshire, the species is fairly common in **Bernwood Meadows**, most notably in the Blackthorn thickets at the western edge of York's Wood (SP 610 110). Good numbers are also present at nearby **Whitecross Green Wood** (SP 600 150). Visitors to the latter site should take great care not to trample the rideside vegetation, as this will damage the breeding areas and the eggs and larvae of the Wood White. Also in Buckinghamshire, the butterfly is common at **Finemere Wood** (park at SP 721 210 and follow the track for 500m to the wood).

Other regions. Absent.

Fig. 95 Dense blackthorn thicket with flowering Privet at Glapthorn Cow Pasture, Northamptonshire

Small Copper

The Coppers
(Lycaenidae, subfamily Lycaeninae)

Small Copper
Lycaena phlaeas (Linnaeus) subspecies *eleus* (Fabricius)

Subspecies type locality and authority
Specimens from Germany were first described as this subspecies by Fabricius (1798), though no specific locality is given. The nominate subspecies is widespread throughout mainland Europe but does not occur in the British Isles.

General distribution and status
Resident. This species is widespread and common throughout most of the British Isles south of a line approximately between southern West Inverness-shire in the west and eastern East Ross in the east. Here it might be expected in all but the more mountainous districts, although it is absent from most of the Western Isles of Scotland and from the Shetlands. In Ireland, it is widespread and fairly common but probably under-

Fig. 96 Small Copper upperside. Holkham, West Norfolk

Small Copper

recorded. Here it is represented by the Irish Small Copper (p. 134). Populations in the Isle of Man also appear to conform to the Irish subspecies, though further research is required to confirm this. It is widespread and common in the Channel Isles. There is evidence of a decline in the species' abundance since the start of the 20th century but it remains a common butterfly throughout most of its range despite great variation in annual numbers.

Flight period
In most of England and Wales there are at least three generations a year flying between late April and the end of October or even early November. The first brood peaks during the last two weeks of May and the second during the first two weeks of August. A third occurs in September and early October and, on rare occasions, a fourth emergence takes place in early November. In northern England and Scotland there are usually two generations. In the south of the region, the first brood flies between early May and late June, peaking during the last week of May and the first week of June, and in the north it is on the wing between mid-May and mid-July, peaking during the second and third weeks of June. The second generation is seen most commonly during the second and third weeks of August in the southern part of its range and in the north it peaks during the last week of August and the first week of September. A third emergence is very rare but may occur during late September and early October.

Larval foodplants
The most common foodplants are Common Sorrel and Sheep's Sorrel. There are occasional records of Broad-leaved Dock being used. Colonies on the coastal shingle of parts of north Norfolk have recently been found to be utilizing Curled Dock.

Habitat requirements
The Small Copper occurs in a wide variety of habitats, including unimproved grassland, moorland and heathland, woodland rides and clearings, coastal dunes and undercliffs, roadside verges, field edges and set-aside, allotments and waste ground. Open sunny situations are preferred and these will usually contain small bare patches and flowers on which the adults can bask and perch during territorial behaviour. In the spring, the females require large sorrel plants in tall vegetation whereas small young plants in sparser sward are chosen in the summer.

Identification characters, variation and similar species.
Average wingspan 30mm. The Small Copper should not be mistaken for any other species found in the British Isles. As a general rule, the forewings of the male are more pointed than those of the female. The spring generation is generally brighter with less black suffusion on the forewings than specimens from later broods. This is a very variable species with many named forms, perhaps the more spectacular being form *schmidtii* Gerhard, where all of the usual copper colour is replaced with white, and form

Small Copper

fuscae Robson, in which the copper areas are heavily and extensively suffused with black. A fairly common form (particularly in the north of Scotland where it may comprise around a half of some populations) has a row of blue spots along the submargin of the hindwing upperside and is known as *caeruleopunctata* Rühl. Thomson (1980) describes a form which he believes to be a geographical race found in central and northern Scotland where the dark outer band of the forewing upperside is narrower than usual and the copper areas are clear of any black suffusion. The copper colour in the band on the hindwing is said to often radiate towards the base of the wing. He does not give this form a name and no further work appears to have been done to clarify its status. The Small Copper is unlike any other extant British or Irish species, and the differences between this and the Irish subspecies are discussed on p. 134.

Field tips

The Small Copper is a very active butterfly, the males vigorously defend territories from selected favoured perches where they bask with their wings open, offering good photographic opportunities. They fly rapidly to intercept any other butterfly that approaches too close and will even on occasion investigate human 'intruders'. If another male Small Copper is encountered a frenetic confrontation takes place that will sometimes lead to the two flying some distance from the original spot and occasionally not returning. However, if a different species is involved, the Small

Fig. 97 Small Copper underside. Holme, West Norfolk

Copper almost invariably returns to its original perch. Flowers of the daisy family (Compositae) are most commonly used for the look-out posts and, in suitable habitats, these plants should be watched for such activity. The females behave differently and are less active. They are most often seen flying low over the vegetation as they search for sorrel plants on which to lay eggs. They settle frequently to inspect potential host-plants and are then fairly easy to observe despite the fact that they tend to walk continuously over the leaves in an apparently erratic way as they 'taste' the plant for suitability. This can be frustrating for the photographer as the viewing angles change again and again.

Regional prime sites

Scotland. Absent from the Highlands, the north-west, the Outer Hebrides and the Shetland Islands. Elsewhere it is widespread and found frequently in suitable habitats.

Small Copper / Irish Small Copper

Northern England. Absent from many mountainous areas but otherwise widespread and fairly common.

Eastern England. Widespread and common apart from in the intensively cultivated areas of South Lincolnshire and Cambridgeshire where it is scarce or absent.

Western and eastern Ireland. Represented by the Irish Small Copper (see below).

Other regions. Widespread and common.

Irish Small Copper
Lycaena phlaeas subspecies *hibernica* Goodson

Subspecies type locality and authority
Specimens from Kerry, Ireland, were first described as a subspecies by Goodson (1948), though no specific locality is given.

General distribution and status
Resident. This endemic subspecies of the Small Copper is widespread throughout Ireland and is likely to be met within any suitable habitat. The few specimens from the Isle of Man examined by the author also appear to conform to this subspecies but study of a larger sample is required for confirmation.

Flight period
There are at least two generations a year flying from early May to late June and late July to late September. The optimum times to see the butterfly are during the last week of May and the first week of June and the last two weeks of August. A third brood might be expected in early October in favourable years.

Larval foodplants and habitat requirements
As for the Small Copper (p 131), but there appears to be no record of the species using Broad-leaved Dock or Curled Dock in Ireland.

Identification characters, variation and similar species
Unlike any other extant species found in the British Isles and differs from the typical Small Copper in the following ways:

1. Hindwing upperside with copper-coloured band broader.
2. Hindwing underside ground colour much greyer and less brown in shade; orange band brighter and more conspicuous.
3. Forewing underside with marginal band much greyer.

The whitish form *schmidtii* Gerhard has been recorded occasionally.

Irish Small Copper

Fig. 98 Irish Small Copper upperside.
Boston, Co. Clare

Fig. 99 Irish Small Copper underside.
Boston, Co. Clare

Field tips
As for Small Copper (p. 131).

Regional prime sites
The Irish Small Copper may be expected in appropriate habitats throughout Ireland but the following sites are useful examples for the first-time visitor.

Western Ireland. Widespread in the Burren district of Clare and South-east Galway but most often found on disturbed or rough ground rather than on the exposed limestone itself. Good examples of such ground are the grazed meadows on the southern shores of **Lough George**, Clare (R 375 924), the viewing point at **Black Head**, Clare (M 135 125) and the lane near the creamery some 0.75km north of **Dingle**, South Kerry, at approximately Q 460 019. Further north, in West Donegal, the species can be found around the golf course near **Clooney** (G 725 990).

Eastern Ireland. In the south, in Wexford, it can be seen beneath the coastal undercliffs at **Rosslare** (T 145 130), in the coastal dunes at the **Raven National Nature Reserve** (T 110 250) and in the open sandy areas around **Carnsore Point** (Y 125 040). Further north, it is present on the rough grassland at **Craigavon Lakes**, Down (park at J 060 580 and search the causeway between the lakes). Any of the golf course edges on the **Ards Peninsula**, Down, are also worth a search (J 60 50).

Other regions. This may be the representative subspecies in the Isle of Man but this needs confirmation. Here the butterfly is widespread and fairly common.

Silver-studded Blue

The Blues
(Lycaenidae, subfamily Polyommatinae)

Long-tailed Blue
Lampides boeticus (Linnaeus)

Status

Scarce immigrant. The Long-tailed Blue is recorded almost annually but usually only as single individuals. Several consecutive years may pass without the species being seen. 1945 and 1990 were the only years of relative abundance, and the first confirmed instance of a 'home-bred' generation occurred in the latter of these two years. There are several reported cases of larvae being imported from continental Europe with vegetable produce such as Mangetout Peas, and many recorded butterflies may originate from such sources. Its superficial resemblance to more common butterflies may have led to the Long-tailed Blue being overlooked by casual observation. The species cannot survive the winter climate of the British Isles. In western Europe, its main breeding grounds are around the Mediterranean from where it migrates northwards each spring through central Europe as far north as France, Germany and The Netherlands. It is absent from Denmark and Fennoscandia.

Distribution of records

A single specimen was seen at Ardrossan, Ayrshire, in 1881 and this remains the only Scottish record (Thomson, 1980). It has not been reported from Ireland or the Isle of Man. Apart from scattered sightings from as far north as Caernarvonshire, Cheshire and Derbyshire, the Long-tailed Blue is rarely seen away from the southernmost counties of England with

Fig. 102 Long-tailed Blue male upperside. Spain

Fig. 103 Long-tailed Blue female upperside. Spain

Long-tailed Blue

a strong bias towards those in the south-east. It is recorded frequently in the Channel Isles. The species was first recorded in the British Isles in 1859 when two were seen on Brighton Downs, East Sussex, and one at Christchurch in South Hampshire (Salmon, 2000). It was not reported again until 1878 and by 1944 fewer than 40 had been recorded in total. 1945 saw the first large-scale immigration of the species with 38 records from West Sussex, South Hampshire and Dorset. In 1952, eggs were found on Broad-leaved Everlasting Pea in a garden in Surrey, but the first instance of successful breeding in Britain did not occur until 1990. During that year, some 100 individuals were recorded in the London area and a second generation was produced. Because their progeny cannot survive a British winter, subsequent annual reports have dropped to the usual frequency of one individual or none.

Flight period
In the Mediterranean region the species is continuously brooded. In the British Isles, it has occasionally been reported earlier, but the majority of records occur during August, September and October with a single late record during November.

Larval foodplants
In Britain, eggs and larvae have been found on Broad-leaved Everlasting Pea, Narrow-leaved Everlasting Pea, Broom and Bladder Senna. Larvae are found almost annually on imported beans and peas, and adult butterflies from such origin have been recorded on several occasions. In mainland Europe, the species has been found feeding on a wide variety of wild and cultivated leguminous plants.

Habitat requirements
Abroad, the species frequents a wide variety of hot nectar-rich habitats. In Britain, it has been recorded mainly from gardens or open downland. Butterflies seen during the large immigration of 1990 occurred in such diverse places as a cemetery, a park and on Ranworth Common in Surrey.

Identification characters, variation and similar species
Average wingspan 37mm. The female appears much darker than the male, as the blue is restricted to only the central part of the forewing and the basal third of the hindwing, the rest of the wings being dark brown. Those of the male are almost entirely purplish blue. On open downland it often flies in company with

Fig. 104 Long-tailed Blue underside.
Spain

Long-tailed Blue / Geranium Bronze

other blues but its large size and generally dark colouration should prevent confusion with all species other than the Common Blue. The Long-tailed Blue has a characteristic rapid jerky flight pattern not unlike that of a hairstreak and this should immediately warrant closer inspection. In other habitats it may be confused with the Holly Blue, but the flashes of silver from the undersides of that species in flight are not evident in the Long-tailed Blue. When settled, the distinctive pale brown and cream lines of the underside and the long 'tail' on the hindwing are diagnostic.

Field tips
Scarce though this species undoubtedly is, its similarity to other blues has almost certainly led to a degree of under-recording. Consequently, during a hot late summer with periods of southerly winds, an observer on the English south coast should always be aware of its possible presence. Extra care should then be taken to examine all blue butterflies seen in gardens, allotments, parks, wastelands and downs where potential foodplants are known to grow. Particular attention should be paid to gardens where Sweet Pea is cultivated as these would almost certainly be of interest to a passing egg-laying female.

Geranium Bronze
Cacyreus marshalli Butler

Status
Introduction. To date this species has only been recorded as an accidental importation on cultivated geraniums. Its status as a horticultural pest following its inadvertent introduction into parts of

Fig. 105 Geranium Bronze upperside.
Spain

Fig. 106 Geranium Bronze underside.
Spain

Geranium Bronze

southern Europe and its subsequent rapid range expansion warrants the species' inclusion here. At present, its foodplants are unable to survive the British winter and are usually protected indoors. However, adaptation to feed on related native plants coupled with climate amelioration may see this situation change. Abroad, the species is established in the Balearic Islands, Spain, France, Italy, Portugal and the Canary Islands. Its usual home is in southern Africa. It is not renowned for its powers of dispersal, and its future occurrence in the British Isles is therefore probably reliant on accidental introduction.

Distribution of records
Several adults were recorded near Lewes, East Sussex, in 1997, and egg-laying was seen in two gardens in the area (Asher *et al.*, 2001). In 1998, three adults emerged in the same district from overwintered geranium plants; a further individual was seen in a nearby garden (Asher *et al.*, 2001). There are further confirmed records from Portland, Dorset, and Little Paxton, Huntingdonshire, in 2001, and Gwithian, West Cornwall, in 2002.

Flight period
In southern Europe, the species appears to be continuously brooded. In East Sussex, it was recorded between September and November and again in February and May.

Larval foodplants
It is restricted to geraniums of the genera *Pelargonium* and *Geranium*. In Europe only the former has so far been recorded as a host-plant.

Habitat requirements
Abroad, the species is most often found in gardens, parks and roadsides where geraniums are planted. It may be found wherever these plants are grown; breeding has even been recorded in window boxes.

Identification characters, variation and similar species
Average wingspan 20mm. The sexes are similar, though the female has slightly more rounded and ample wings and is slightly larger than the male. The uniform bronze-brown upperside, white and dark brown chequered wing fringes, distinctive striped underside and long 'tail' on the hindwing prevent confusion with other species.

Field tips
The Geranium Bronze is most likely to be encountered in gardens where geraniums are cultivated. Once the butterflies emerge they tend to be rather sedentary and remain close to the foodplants. Any small dark butterfly with a low lazy flapping flight seen in such circumstances should be inspected carefully. If it is identified as this species the Department for Environment, Food and Rural Affairs (DEFRA) should be contacted immediately (see Appendix II). The males are more active than the females, their flight pattern resembling that of a hairstreak.

Small Blue
Cupido minimus (Fuessly)

General distribution and status

Resident; protected from sale (GB); fully protected (NI). In Scotland, northern England, Wales and most of Ireland, the Small Blue is found mainly in coastal localities, although a few inland sites exist. It is absent from the Isle of Man, the western and northern isles of Scotland and the Channel Isles. The species is found most commonly on the chalk and limestone grasslands of central southern England. Populations are usually small and discrete, though there are some large colonies in which the butterfly is abundant. It appears to be generally in decline throughout its range and, during the 20th century this led to its extinction in most of northern England. Even in some of its former strongholds in the south, such as those on the North Downs of Surrey, numbers have fallen dramatically. This decline appears to have been caused mainly by agricultural intensification and urban development; however, losses on managed nature reserves have occurred in recent years and these may be due to unchecked natural vegetative succession.

Flight period

Usually single brooded, flying from late May until late June with the optimum time for seeing the butterfly during the first two weeks of June. In southernmost

Fig. 107 Small Blue upperside. Portland, Dorset

Small Blue

Fig. 108 Small Blue underside. Portland, Dorset

localities there is a partial second emergence during late July and August. The best chance of seeing it is during the second week of August. In northern Scotland, it flies somewhat later with a peak during the last two weeks of June.

Larval foodplants
The larvae feed solely on Kidney Vetch.

Habitat requirements
The Small Blue requires warm sheltered situations where Kidney Vetch is common (Figs. 8 and 14). These may be on chalk, limestone or coastal grasslands or dunes, woodland clearings and coastal undercliffs. Man-made habitats such as golf courses, quarries, disused railway lines and roadside cuttings, verges and embankments are also frequented. It requires a mixture of short turf in which the foodplant can grow amongst bare patches of ground, longer grasses in which to roost and small areas of shelter formed by light scrub. It appears to do best on disturbed ground where patches of exposed soil, in which the foodplant can reproduce successfully, are created by erosion or the activities of rabbits and other animals.

Identification characters, variation and similar species
Average wingspan 21mm. The female lacks the dusting of pale blue scales found at the base of the males' wings. Significant variation is rare. This is the smallest resident butterfly in Britain and Ireland and its tiny size and dark colouration make confusion with other species unlikely.

Field tips
In a known general locality one should try to find areas where Kidney Vetch grows in abundance: its large pale yellow flower-heads are conspicuous and easy to spot (Fig. 109). The host plant blooms from late April, and likely habitat can therefore be sought before the butterfly's flight period and noted for later inspection. The males spend most of their time perching and basking, though they do not appear to be actively territorial. Several can often be seen sharing the same grass tussock or shrub, and specific perches do not seem to be chosen and defended by each individual. Other small butterflies and female Small Blues are intercepted as they approach the perching sites; it is here that mating takes place. These sites are usually found at the foot of a south-facing slope and can sometimes be a considerable distance from where the

Small Blue

foodplant grows. Having mated, the females rarely return to them and thereafter spend most of the rest of their lives basking amongst the foodplant, feeding and laying eggs. Both sexes usually bask with their wings held half-open and flights are invariably short and low to the ground. In late afternoon and early morning, and during dull weather, the butterflies can be found at communal roosts. Here they rest head down some 50cm above the ground on the stems of taller grasses and herbaceous plants. Small Blues can often be seen feeding from the flowers of Kidney Vetch, Common Bird's-foot Trefoil, and Horseshoe Vetch, and the males regularly visit mud patches, animal droppings and carrion.

Regional prime sites

Scotland. Restricted to the eastern side of the country where it is mostly coastal in distribution. In the north, it occurs along the coast at **Dunnet Head** in Caithness (from the Visitor Centre at ND 218 705 search the area north adjacent to the beach at about ND 218 718). Further south, it is fairly widespread along the coast of the Moray Firth and can be seen in good numbers at the Scottish Wildlife reserve at **Lein of Garmouth** in Moray (NJ 333 657). Nearby, in East Inverness-shire, there is an inland colony just east of **Boat of Garten** along the verges of the B970 at NH 952 190, although numbers have dropped in recent years and hence it can probably no longer be regarded as reliable there. On the east coast, the species can be found at **Seaton Cliffs**, Angus (park at NO 658 412 and follow the nature trail north-east). There is a single known site in the south of the country but it is not considered appropriate to publish its whereabouts.

Northern England. It is now found only in Cumberland. Here it can be seen near the marina at **Maryport Harbour** (park at NY 029 363 and search the area between the sea wall and the sandhills) and at **Workington** where it inhabits the area below the wind turbines at NX 995 303.

Central England. Very scarce; most site owners have understandably asked that the locations are not publicized. However, Hill & Twist (1998) note that public access is available at **Ufton Fields** in Warwickshire (SP 378 615).

Eastern England. There is a single isolated colony near Newmarket, Cambridgeshire, at **Devil's Dyke** (on

Fig. 109 Kidney Vetch. Narborough, West Norfolk

Small Blue

the roundabout at the junction of the A1303 and A1304 take the turning signposted for the National Stud, park at the end of the road near Gate 3 and follow the marked footpath north-west from TL 617 613). On the border with south-east England it is fairly common in Bedfordshire at the base of the northern part of **Whipsnade Downs** (TL 008 197), **Sewell Cutting** (TL 994 228) and the western section of **Totternhoe Knowles** (SP 986 217).

South-east England. Of scattered distribution throughout the region on calcareous grassland. In Hertfordshire, it is very common at **Upper Sundon Quarry** (TL 045 275). In Oxfordshire, it is present in large numbers at **Swyncombe Down** (park at SU 666 914 and follow the path through the wood to the top of the down to approximately SU 678 915, though one must keep to the paths as much of this site is privately owned) and, at **Greenham Common** in Berkshire, it can be found in the vicinity of the control tower car park (SU 499 651). In Surrey, it has declined over much of the North Downs but can still be seen in suitable areas of **Epsom Downs** (access at TQ 218 587). In the east of the region, it is found in East Kent at **Western Heights**, Dover (TR 313 410) and **Lydden Down** (TR 277 453). In the south of the region, it can be seen in good numbers at **Pitt Down**, South Hampshire (SU 418 293) and on the coastal chalk grasslands around **Compton Down** in the Isle of Wight (SZ 366 855). It is very common along Bokerley Ditch on **Martin Down**, South Hampshire (1km south-west of the car park at SU 058 192).

South-west England. The butterfly is absent from Cornwall and most of Devon, but in North Devon it may still be present at **Braunton Burrows** (SS 463 351)(although it has not been recorded there since 2003) and, in South Devon, it is found at **Lummaton Quarry**, Torquay (SX 913 665). In the north of the region, it is present at **Prestbury Hill**, East Gloucestershire (SO 993 248) and **Stoke Camp** (park at ST 486 513 and walk 300m east to the reserve entrance at ST 489 512) in North Somerset. It is plentiful in many of the disused quarries at Portland in Dorset (e.g. **Broadcroft Quarry** at SY 697 720) and, in the same county, it is common on **Ballard Down** (from just north of the lay-by at SZ 022 808 follow the path east along the south-facing slope).

Wales. Present only in coastal localities in the south of the country, for example in Glamorgan at **Kenfig** (grassland west and south-west of the visitor centre at SS 802 810) and **Whiteford Burrows** (park at SS 440 935 and walk north through the reserve).

Western Ireland. Very common in the limestone district of the **Burren**, Clare, and South-east Galway, and can be expected here in most sheltered localities where the foodplant is abundant.

Small Blue / Short-tailed Blue

Eastern Ireland. In the north, it is seen in good numbers at **North Bull Island**, Dublin (O 234 360) and in the south, in Wexford, along the coastal edge of the **Raven NNR** at T 110 250 and in the dunes and grassy undercliffs near **Rosslare Harbour** (T 140 129).

Short-tailed Blue
Everes argiades (Pallas)

Status

Scarce immigrant. The Short-tailed Blue is amongst the rarest immigrant species recorded in the British Isles. There are fewer than 20 reliable sightings, all of which come from the counties of southern England. Abroad, the species ranges westwards from northern Spain through most of central and southern Europe northwards to a line approximately between northern France in the west and the Baltic states in the east. It occurs in southern Scandinavia as a scarce migrant.

Distribution of records

A specimen was recorded from Blackpool, West Lancashire, in around 1860, but doubt has been expressed regarding its authenticity (Emmet & Heath, 1989). In 1874, a pair were caught at Frome, North Somerset, but were not identified correctly for several years (Salmon, 2000). The first official record was of a male and female caught at Bloxworth Heath in Dorset in 1885; it was from this locality that the original name of 'Bloxworth Blue' came from (Salmon, 2000). In the same year, a specimen was caught near Bournemouth on the Dorset/South Hampshire border. Subsequent records can be summarized as follows: Wrington, North Somerset,

Fig. 110 Short-tailed Blue upperside.
France (W. Powell)

Fig. 111 Short-tailed Blue underside.
France (W. Powell)

Short-tailed Blue / Silver-studded Blue

1895 or 1896; New Forest, South Hampshire, 1921; Framfield, East Sussex, 1931; Falmouth, West Cornwall, St Austell, East Cornwall, Branksome and Peveril Point, Dorset, 1945; Purbeck coast, Dorset, 1952; Rogate, West Sussex, 1958 and Beachy Head, East Sussex, 1977. In 1994, there was a record from Kent and, in 1998, it was reported from Derbyshire and Warwickshire. Unfortunately, the authenticity of these last three records cannot be confirmed. In the Channel Isles it has been recorded twice, in 1942 and 1944.

Flight period
In mainland Europe, the species is double brooded, flying during May and June and again from July to September. All of the English records are of second generation individuals.

Larval foodplants
Several species of leguminous plants are used abroad, including some that are common in the British Isles such as Common Bird's-foot Trefoil, Red Clover and Tufted Vetch.

Habitat requirements
It is usually found in flower-rich meadows, downland, heaths and woodland edges and clearings.

Identification characters, variation and similar species
Average wingspan 25mm. The upperside of the male is almost entirely violet blue, whereas the female is predominantly dark brown with only a slight blue suffusion near the base of the wings. In flight, the species could easily be overlooked as the Small Blue or Silver-studded Blue with which it may share similar habitats. When settled, the short but conspicuous 'tails' on the hindwings are diagnostic.

Field tips
The chances of finding a specimen of this extremely scarce immigrant are slim but its similarity on the wing to the Silver-studded Blue and Small Blue may have led to a degree of oversight. There-fore, on southern English grasslands and commons during August and September, whenever possible, check carefully every dark blue butterfly encountered.

The Silver-studded Blue group
Plebejus argus (Linnaeus)

Introductory notes
In the British Isles, there are presently three recognized subspecies of the Silver-studded Blue which differ in appearance from the typical form. Their subspecific status requires more detailed examination as some authorities believe their validity is questionable (e. g. Emmet & Heath, 1989). Recognition and study of these geographically isolated forms is important for the conservation of genetic diversity and their distinct external morphology

warrants inclusion in this book. For these reasons, and in order to comply with current nomenclature, their status as subspecies is hereby maintained. For detailed accounts of the ecological requirements and conservation of this highly localized species, the reader is referred to the works of Thomas *et al.* (1999), Joy (1995), Ravenscroft (1990) and Thomas (1985).

Silver-studded Blue
Plebejus argus subspecies *argus* **(Linnaeus)**

General status and distribution

Resident; protected from sale (GB). The Silver-studded Blue is locally common in parts of southern and eastern England. Elsewhere the species is extremely localized with many colonies isolated and vulnerable to extinction. It is extinct in most of central and northern England and Scotland and, in Wales, is restricted mainly to the north and south of the country. It is absent from Ireland and the Isle of Man and, in the Channel Isles, is present only on Sark. The species' main habitat is acid heathland and up to 60 per cent of this was lost during the last century through neglect, agricultural intensification and urban development. Although this trend may have slowed, the butterfly is still under threat in many areas and is considered generally to be in decline. On the Great Orme, Caernarvonshire, it is represented by the Western Silver-studded Blue (p. 156), in Shropshire by the Northern Silver-studded Blue (p. 153) and at Portland, Dorset, by the Southern Silver-studded Blue (p. 152).

Flight period

The usual flight period for this single

Fig. 112 Silver-studded Blue male upperside. Chobham Common, Surrey

Fig. 113 Silver-studded Blue female upperside. Arne, Dorset

Silver-studded Blue

Fig. 114 Silver-studded Blue male underside. Kelling, East Norfolk

Fig. 115 Silver-studded Blue female underside. Arne, Dorset

brooded species is throughout July and August with an optimum period for seeing the butterfly during the last two weeks of July and the first week of August. Populations in north Wales, including those of the Western Silver-studded Blue (p. 156), and eastern England emerge earlier; the best time to see these is during the last week of June and the first two weeks of July.

Larval foodplants
On acid heathland, the most commonly used foodplants are Heather, Cross-leaved Heath, Bell Heather and Gorse. On calcareous grassland, the species usually uses Common Rockrose, Common Bird's-foot Trefoil and Horseshoe Vetch.

Habitat requirements
Throughout most of its range the butterfly is usually associated with lowland acid heathland but can also be found on calcareous grassland and coastal dunes. On heathland, it requires short sparse vegetation where fire or other disturbance encourages fresh growth of the foodplants in open situations (Fig. 16). A great deal of work is currently being undertaken by conservation organizations to maintain and extend such habitats through scrub clearance and rotational burning regimes. On calcareous sites, it thrives on thin crumbling or eroding soils. In such situations, warm south-facing slopes and sheltered sun-traps are preferred.

Identification characters, variation and similar species
Average wingspan 29mm. The depth of violet hue and the width of the dark wing borders of the male can vary extensively, and the amount of blue on the female upperside is also variable. Such features are used to separate the other three subspecies of Silver-studded Blue and are discussed under their individual accounts.

Silver-studded Blue

Although the Silver-studded Blue could be confused with other species, there are certain key features that will offer immediate help. On heathlands, any blues seen flying low over the dominant vegetation are likely to be this species. On closer inspection, the rounded ample shape of the forewings will then allow for confident identification. In addition, examination of the hindwing underside should reveal a series of small silver-white dots along the outer edge of the orange markings that is present in most individuals; it is from this that the species derives its English name. It is possible to confuse the female with the Brown Argus or either sex with those of the Common Blue, but in both of these species there is a prominent white inward-pointing triangle in the centre of the outer third of the hindwing underside. Where Holly Blues occur on the edges of heathlands they can sometimes be seen flying low over the open vegetation and can then present problems in species recognition. However, as can be seen from Fig. 153, the underside of this species is quite unlike that of the Silver-studded Blue.

Field tips

Silver-studded Blues will fly in dull weather provided it is warm and fairly still, but windy conditions are not generally suitable for seeing the butterfly. On calcareous sites, it should be sought in sheltered spots such as small valleys and it has a distinct preference for south-facing aspects. During the late afternoon the species usually congregates in large numbers around short bushes or dense tussocks of grass in which the butterflies roost communally. If such places can be located and visited in the early morning, excellent opportunities to photograph the insects will be available as both sexes bask with their wings wide open. On heathlands there is little substitute for simply walking through the heathers and watching for the brightly-coloured males as they take off for their brief but frequent low exploratory flights. Attention should be directed towards areas containing taller vegetation that provides sites for perching and roosting.

Regional prime sites

Scotland and northern England. Absent.

Central England. There is one site in Shropshire where the species is represented by the Northern Silver-studded Blue (p. 153).

Eastern England. In East Norfolk, the species flies in good numbers at **Buxton Heath** (TG 172 220) and at the reintroduction site at **Kelling Heath** (near the railway level crossing at TG 102 415). In East Suffolk, it is common on **Westleton Heath** (TM 453 695).

South-east England. Widespread and common on the heathlands of the New Forest, South Hampshire (SU 20/30). There are also strong colonies on several of the Surrey heaths, including **Chobham Common** (SU 975 646), **Blackheath Common** (TQ 035 456)

Silver-studded Blue / Southern Silver-studded Blue

and **Thursley Common** (SU 900 417). In East Sussex, it abounds in the open areas of heathland adjacent to the many car parks in **Ashdown Forest** (visitor centre at TQ 432 325).

South-west England. In the east of the region, it is common in Dorset at **Studland Heath** (park at SU 034 835 and follow trails north-west) and at the RSPB reserve at **Arne** (SY 972 878). At **Portland**, also in Dorset, it is represented by the Southern Silver-studded Blue (see below). Further west, in South Devon, it can be found at **Start Point** (south-east along the coastal path from the car park at SX 821 377) and at **Bolt Head** (SX 713 376). In the far west of the region, Cornwall offers some interesting sites where the butterfly occupies three different habitats. In West Cornwall, it is common on the coastal heaths between **Botallack** (SW 363 337) and **Pendeen** (SW 378 355), and between **Riviere Towans** (SW 555 380) and **Gwithian Towans** (SW 579 413) it is abundant on the calcareous dune systems. At **Breney Common** in East Cornwall (SX 054 610) there is a strong inland heathland colony. Perhaps the best site in West Cornwall for this species is at **Cudden Point** (SW 552 278) where very large numbers can sometimes be found.

Wales. In the north, the butterfly has been the subject of several introduction schemes involving this subspecies and the Western Silver-studded Blue (p. 156). However, in Anglesey, the typical Silver-studded Blue occurs naturally on Holy Island at RSPB **South Stack** (SH 205 823 and the heaths to the south). In the south of Wales, the species is present at **St Govan's Head** in Pembrokeshire (north and east of the car park at SR 967 930), although much of this is Ministry of Defence land that is only open to the public at the weekends, and at **Stackpole Warren** (SR 992 958).

Western and eastern Ireland. Absent.

Southern Silver-studded Blue
Plebejus argus subspecies *cretaceus* Tutt

Subspecies type locality and authority
Specimens from Dover in East Kent, England, were first described as a subspecies by Tutt (1909).

General distribution and status
Resident; protected from sale (GB). Formerly locally widespread on the calcareous downland in parts of Kent, Surrey and Essex but these colonies are all now extinct. It is presently restricted to one locality in Dorset where it remains fairly common.

Southern and Northern Silver-studded Blue

Flight period
Single brooded, flying slightly earlier than the typical Silver-studded Blue, with a peak during the last week of June and the first two weeks of July.

Larval foodplants
The most commonly used plants are Common Bird's-foot Trefoil and Common Rockrose.

Habitat requirements
Restricted to warm sheltered parts of abandoned limestone quarries on thin soil where the foodplants grow next to bare ground or rocks (Fig. 9).

Identification characters
Individuals formerly found in south-east England were slightly larger than the typical subspecies, but this seems not to be the case with those from Dorset. The justification for subspecific status of the Dorset populations has consequently been called into question by some authorities (e. g. B. Skinner, pers. comm.). However, the brighter blue of the male forewings and the reduced width of their dark borders remain characteristic features of the Southern Silver-studded Blue.

Prime sites and field tips
South-west England. The abandoned limestone quarries of Portland in Dorset provide the ideal warm sheltered habitats for this butterfly and these should be searched. Perhaps the best-known is the Butterfly Conservation reserve at **Broadcroft Quarry** off Grove Road, Easton (SY 697 720).

Other regions. Absent.

Fig. 116 Southern Silver-studded Blue male upperside. Portland, Dorset

Northern Silver-studded Blue
Plebejus argus subspecies *masseyi* Tutt

Subspecies type locality and authority
Specimens from Witherslack Moss in Westmorland, England, were first described as a subspecies by Tutt (1909).

General distribution and status
Resident; protected from sale (GB). Formerly found on the mosses of Lancashire and Westmorland but has been extinct in the region since about 1947. However, a form conforming

Northern Silver-studded Blue

Fig 117 Northern Silver-studded Blue male upperside. Prees Heath, Shropshire

Fig. 118 Northern Silver-studded Blue female upperside. Prees Heath, Shropshire

closely to the Northern Silver-studded Blue can still be seen at one locality in Shropshire. Here the single small colony is surrounded by agricultural land and is under continuous threat from development.

Flight period
The optimum time to see the Northern Silver-studded Blue is during the last two weeks of July and the first week of August.

Larval foodplants
Mainly Cross-leaved Heath and Gorse.

Habitat requirements
The remaining colony inhabits a small piece of heathland where scrub clearance has been undertaken to increase the availability of suitable breeding areas (Fig. 121).

Fig. 119 Northern Silver-studded Blue male underside. Prees Heath, Shropshire

Fig. 120 Northern Silver-studded Blue female underside. Prees heath, Shropshire

Northern Silver-studded Blue

Identification characters
Differs from the nominate subspecies as follows:

1. Male upperside brighter blue with less violet tinge; dark border much narrower, revealing a clear row of black spots around the margins of the hindwings.
2. Male underside of most individuals much paler, chalky-grey.
3. Female upperside of many individuals with blue flush over most of hindwings and base of forewings.

Field tips and prime sites
Central England. The Northern Silver-studded Blue is restricted to a single locality at **Prees Heath** in Shropshire (Fig. 121) where the colony is situated immediately north of the small car parking area at SJ 558 365.

Other regions. Absent.

Fig. 121 Habitat of Northern Silver-studded Blue at Prees Heath, Shropshire

Western Silver-studded Blue
Plebejus argus subspecies *caernensis* Thompson

Fig. 122 Western Silver-studded Blue male **upside.** Great Orme, Caernarvonshire

Fig. 123 Western Silver-studded Blue female **upside.** Great Orme, Caernarvonshire

Subspecies type locality and authority
Specimens from the Great Ormes Head in Caernarvonshire, Wales, were first described as a subspecies by Thompson (1937).

General distribution and status
Resident; protected from sale (GB). Restricted to limestone areas of north Wales. The Western Silver-studded Blue remains common at its original home on the Great Orme and populations established using stock from this site in 1942 are still present in the area around Rhyd-y-foel. Three of these sites were visited by the author in June 2006, and the butterfly was found to be common and identical in appearance to those on the Great Orme.

Flight period
This subspecies flies up to a month earlier than the typical Silver-studded Blue. The best time to see it is during the last week of June and the first two weeks of July.

Larval foodplants
Mainly Common Bird's-foot Trefoil and Common Rockrose.

Habitat requirements
The butterfly is usually found on south-facing slopes, where the thin soil is prone to erosion, and in abandoned quarries (Fig. 9).

Identification characters
Differs from the nominate subspecies as follows:

1. Generally smaller (average wingspan 26mm).
2. Male upperside with dark borders usually much narrower.
3. Male underside usually paler.
4. Female upperside of many individuals with extensive blue flush on hindwings and base of forewings.

Western Silver-studded Blue / Brown Argus

Fig. 124 Western Silver-studded Blue male underside. Great Orme, Caernarvonshire

Field tips and regional prime sites
Wales. Strictly speaking, those wishing to see this subspecies should concentrate their efforts on the Great Orme, Caernarvonshire, as populations from this origin established elsewhere may be slightly different in appearance and behaviour as a result of differing environmental and selective influences. On the Great Orme, the Western Silver-studded Blue is common on the south-facing slopes to the north-west of **Llandudno** (take the footpath from Abbey Road 20m north-east of Abbey Court to SH 773 824), **Happy Valley** (SH 780 832) and in old limestone quarries such as that at **Great Orme Mine** (SH 763 831). Colonies established from Great Orme stock can be seen at the bases of the limestone cliffs around **Rhyd-y-foel** (e.g. at the original release site at SH 913 764). One should concentrate on areas where the yellow flowers of Common Rockrose are abundant.

Other regions. Absent.

Brown Argus
Aricia agestis ([Denis & Schiffermüller])

General distribution and status
Resident. Widespread and fairly common south of a line approximately between South-east Yorkshire in the east and South Devon in the west. Elsewhere in England there are scattered colonies in Derbyshire, North Devon and East and West Cornwall. In Wales, it is locally common in the north and south of the country but absent elsewhere. It is not found in Scotland, Ireland or the Isle of Man. In the Channel Isles, it is locally common but apparently absent from Guernsey. During the 20th century, the Brown Argus declined dramatically but during the 1990s an equally dramatic expansion of range began, particularly in the east and the north, and many areas have been newly colonized or recolonized after a long absence. The presence of set-aside areas on arable land is thought to have been greatly beneficial to this species.

Flight period
Over most of its range, the species is double brooded flying from early May

Brown Argus

Fig. 125 Brown Argus upperside.
Whipsnade Downs, Bedfordshire

Fig. 126 Brown Argus underside.
Whipsnade Downs, Bedfordshire

to the end of June, peaking during the last week of May and the first week of June, and again from mid-July to mid-September with a peak during the second and third weeks of August. In north Wales and parts of northern England, there are populations with only one generation, flying during June and July. The optimum time to see the butterfly here is during the last week of June and the first week of July. A partial second emergence during August and early September has occasionally been recorded at these northern localities.

Larval foodplants
On calcareous sites, Common Rockrose is the usual foodplant. In other habitats Common Stork's-bill and Dove's-foot Crane's-bill are the most commonly used plants, although several other species of Crane's-bill have been recorded.

Habitat requirements
This butterfly is traditionally associated with calcareous grassland, coastal dunes, heaths and open woodland rides and clearings (Figs 6, 8, 13 and 16). The recent range expansion has seen the species spread to roadside verges, disused railway lines and non-rotational set-aside land. On open grassland it thrives best where there is short turf on south-facing slopes with taller vegetation at their base to provide roosting sites. In other localities it requires sheltered areas with disturbed or exposed soil where its annual or biennial foodplants can regenerate.

Identification characters, variation and similar species
Average wingspan 28mm. The female has more prominent orange spots on the upperside – particularly on the forewing – where, in the male, they are often absent towards the tip. Major variation is rare. This species is similar to the Scottish subspecies of the Northern Brown Argus (p. 161) but lacks the prominent central white spot on both

Brown Argus

the upper- and underside of the forewings. It is also similar to the female Common Blue (p. 165) but invariably lacks the traces of blue that are almost always present near the base of the wings of that species. There is also a difference in the pattern of spots on the hindwing underside that is shown in Figs. 127a & b. Female Adonis and Chalkhill Blues share the same basic pattern of orange marginal spots on a dark brown background but both are much larger than the Brown Argus. It could easily be confused with the English subspecies of the Northern Brown Argus (see Castle Eden Argus, p. 163) but differs in the following ways:

1. Geographical range extends northwards only as far as Derbyshire in the west and North-east Yorkshire in the east. The southernmost limit for the Northern Brown Argus is West Lancashire and Mid-west Yorkshire in the west and Durham in the east. The two populations do not appear to overlap.
2. Upperside with orange spots usually much brighter and more conspicuous – particularly on the forewing.
3. Underside with black spots usually larger and more prominent.

Field tips
Towards evening, and during dull weather, the Brown Argus forms communal roosts on grass flower-heads and other tall vegetation at the base of south-facing slopes, sheltered hollows and in open woodland clearings. These are often shared with Common Blues. If such sites can be located and visited at around 8am, excellent photographic opportunities will be available as the butterflies bask in the early morning sun. During very warm weather these visits may have to be made earlier in the day.

Regional prime sites
Scotland. Absent.

Northern England. Very localized and

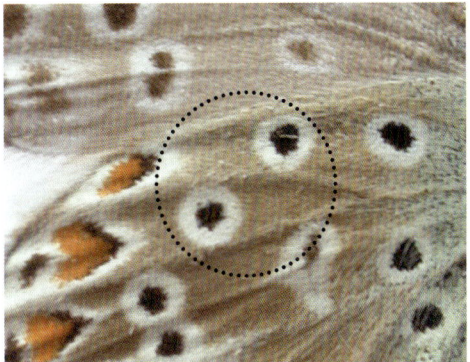

Fig. 127a Common Blue hindwing underside details

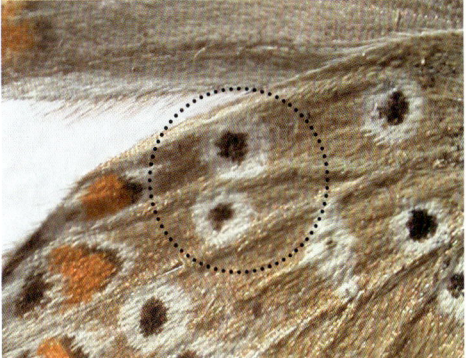

Fig. 127b Brown Argus hindwing underside details

Brown Argus

restricted to a few sites in Yorkshire. Here it can reliably be seen in North-east Yorkshire at **Ellerburn Bank** (SE 853 848) and nearby **Pexton Bank** (SE 843 850). In South-west Yorkshire, it is present at **Potteric Carr** (park at SE 589 007 and walk south-east to the reserve) and, in South-east Yorkshire, it can be found at **Thixendale** (SE 838 612) and along the **Spurn Peninsula** (access from the car park at TA 416 155).

Central England. In the north-western half of the region, it is very localized and restricted to only a few sites. It flies in fair numbers over the limestone at **Llanymynech** in Shropshire (SJ 266 221) and at **Lathkill Dale**, Derbyshire. One can approach the latter site from the west, parking at SK 157 665, or from the east at Over Haddon village (SK 203 664). In the south-east, the species is widespread and locally common and can be found at **Ufton Fields**, Warwickshire (SP 387 615), **Trench Wood**, Worcestershire (SO 925 587) and **Twywell Hills**, Northamptonshire (explore the Whitestones area north of the car park at SP 945 775).

Eastern England. Widespread and locally common. It can be found reliably at the following sites: **Risby Warren** (SE 929 144) and **Chamber's Farm Wood** (TF 149 739) in North Lincolnshire, **Devil's Ditch** (TL 617 613) and **Barnack Hills** (TF 074 048) in Cambridgeshire, **Foulden Common** (TL 765 999) and **Holkham Meals** (TF 891 448) in West Norfolk and the coasts near **Dunwich Heath** (TM 477 677) and **Landguard** (TM 285 315) in East Suffolk.

South-east England. Widespread and locally common. Some reliable sites are, for example, on the border with eastern England – the chalk downland of Bedfordshire such as **Whipsnade Downs** (TL 999 084), **Sharpenhoe Clappers** (TL 065 296), **Barton Hills** (TL 085 303) and **Totternhoe Knowles** (SP 986 217), **Aston Rowant**, Oxfordshire (SU 730 970), **Box Hill**, Surrey (TQ 182 523), **Malling Down**, East Sussex (access from the B2192 at TQ 434 115), **Lydden Down**, East Kent (TR 277 453) and **Magdalen Hill Down** (SU 505 292), and **Martin Down** (SU 058 192) in South Hampshire.

South-west England. Locally common in the eastern half of the region at sites such as **Prestbury Hill** in East Gloucestershire (SO 992 242), **Ubley Warren** (ST 505 557) and **Collard Hill** (ST 484 345) in South Somerset and **Hod Hill** (ST 852 112) and **Ballard Down** in Dorset (from just north of the lay-by at SZ 022 808 walk east along the south-facing slope). In the west, the species becomes more localized and is found most commonly at coastal sites such as **Braunton Burrows** in North Devon (SS 463 351), between **Prawle Point** and **Start Point** in South Devon (access from SX 802 372) and **Penhale Sands** (SW 767

570) in West Cornwall.

Wales. Restricted to the north and south of the country. In the north, it is present on the **Great Orme**, Caernarvonshire (SH 766 833) and **Eyarth Rocks**, Denbighshire (SJ 121 540). In the south, it can be found at **Whiteford Burrows** (SS 440 935) and **Oxwich Burrows** (SS 502 865), Glamorgan.

Western and eastern Ireland. Absent.

Northern Brown Argus
Aricia artaxerxes subspecies *artaxerxes* **(Fabricius)**

Subspecies type locality and authority
Specimens from Edinburgh in Midlothian, Scotland, were first described as a subspecies by Fabricius (1793).

General distribution and status
Resident; protected from sale (GB). This nominate subspecies of the Northern Brown Argus is found only in Scotland. Its distribution is very localized and restricted to the south-west and the eastern half of the country. Colonies are usually discrete and small and the butterfly is rarely seen in large numbers. In England, the species is represented by the Castle Eden Argus (p. 163).

Flight period
Single brooded, usually flying between early June and the end of July with a peak during the last week of June and first two weeks of July. This may be slightly later in the north, and, on north-easterly coastal sites, the flight peaks during the last three weeks of July.

Fig. 128 Northern Brown Argus upperside.
Port O' Warren, Kirkcudbrightshire

Fig. 129 Northern Brown Argus underside.
Port O' Warren, Kirkcudbrightshire

Northern Brown Argus

Larval foodplants
This species feeds solely on the Common Rockrose.

Habitat requirements
Usually found on well-drained flower-rich grassland where the foodplant grows amongst bare patches of ground (Fig. 17). This may be on open grassy areas with limestone outcrops, south-facing slopes near the sea, coastal valleys and cliffs, quarries and limestone pavement. Typical sites contain an abundance of flowers such as Wild Thyme and Common Bird's-foot Trefoil.

Identification characters, variation and similar species
Average wingspan 30mm. The bright white central spot on the forewing upperside and underside should prevent confusion with any other species. Also, the white spots on the hindwing underside usually lack the black 'pupils' found in all other British blues.

Field tips
During periods when the sun is not shining, the butterflies can be found easily as they roost conspicuously, head downwards, on grass stems. They should then be watched until the sun comes out when they usually bask for a while with their wings held open. They feed regularly from various flowers, often Wild Thyme and Common Bird's-foot Trefoil, and can then be approached with caution. Most colonies are small, and the observer should be prepared to spend some time searching likely habitats. Some of the sites detailed below are potentially dangerous as they are on rugged coastal undercliffs. Extreme care should be taken when working such localities.

Regional prime sites
Scotland. In the south-west, the Northern Brown Argus can be seen along the coast of Kirkcudbrightshire. The best area is probably between **Port O' Warren** (NX 880 535) and **Castlehill Point** (from car park at NX 851 535). Here the butterflies can be found along the coastal path by searching sheltered undercliffs where the foodplant grows. In the north-west, it can be seen in good numbers at **Creag Dhubh**, near Newtonmore, East Inverness-shire (along the southern base of the cliffs at approximately NN 672 957). In South Aberdeenshire, it is present at **Muir of Dinnet** (visitor centre at NO 429 996). It may be found throughout the reserve but the best places to try are along the tracks to the south-west of **Loch Kinord** (NO 445 988) and south of **Loch Davan** (NJ 440 003). Near **Muchalls**, Kincardineshire, the butterfly occurs along the coast at NO 902 917 but the rocky terrain here is difficult to negotiate. The subspecies is relatively easy to find at **Balkello Common Woods**, Angus, along the track running west from NO 370 390. Here one should search the south-facing slopes and rocky outcrops to the north. In Berwickshire, it is found at **East**

Northern Brown Argus / Castle Eden Argus

Lammamuir Deans (NT 703 700) and **St Abb's Head** (NT 912 775) and in East Perthshire on the **Jubilee Rifle Range** (NN 874 663).

Northern England. Represented by the Castle Eden Argus (see below).

Other regions. Absent.

Castle Eden Argus
Aricia artaxerxes subspecies *salmacis* (Stephens)

Subspecies type locality and authority
Specimens from Castle Eden Dene in County Durham, England, were first described as a subspecies by Stephens (1828).

General distribution and status
Resident; protected from sale (GB). This subspecies of the Northern Brown Argus is found only in northern England. It is restricted to a band running between Westmorland and Mid-west Yorkshire in the west and Durham in the east and here it is locally fairly common but rarely seen in large numbers. It is absent from the Isle of Man. Its former English name of Durham Argus is often still used and, at localities in the west of its range, it is usually referred to simply as 'Salmacis' or, perhaps more accurately, as 'Salmacis Northern Brown Argus'. In order to conform to the established current nomenclature the name Castle Eden Argus is adhered to here.

Flight period
Single brooded, flying from early June to early August with a peak during the last week of June and the first and second weeks of July.

Fig. 130 Castle Eden Argus upperside.
Gait Barrows, West Lancashire

Fig. 131 Castle Eden Argus underside.
Gait Barrows, West Lancashire

Castle Eden Argus

Larval foodplants
Exclusively Common Rockrose.

Habitat requirements
Limestone grassland with rocky outcrops, disused quarries (Fig. 9) and limestone pavement are the favoured localities (e.g. Fig. 198).

Identification characters, variation and similar species
Very similar to the Brown Argus and some female Common Blues. The identification features are discussed under the former species (p. 157). Approximately five per cent of individuals found in Durham have a white forewing spot and cannot be distinguished visually from the Scottish subspecies of Northern Brown Argus.

Regional prime sites and field tips
Northern England. When searching for the Castle Eden Argus the first thing to look for is the larval foodplant, Common Rockrose. Its large conspicuous yellow flowers make it easy to locate (Fig. 132).

In the west, the butterfly abounds in Westmorland and West Lancashire at **Whitbarrow Scar** (access from SD 458 867), **Arnside Knott** (SD 450 775) where it inhabits the limestone grassland, often favouring the bases of south-facing

Fig. 132 Common Rockrose at Gait Barrows, West Lancashire

slopes, **Gait Barrows** (car park at SD 482 777), though a permit to visit must be obtained from Natural England (see Appendix II under Gait Barrows), and **Smardale Gill** (from the car park at NY 740 082 search the disused railway line south-west). Also in the western part of its range it can be seen at **Bastow Wood** (SD 990 660) in Mid-west Yorkshire. In the east, in County Durham, the butterfly is still found in its place of discovery at **Castle Eden Dene**, though only in small numbers. The north and south headlands are the best places to try (NZ 456 407 and NZ 458 406, respectively). Also in Durham there is an excellent site at the disused quarry at **Bishop Middleham** (from NZ 335 318 follow the footpaths north and then west past Farnless to NZ 332 326).

Other regions. Absent.

Common Blue
Polyommatus icarus subspecies *icarus* (Rottemburg)

General distribution and status
Resident. Widespread and common throughout the British Isles with the exception of the Shetlands from which it is absent. In Ireland, it is represented by the Irish Common Blue (p 168).

Flight period
In southern and central England, Wales and most of Ireland, the Common Blue has two generations a year, flying in May and June and late July to September. The optimum time to see the species is during the last week of May and first week of June and the last two weeks of August. In northern England, Scotland and the north and north-west of Ireland, there is a

Fig. 133 Common Blue male upperside.
Stiffkey, West Norfolk

Fig. 134 Common Blue female upperside.
Narborough, West Norfolk

Common Blue

Fig. 135 Common Blue female f. *caerulea*. Syderstone, West Norfolk

Identification characters, variation and similar species

Average wingspan 33mm. Variation in the male is confined mainly to the depth of the blue colouration. In some this may approach that hue of the Adonis Blue. The female can vary greatly in the amount of blue present. In some cases this may be almost absent or, as in form *caerulea* Fuchs, may be extensive (Fig. 135). The development of the marginal orange spots also varies extensively and in some specimens may be very large and bright. The combination of extensive blue colouration and large orange spots is one of the characteristics of the Irish Common Blue but can occasionally be seen in specimens from elsewhere. Confusion may arise with the Silver-studded Blue, Brown Argus, Castle Eden Argus, Adonis Blue and female Chalkhill Blue but in comparison with these, the Common Blue displays the following characteristics:

Silver-studded Blue
1. Forewing more angular and pointed.
2. Male upperside paler violet blue; lacks broad dark margins to all wings; hindwing with row of black marginal spots absent.
3. Female upperside, where blue present, paler violet.
4. Hindwing underside of both sexes with white central inward-pointing triangle in outer third.
5. Hindwing underside of both sexes with row of silver-blue dots along outer edge of orange spots absent.

protracted single brood flying between early June and early September, peaking throughout July. There is an occasional partial third emergence in southern England in October and, in late September and October, there may be a partial second emergence in single brooded populations.

Larval foodplants
Many leguminous plants have been recorded but by far the most commonly used is Common Bird's-foot Trefoil. Others include Greater Bird's-foot Trefoil, Rest-harrow, White Clover, Lesser Trefoil and Black Medick.

Habitat requirements
A wide range of grassy habitats are used including downland, coastal dunes and shingle, heaths and commons, roadside verges, disused railway lines, woodland rides and clearings, parks, golf courses and gardens (see also Fig. 5).

Common Blue

Brown Argus and Castle Eden Argus
1. Female upperside with blue shading at the base of the wings.
2. Hindwing underside spotting pattern differs as in Figs. 127 a & b. Two spots in the centre of leading edge placed much further apart.

Adonis Blue
1. Male upperside deeper violet blue.
2. Female upperside where blue present deeper violet.
3. Wing fringes of both sexes lacking distinctive white and dark-coloured chequered pattern.
4. Underside of both sexes usually with smaller black spots.

Chalkhill Blue
1. Female upperside fringes lacking white and dark coloured chequered pattern.
2. Female upperside where blue present deeper violet.
3. Female underside with smaller black spots.

In flight, the species may also be confused with the Holly Blue, but Common Blues generally fly more strongly and lower to the ground, rarely venturing to tree level. The undersides of the Common and Holly Blue are completely dissimilar (see Fig. 153).

Field tips
The Common Blue might be expected to occur wherever its foodplants grow. In the late afternoon and during dull weather the butterflies rest communally on grass stalks and can then be found easily. Here they will bask openly when the sun comes out and at sunrise. Several males flying close together over a particular spot usually indicates the presence of a female amongst the vegetation below.

Regional prime sites
Scotland. Widespread and common on all but the high ground. Absent from the Shetlands.

Fig. 136 Common Blue male underside.
Holkham, West Norfolk

Fig. 137 Common Blue female underside.
Narborough, West Norfolk

Common Blue / Irish Common Blue

Northern and central England and Wales. Apart from on the high ground, widespread and common.

Eastern, south-east and south-west England. Widespread and common throughout. The form *caerulea* is frequent on the shingle sea defences of West and East Norfolk.

Western and eastern Ireland. Represented by the Irish Common Blue (see below).

Irish Common Blue
Polyommatus icarus subspecies *mariscolore* (Kane)

Subspecies type locality and authority
Specimens from Ireland were first described as a subspecies by Kane in 1893, but no specific locality is given.

General distribution and status
Resident. Restricted to Ireland where it is widespread and common.

Flight period, habitat requirements and larval foodplants
As for the Common Blue (p. 165).

Identification characters, variation and similar species
Average wingspan 34mm. The Irish Common Blue differs from the nominate subspecies in the following ways:

1. Female generally larger.
2. Male forewing more pointed.
3. Female upperside with extensive blue area on fore- and hindwings; orange marginal spots larger and brighter.

Confusion with other species is unlikely as none of those for which comparative details

Fig. 138 Irish Common Blue male. Boston, Co. Clare

Fig. 139 Irish Common Blue female. Boston, Co. Clare

Irish Common Blue / Chalkhill Blue

are given for the nominate subspecies occur in Ireland. In flight the male may be mistaken for the Holly Blue (p. 176).

Field tips
As for the Common Blue (p. 165).

Regional prime sites
Western and eastern Ireland. Widespread and common, especially in coastal localities.

Other regions. Absent.

Chalkhill Blue
Lysandra coridon (Poda)

General distribution and status
Resident; protected from sale (GB). Restricted to the chalk and limestone grasslands of southern England southeast of a line approximately between West Gloucestershire in the west and Cambridgeshire in the east. It is absent from Wales, northern and most of central England, Scotland, Ireland, the Isle of Man and the Channel Isles. During the last century, the Chalkhill Blue declined severely due to habitat loss caused by agricultural intensification, cessation of traditional grazing practices and the reduction of rabbit numbers caused by myxomatosis. Subsequent habitat conservation management on nature reserves and the partial recovery of rabbit populations has halted this trend and the butterfly remains locally common in some areas.

Flight period
Single brooded, flying between early July and early September. The optimum time to see the butterfly is during the first two weeks of August.

Fig. 140 Chalkhill Blue male upperside.
Portland, Dorset

Fig. 141 Chalkhill Blue female upperside.
Martin Down, South Hampshire

Chalkhill Blue

Larval foodplants
This species feeds exclusively on Horseshoe Vetch.

Habitat requirements
The Chalkhill Blue is found only on calcareous grassland where it requires short turf maintained by grazing. Sheltered south-facing slopes are preferred, though seemingly not essential and longer vegetation at the bases of slopes is needed for roosting and basking (Fig. 7).

Identification characters, variation and similar species
Average wingspan 36mm. The large size and pale silvery blue upperside of the male makes confusion with other species unlikely. However, the female is very similar to that of the Adonis Blue but differs in the following ways:

1. Forewing underside with black spots generally larger; orange marginal markings inconspicuous or absent.
2. Upperside blue shading, if present, much paler, resembling that of the male upperside.
3. Hindwing upperside with pale crescents on outer edges of orange marginal markings white rather than blue (Figs. 143a and 143b).
4. Forewing upperside with central black spot often 'C' shaped rather than oval and with outer edge often defined white (Fig. 144a and 144b).

The female is also similar to that of the Common Blue but in that species the white wing fringes are not chequered.

Variation in the male is usually restricted to the pattern and size of the underside

Fig. 142 Chalkhill Blue female and male underside. Portland, Dorset

Chalkhill Blue

Fig. 143a Chalkhill Blue female hindwing

Fig. 143b Adonis Blue female hindwing

Fig. 144a Chalkhill Blue female forewing

Fig. 144b Adonis Blue female forewing

spotting. The amount of blue colouring on the usually brown female varies considerably and can be almost as extensive as that of the male.

Field tips

During dull weather and in the late afternoon the butterflies roost openly on the stalks of long vegetation at the bases of slopes. In such places they can also be seen basking in the early morning sun. The Chalkhill Blue is a conspicuous species and the males are difficult to miss as they fly rapidly over their chosen habitat. Early morning and periods of intermittent brightness offer the best photographic opportunities as short sessions of basking usually follow the reappearance of the sun.

Regional prime sites

Scotland and northern England. Absent.

Central England. A recent unauthorized introduction attempt at a site in South Lincolnshire has apparently failed. Elsewhere the species is found only at **Barnack Hills** in Northamptonshire (TF 074 048).

Eastern England. The species reaches its north-easterly extreme at **Devil's Ditch** near Newmarket racecourse, Cambridgeshire, (TL 617 613) where it abounds. In south-east England, it is common at **Whipsnade Downs** (SP 999 084) and **Pegsdon Hills** (TL 120 295) in Bedfordshire.

Chalkhill Blue / Adonis Blue

South-east England. Widespread on calcareous downland and seen in small numbers at **Therfield Heath**, Hertfordshire (TL 333 380). Elsewhere it can be found reliably at **Lydden Down** in East Kent (TR 277 453), **Malling Down**, East Sussex (access from the B2192 at TQ 434 115), **Box Hill**, Surrey (TQ 182 523) and **Aston Rowant** (SU 730 970) and **Watlington Hill** (SU 708 937) in Oxfordshire. In neighbouring Berkshire it is common at **Lardon Chase** (access from SU 583 807). In North Hampshire, it is common at **Magdalen Hill Down** (SU 505 292) and, in South Hampshire, can be seen in good numbers at **Broughton Down** (SU 291 328) and **Martin Down** (SU 058 192). In the Isle of Wight, it is abundant on the coastal chalk grasslands around **Compton Down** (SZ 366 855).

South-west England. In the north of the region, it is found at **Prestbury Hill**, East Gloucestershire (SO 993 248) and **Stoke Camp,** North Somerset (park at ST 486 513 and walk 300m east to the reserve entrance at ST 489 512). In the south, it is common in Dorset at **Hod Hill** (south of car park at ST 852 112), **Ballard Down** (from just north of the lay-by at SZ 022 808 walk east along the south-facing slope) and on the limestone grasslands of **Portland** (e.g. SY 693 704).

Wales and Ireland. Absent.

Adonis Blue
Lysandra bellargus (Rottemburg)

General distribution and status
Resident; protected from sale (GB). Confined to the calcareous grasslands of southern England but absent in the south-west. Its precise habitat requirements make its distribution extremely localized, but it is fairly common in areas such as the chalk downlands of Dorset, South Wiltshire, East and West Sussex and East Kent. It is absent from central and northern England, Wales, Scotland, Ireland, the Isle of Man and the Channel Isles. During the last century, the Adonis Blue underwent a severe decline due to habitat loss caused mainly by the cessation of traditional grazing regimes and the fall in rabbit populations following the introduction of myxomatosis. By the beginning of the 1980s there were only about 75 remaining colonies, but subsequent successful habitat management has reversed this trend and it is now estimated there are more than double that number (Asher *et al.*, 2001). Numbers of individuals can fluctuate greatly from year to year and populations can fall dramatically during periods of drought as the larval foodplant cannot tolerate such conditions.

Adonis Blue

Flight period
Double brooded, flying during May/June and August/September. The best times to see the species are during the last week of May and the first week of June, and the last week of August and the first week of September. The second generation is always considerably more numerous than the first.

Larval foodplants
It feeds exclusively on Horseshoe Vetch.

Habitat requirements
In the British Isles, this species reaches the northern limit of its European range and, as is often the case in such circumstances, its habitat requirements are rather precise. It is restricted to dry well-grazed calcareous grassland where warm south-facing slopes are preferred (Fig. 7). The turf needs to be very short; the females will not lay their eggs where it grows to more than about 5cm. As well as open grassland, the butterfly can be found in abandoned chalk and limestone quarries. Areas of taller grasses at the base of slopes or in sheltered hollows are required as roosting sites. An abundance of the foodplant is needed, as it is also an important nectar source for the spring generation adults.

Identification characters, variation and similar species
Average wingspan 35mm. The dazzling cobalt blue of the male makes confusion with other species unlikely. It could be mistaken for a Common Blue but it lacks the violet tinge of that species. At rest the chequered black and white margins to the wings are diagnostic. The female is very similar to that of the Chalkhill Blue and Common Blue; the identification features are discussed under those species (pp. 169 and 165, respectively). Variation in the amount of blue present on the female is extensive and may cover most of the wings or be almost absent.

Field tips
During dull weather the butterflies can

Fig. 145 Adonis Blue male upperside.
Martin Down, South Hampshire

Fig. 146 Adonis Blue female upperside.
Martin Down, South Hampshire

Adonis Blue

easily be found as they rest on tall grass stems. In the late afternoon they congregate at their roosting sites amongst tall vegetation. If these can be found, a visit during the early morning will provide good photographic opportunities as the butterflies then bask with their wings open. A variety of nectar sources are used, the first generation regularly visiting flowers of the larval foodplant, Horseshoe Vetch.

Regional prime sites
Scotland, northern, central and eastern England and Wales. Absent.

South-east England. Very localized and restricted to chalk grassland. In East Kent, it is fairly common on **Lydden Down** (TR 277 453) and in Surrey, despite a general decline over the last 50 years, it still flourishes at **Ranmore Common** (TQ 142 505), **Colekitchen Down** (TQ 084 488) and **Box Hill** (TQ 182 523). In the north of the region, after a period of scarcity, numbers have increased recently at its long-standing site at **Lardon Chase**, Berkshire (access from SU 583 807). In the south, it can be seen at **Malling Down** in East Sussex (access from the B 2192 at TQ 434 115), **Martin Down**, South Hampshire (SU 058 192), and on the Isle of Wight where it is common on the chalk grasslands around **Compton Down** (SZ 366 855).

South-west England. The county of Dorset is a stronghold of the species. Here it can be seen in good numbers from the coastal footpath at **Ballard Down** (from just north of the lay-by at SZ 022 808 walk east along the south-facing slope) and the nearby **Durlston Country Park** (SZ 033 773), **Fontmell Down** (park at ST 888 185 and cross the road west to the reserve) and **Hod Hill** (ST 852 112). At **Portland** it frequents many of the disused limestone quarries (e.g. SY 693 704).

Western and eastern Ireland. Absent.

Fig. 147 Adonis Blue male underside.
Martin Down, South Hampshire

Fig. 148 Adonis Blue female underside.
Martin Down, South Hampshire

Mazarine Blue
Cyaniris semiargus (**Rottemburg**)

Fig. 149 Mazarine Blue upperside.
Switzerland (R. Harrington)

Fig. 150 Mazarine Blue underside.
Switzerland (R. Harrington)

Status

Extinct resident. The butterfly was first mentioned in the British literature in 1710 (Salmon, 2000) and subsequently recorded from at least 24 vice-counties in England and Wales. It was found in England as far north as North-east Yorkshire, but the bulk of records are from more central and southern counties. The best documented colonies were at Glanville's Wootton in Dorset where approximately 290 individuals were seen between 1811 and 1841, Penarth and Llantrisant, Glamorgan, in plenty between 1835 and 1877, several localities in Gloucestershire until 1865, and Epworth in North Lincolnshire until 1903. Since 1900, there have been several scattered records of presumed migrants and these are summarized below. However, the presence of so many records from East Suffolk raises the possibility that the species may have been resident in the Gorleston area between 1900 and 1913.

1900: two in East Suffolk near Gorleston.
1901: three in East Suffolk near Gorleston.
1902: one in East Sussex at Beachy Head.
1907: two of dubious origin in north Wales.
1908: one of dubious origin in Berkshire at Mortimer.
1910-1913: singletons in East Suffolk near Gorleston.
1917: one in East Sussex at Eastbourne.
1918: one in East Sussex at Hastings.
1934: one in East Cornwall at Fowey.
1942-1946: six in Jersey in the Channel Isles.
1958: one in West Sussex at Rogate.

The reason for the demise of the Mazarine Blue is not clear. Changing climate may well have played its part, but the widespread use of clover (the larval foodplant) as a crop in the late 19th century and its subsequent harvesting before the completion of larval development may also have had an effect. No attempt has been made to re-establish the butterfly in Britain, although the author believes this warrants serious consideration as, by comparison with, for example, the Large Copper, satisfying its ecological requirements appears far more attainable.

Flight period
Mid-June to mid-July in a single brood.

Foodplants
There is no record of the early stages in Britain, but the usual foodplant is believed to have been Red Clover. (Asher *et al.*, 2001).

Habitat
Flower-rich meadows and unimproved grassland are favoured in mainland Europe.

Holly Blue
Celastrina argiolus (Linnaeus) subspecies *britanna* (Verity) 1919

Subspecies type locality and authority
Specimens from Epping Forest in South Essex, England, were first described as a subspecies by Verity (1919). The nominate continental subspecies does not occur in the British Isles.

General distribution and status
Resident; fully protected (NI). Widespread and fairly common in England as far north as Cumberland and the Isle of Man in the west and Durham in the east. It is most common in the southern half of England and the Channel Isles. Its status in Scotland is at present uncertain. It has usually been regarded as a scarce vagrant there but breeding was confirmed in Kirkcudbrightshire in 2004 (J. MacKay, pers. comm.). In Ireland, the species is very localized but widespread and fairly common at known localities. Annual numbers vary considerably and there appears to be a six- or seven-year cycle of abundance (Asher *et al.*, 2001).

Flight period
In the south, including that of Ireland, the species is double brooded, flying between late March and late June and again between late July and early September; the optimum times are the first two weeks of May and the second and third weeks of August. There is an occasional and partial third emergence in southernmost localities, for example in the Isles of Scilly, West Cornwall, during October. In the north, it is usually single brooded and flies between early April and early July, peaking during the last two weeks of May. There is an occasional second generation during August and early September.

Holly Blue

Fig. 151 Holly Blue male upperside.
Cley, East Norfolk

Fig. 152 Holly Blue female upperside.
Kelling, East Norfolk

Larval foodplants
Spring generation females usually lay their eggs on Holly whilst those of the summer brood use Ivy. A variety of other foodplants has been recorded, most notably Gorse which can be used by both generations. Other plants, including Snowberry, dogwoods and brambles, are also used occasionally.

Habitat requirements
Various habitats are used, including woodland rides and clearings, hedgerows, parks, gardens and churchyards. It is often a regular sight along country lanes.

Identification characters, variation and similar species
Average wingspan 30mm. The female has a much broader dark border to the wings, particularly in the second generation. Females of this later brood also have a row of dark spots around the edge of the hindwing and an obvious dark central spot on the forewing. These features are lacking in the male. The Holly Blue may be confused in flight with the Common Blue, but examination of the underside will reveal the lack of orange spots found around the wing margins of that species. The flight pattern of the Holly Blue is more like that of hairstreaks than other blues as it usually flits actively along the top of hedges and trees whereas most blues fly low near the ground. This can be a useful guide to identification in the field. Where woodland borders heathlands, the butterflies can sometimes be seen feeding from the flowers of heathers, and confusion with the Silver-studded Blue is possible. However, the Holly Blue is significantly larger and, again, the plain silvery-white underside and lack of orange marginal markings are diagnostic.

Field tips
Both sexes are very active fliers and chances to photograph them can be

Holly Blue

Fig. 153 Holly Blue underside. Cley, East Norfolk

frustratingly few and far between. Churchyards provide good opportunities as both of the main larval foodplants are often found there. Old country tracks where Holly and Ivy are present are also good places to try, particularly where Snowberry grows as a garden escape. Once such localities have been found, the observer must simply be patient and alert. The females can usually be spotted as they search for egg-laying sites and, as they alight, brief opportunities for close examination will arise. Both sexes often bask with their wings held half open during the early part of the day, and shiny leaf surfaces, such as those of Holly or Ivy, are preferred. Males often visit damp ground, puddles and animal droppings and can here be approached closely as they tend to become rather preoccupied with feeding. Both sexes also regularly visit flowers, particularly those of Snowberry, brambles and Holly.

Regional prime sites
Scotland. Usually regarded as a vagrant but a colony was found in 2004 at a private site in Kirkcudbrightshire.

Northern England. Widespread and fairly common throughout the southern part of the region. In the northern part

Holly Blue / Large Blue

of its range, where it is more localized, it can be seen most reliably at **Arnside Knott**, Westmorland (SD 453 774) and, in Mid-west Yorkshire, at **Sun Lane Nature Park** near Burley in Wharfedale (SE 154 467).

Central, eastern, south-east and south-west England and Wales. Widespread and fairly common.

Western Ireland. Very localized and most common in the south-west where it can be seen in Mid Cork at **Cork City** (e.g. W 663 714) and **Curraghbinny Wood** (W 797 618).

Eastern Ireland. Widespread but very localized. In the north, it is present at **Bohill Forest**, Down (J 395 458). In County Dublin, it can be seen in Dublin City at localities such as **Blackrock** (O 212 297) and **St Stephen's Green** (O 162 334) and in the south, in Wicklow, it is present at **Enniskerry Glen** (O 235 164).

Large Blue
Maculinea arion subspecies *arion* (Linnaeus)

General distribution and status

Extinct resident; reintroduced resident; fully protected (GB). The endemic British subspecies *eutyphron* (Fruhstorfer) became extinct in 1979, and attempts to reintroduce the Large Blue, using Swedish stock similar in appearance to original British specimens, began in 1983. After painstaking preparation of the habitat the first full scale release took place in 1986, and subsequent monitoring has shown very promising results. At the time of writing it is present at about nine managed localities

Fig. 154 Large Blue male upperside.
Collard Hill, South Somerset

Fig. 155 Large Blue female upperside.
Collard Hill, South Somerset

Large Blue

Fig. 156 Large Blue male underside.
Collard Hill, South Somerset

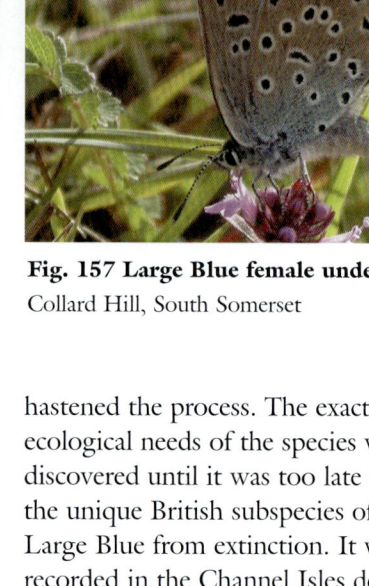

Fig. 157 Large Blue female underside.
Collard Hill, South Somerset

in south-west England, and so successful has its reintroduction been that public access is now permitted at certain sites. The species was formerly locally abundant on close-grazed grassland at around 90 known sites in southern England. Most of these were in the south-west with outlying colonies in the region of Barnwell Wold in Northamptonshire. The diaries of Victorian collectors reveal that the species was greatly prized and many thousands of specimens were taken and still exist in old collections. Towards the end of the species' tenure in England this may have had a significant effect in accelerating its eventual demise, but the single major reason was certainly habitat loss. This resulted from agricultural 'improvement', ploughing and abandonment of suitable sites and cessation or relaxing of grazing. By 1950, most of its remaining sites relied exclusively on rabbit grazing and the introduction of myxomatosis and the subsequent collapse of rabbit populations simply hastened the process. The exact ecological needs of the species were not discovered until it was too late to save the unique British subspecies of the Large Blue from extinction. It was never recorded in the Channel Isles despite being widespread in nearby northern France. For detailed accounts of the decline and extinction of this species in Britain see Salmon (2000) and Thomas & Lewington (1991).

Flight period
Mid-June until late July in a single brood, peaking during the last week of June and the first week of July.

Larval foodplants
The eggs are laid on Wild Thyme and the young larvae feed on the flowers and developing seeds until their fourth instar. They then drop to the ground where they secrete a sweet-tasting substance that is attractive to a particular species of red ant (*Myrmica sabuleti* Meinert). The larvae are

Large Blue

carried underground to the brood chamber and here they complete their growth feeding on ant grubs. Pupation takes place within the ants' nest and the butterflies emerge the following summer.

Habitat requirements
The red ant on which this butterfly is dependent for its development requires very short turf on thin, nutrient-poor soils (Fig. 7). If grazing is relaxed, even for a single year, the site very quickly becomes unsuitable and the ants, and consequently the Large Blue, will disappear. Strict grazing regimes are therefore required and specific breeds of animal stock that can thrive in such nutrient-deficient habitats must be used. Preferred sites are characteristically on warm south-facing slopes with longer vegetation at their bases amongst which the butterflies can roost and mate. Scattered shrubs are also usually a feature and these are used for shelter. For a detailed account of the ecological requirements of the Large Blue the reader is referred to Mouquet *et al*. (2005).

Identification characters, variation and similar species
Average wingspan 45mm; the female is slightly larger than the male. Apart from their wingspans the sexes are similar and major variation is rare. The large size and distinctive upperside spotting of the insect make confusion with other species very unlikely.

Field tips
The females are most commonly seen flying low over the hillsides searching for Wild Thyme plants on which to lay eggs and take nectar. The males spend much of their time at the bases of the slopes amongst taller vegetation where they bask in the early morning sun and patrol in search of females. The females fly to these sites soon after emergence and it is here where mating takes place. Most activity at these locations is during the morning; it is then that they should be visited by those wishing to photograph the species. During the afternoon, males spend long periods resting with their wings closed, and during egg-laying the females rarely settle with their upsersides exposed.

Regional prime sites
South-west England. At the time of writing there are a few sites open to visitors but most require a pre-arranged permit. The public is allowed free access to **Collard Hill** in South Somerset. From the car park near the Youth Hostel at ST 484 345 a footpath leading to the reserve to the south-east is marked out during the flight period and a warden is usually on hand to offer advice.

Other regions. Absent.

Duke of Burgundy

The Metalmarks
(Lycaenidae, subfamily Riodininae)

Duke of Burgundy
Hamearis lucina (Linnaeus)

General distribution and status
Resident; protected from sale (GB). Outside the calcareous grasslands of central southern England this species is extremely localized and scarce. Even in its southern strongholds most colonies are very small and vulnerable. The Duke of Burgundy is extinct in Scotland and Wales, and in northern, central and eastern England is a species of great conservation concern. It is absent from Ireland, the Isle of Man and the Channel Isles.

Flight period
There is one generation per year flying from early May to mid-June, though more northerly populations tend to fly approximately a week later. The best times to see the species are during the last two weeks of May in the south, and the last week of May and first week of June in the north.

Larval foodplants
On calcareous grasslands the main foodplant is the Cowslip and, in woodlands, Primrose.

Habitat requirements
Traditionally a species of wide woodland rides and clearings (Fig. 12), the Duke of Burgundy has been in continuous decline since the beginning of the 20th century, as changes in forestry management destroyed most suitable woodland habitat. The cessation of traditional rotational coppicing and the replacement

Fig. 158 Duke of Burgundy upperside.
Whipsnade Downs, Bedfordshire

Fig. 159 Duke of Burgundy underside.
Whipsnade Downs, Bedfordshire

Duke of Burgundy

of broad-leaved woodlands with coniferous plantations are mostly to blame. It is estimated that approximately 98% of woodland colonies were lost between 1950 and 1990 (Asher *et al.*, 2001). Most species of butterfly associated with calcareous grassland declined during this period, as grazing practices were relaxed and rabbit populations collapsed after the introduction of myxomatosis. However, the Duke of Burgundy was able to take advantage of the resulting conditions as it requires a taller tussocky sward where its foodplant can grow in sheltered situations with minimal grazing. As a consequence of these seemingly complementary changes in land use the species is now predominantly associated with chalk and limestone grassland. Typically it inhabits sheltered gullies and hollows with scrubby edges, with north- and west-facing aspects often preferred (Fig. 8).

Identification characters, variation and similar species

Average wingspan 31mm. The female is brighter than the male with less intense black markings and has more rounded and ample forewings. Variation is rare. Confusion with other butterfly species is unlikely, but it can be mistaken on the wing for the Burnet Companion moth (Fig. 41) which flies in similar habitats and at the same time of the year.

Field tips

The males are easy to find as they are highly territorial and spend long periods defending sunny patches along scrub edges, hollows and glades or ride intersections. Here they bask conspicuously on vegetation and pursue intruders with great vigour. When two males meet they occasionally battle in an upward spiral until, even through binoculars, they become tiny dots in the sky or disappear completely. On the other hand, the females are more secretive and fly low to the ground in search of the larval foodplants. Neither sex visits flowers regularly, but both may occasionally feed from Tormentil, Hawthorn or Bugle.

Regional prime sites

Scotland. Absent.

Northern England. The butterfly is now thought to occur at fewer than 25 colonies, most of which are rightly considered to be too sensitive for publication here. It can be seen at its most northerly location in England on the north-western slopes of **Whitbarrow Scar** in Westmorland (access from SD 458 867). Two sites where prior permission to visit must be obtained are at **Ashberry Pasture**, North-east Yorkshire (Hill & Twist, 1998) and **Gait Barrows**, West Lancashire (SD 482 777). For site permits see Appendix II under Gait Barrows and Ashberry Pasture.

Central England. Restricted to perhaps one remaining colony on the borders of Leicestershire and Northamptonshire; it is thus not considered appropriate to publish details of the site.

Eastern England. Found at one remaining private site in South

Duke of Burgundy

Lincolnshire, details of which should not be made public. Further south, it can reliably be seen at **Whipsnade Downs**, Bedfordshire (park at SP 998 186 and explore the scrubby sunken trails and valleys to the north-east).

South-east England. In the east, it is present in **Denge Wood**, East Kent, in the area known as 'Bonsai Bank' (TR 096 505), whilst in the south it can be found in North Hampshire on the chalk grasslands at **Noar Hill** (SU 741 320).
South-west England. In the north of the region, it occurs in fair numbers at **Prestbury Hill**, East Gloucestershire (SO 993 248) and, in the south-west, is fairly common at **Buckland Wood** (ST 185 175) and in the area around Section marker 3 at **Thurlbear Quarry** (ST 272 210), South Somerset. In the south, it is seen in small numbers at **Fontmell Down**, Dorset (park at ST 888 185 and cross the road for the reserve to the west). Also in Dorset it is present at **Clubmen's Down** (ST 887 188).

Wales and Ireland. Absent.

White Admiral

The White Admirals
(Nymphalidae, subfamily Limenitinae)

White Admiral
Limenitis camilla (Linnaeus)

General distribution and status
Resident. Locally common at low density south-east of a line approximately between South Devon in the west and North Lincolnshire in the east, though it is of scattered distribution and generally uncommon in much of eastern England. Its distribution becomes very localized in south-west England and it is absent from Cornwall. It is not present in northern England, the Isle of Man, Scotland or Ireland, and in Wales it is confined to isolated localities in the south where it is scarce. In the Channel Isles, it has been recorded only twice. The species is presently in a period of range expansion which began in the 1920s (Asher *et al.*, 2001).

Flight period
Single brooded, flying between mid-June and mid-August with the optimum viewing period during the second and third weeks of July. On rare occasions, such as in 2006, there is a partial second emergence during late September.

Larval foodplants
The sole foodplant is Honeysuckle.

Habitat requirements
The White Admiral is truly a woodland butterfly. Its traditional home is ancient deciduous woodland (Fig. 12) but it has been able to adapt to thrive in coniferous plantations that are interspersed with sections, rides or edges comprising broad-leaved trees. Honeysuckle growing in shade is usually required for egg-laying, and a good supply of flowering brambles is needed as a nectar source for the adults. The butterfly is occasionally seen some distance from its usual habitat; this suggests a ready ability to find and colonize suitable new localities.

Identification characters, variation and similar species
Average wingspan 60mm. The female differs from the male in having a more conspicuous chestnut-coloured patch at the hind corner of the hindwings. Variation is generally rare but a prized sighting is that of the scarce black form *nigrina* Weymer in which the white markings are almost or entirely absent. Figure 162 shows a similar form known as *obliterae* Robson and Gardner. The only similar species is the Purple Emperor (p. 191) from which it differs in the following ways:

1. Wingspan significantly smaller (average for the Purple Emperor 76mm).
2. Outer margin of forewing straight or slightly convex rather than deeply

White Admiral

concave (a useful feature in flight).
3. Purple sheen on fore- and hindwings absent.
4. Usually flies at lower elevation (though often flies to the canopy to roost in the evening).
5. Habitually visits bramble blossom – a habit never shared by the Purple Emperor.

Field tips
The characteristically elegant flashing and gliding flight is easy to identify at distance, but the easiest way to find the White Admiral (as is the case for many woodland butterflies) is to find a patch of flowering brambles at a known locality and simply await its arrival. When feeding, they can be approached and photographed with ease. The butterflies are also attracted to animal droppings and damp patches of ground. Aphid honeydew from the tree canopy is an important part of their diet.

Regional prime sites
Scotland and northern England. Absent.

Central England. Locally frequent in the south-east corner of the region, most notably in the **Wyre Forest**, Shropshire (especially near **Cooper's Mill** at about SO 758 768). It is common in **Fermyn Woods**, Northamptonshire (e.g. SP 966 859) and **Monk Wood**, Worcestershire (SO 804 607).

Eastern England. Absent from much of the region but locally quite common in some of the larger woods such as **Chamber's Farm Woods** (TF 149 739) and **Southery Wood** (TF 127 682) in North Lincolnshire, **Foxley Wood** (TG 050 229), **Holt Country Park** (TG 083 376) and **Horsford Woods** (TG 192 183) in East Norfolk, **Great Hockham** (TL 934 923) in West Norfolk, **Dunwich Forest** (TM 461 711), East Suffolk, **Stour Wood** (TM 192 311), North Essex and, just north-east of Grafham Water, at **Brampton Wood** in Cambridgeshire (TL 185 698).

South-east England. Widespread and

Fig. 160 White Admiral upperside. Foxley Wood, East Norfolk

Fig. 161 White Admiral underside. Fermyn Woods, Northamptonshire

White Admiral

Fig. 162 White Admiral form *obliterae*. Fermyn Woods, Northamptonshire (G. McLennan)

locally frequent in many of the larger woods. A few examples are: the **New Forest**, South Hampshire (e.g. **Pondhead Inclosure** (SU 308 070) or the woodlands around **Standing Hat** (SU 315 037)), **Alice Holt Forest**, North Hampshire (e.g. from SU 801 432), **Bernwood Forest**, Buckinghamshire (main car park at SP 611 117), **Ashdown Forest** (e.g. from TQ 432 325) and **Rowland Wood** (access from TQ 515 147) in East Sussex and **Hamstreet Forest**, East Kent (e.g. from TQ 988 346).

South-west England. Less widespread than in south-east England and absent from much of the central area and the south-west. However, it is not uncommon at **Lydlinch Common** (ST 737 137) and **Eastcombe Wood** (ST 827 098) in Dorset. In **Bentley Woods**, South Wiltshire (SU 258 292), it is common. At **Nagshead** (SO 606 085) in West Gloucestershire and **Meare Heath** (ST 441 402) and **Shapwick Heath** (park at ST 424 412 and follow the tracks 200m south-east, 100m south west, 70m south-east and then about 200m south-west) in North Somerset it can be found in small numbers, whilst in South Devon it can be seen reliably in **Plymbridge Woods** (SX 523 582) and **Haldon Woods** (SX 882 847).

Wales. Very scarce and restricted to a handful of sites. It is considered inappropriate to publish the details here.

Western and eastern Ireland. Absent.

Purple Emperor

The Emperors
(Nymphalidae, subfamily Apaturinae)

Purple Emperor
Apatura iris **(Linnaeus)**

General distribution and status
Resident; protected from sale (GB). The main strongholds of the Purple Emperor are in the southern English vice-counties between South Wiltshire and South Hampshire in the west, Surrey and West Sussex in the east and Oxfordshire and Hertfordshire in the north. There are several scattered localities elsewhere and at some the butterfly is recorded regularly, although at most it is scarce. Its usually secretive nature makes estimating population sizes very difficult. It may well be more common and widely distributed than is presently assumed. It is absent from northern England, Scotland, Ireland, the Isle of Man and the Channel Isles. There are historical records for Wales, but it has not been recorded there since the 1930s. Following a widespread and serious decline since the 1950s, the species now appears to be in a period of range expansion both in Britain and elsewhere in mainland Europe. However, fragmentation of suitable woodland habitat will probably slow natural recolonization.

Flight period
Single brooded, usually flying between late June and mid-August. The best time to see the species is during the second and third weeks of July. The males emerge about a week to ten days before the females.

Larval foodplants
Goat Willow is the main foodplant, although Grey Willow and, more rarely, Crack Willow are sometimes used. Eggs are usually laid on parts of the bush growing in at least partial shade.

Habitat requirements
The Purple Emperor is truly a denizen of large deciduous woodlands and forests (Fig. 12), although large areas comprising blocks of smaller woods are also suitable. In such situations the butterfly can sometimes be seen flying along hedgerows or even crossing agricultural fields from one wood to another. Rides, clearings or areas of scrub where the foodplant grows commonly, preferably in partial shade, are essential but these often fall victim to attempts at 'tidying-up'. Fortunately, many important sites are now being managed with the ecological needs of this magnificent butterfly specifically in mind.

Identification characters, variation and similar species
Average wingspan 76mm. The female is larger than the male and lacks the purple

Purple Emperor

Fig. 163 Purple Emperor male upperside. Fermyn Woods, Northamptonshire

sheen on the upperside. Variation is rare but a spectacular melanic form *iole* (Denis & Schiffermüller) has been recorded where the white markings are absent. Its large size and the spectacular iridescent purple flush on the upperside of the male make confusion with other species unlikely, although in some circumstances, particularly when flying at high elevation, it could be mistaken for a White Admiral; the diagnostic features are discussed under that species (p. 187).

Field tips
This most enigmatic of insects has been the subject of more written words than probably any other British butterfly. Observations of, and speculation about, the Purple Emperor's habits litter the entomological literature and an entire book discussing its behaviour was written in 1964 (Heslop, Hyde & Stockley, 1964). The early collectors were somewhat in awe of the creature and it was often referred to as 'His Imperial Majesty', was described as wearing '...a royal velvet cloak...' and a favoured tree on which the butterfly might perch would be known as 'The Emperor's Throne'. Fortunately the compulsion to catch and pin the butterfly is largely confined to the past,

Purple Emperor

but to see it remains as potent a desire as ever it was. For the butterfly-watcher the first view of the secretive and spectacular Purple Emperor is something one will surely never forget.

An essential piece of equipment is a pair of good quality binoculars as the butterflies are often around the tree canopy and searching for them is then akin to birdwatching. There are usually favoured groups of trees, traditionally known as 'master trees' about which the males defend favoured perches and feed on aphid honeydew. These assembly points are occupied each afternoon from about midday and are usually located along north- and east-facing woodland edges on relatively high ground or along similar aspects of prominent trees where the topography is flat. Activity is curtailed during dull or windy weather, and shelter from the wind is usually provided by high ground or tall trees immediately to the south and west of the 'master area' itself. Patient observation at such localities during the afternoon should reveal combative males flying acrobatically around and amongst the canopy.

Seeing Purple Emperors is one thing but photographing them in the wild is altogether a different matter. Fortunately, the males descend regularly to the ground, usually during the morning, to visit damp earth, animal droppings and carrion from which they take moisture and minerals. This habit is often exploited by using various 'baits' such as over-ripe fruit, molasses, urine and faeces. The butterflies have sometimes been noted taking sweat from human skin or probing clothing with the proboscis. At one site, during 2004, travelling families had left piles of discarded babies' nappies at a ride intersection and these were visited regularly and in some numbers by Purple Emperors! They also appear to be rather inquisitive animals and are sometimes seen visiting shiny or bright white objects such as tinfoil, chromium on motor cars and also lights that are left turned on during the day. Along rides they will often inspect white stones amongst the track aggregate. Unless there is a particular attraction, such as those described, their visits to ground level are unpredictable. However, with patient patrolling of the rides and clearings, one may be rewarded with wonderful photographic opportunities, as the butterflies can become extremely engrossed with feeding and many minutes may be available for 'the perfect shot'. If possible, photographs from several different angles to the light should be taken as the amount of purple on display will vary accordingly. Females are far more secretive and very rarely visit the ground but will take sap from damaged trees. Most of their time is spent skulking amongst the foodplants and they are very difficult to find.

Regional prime sites
Scotland and northern England.
Absent.

Purple Emperor

Fig. 164 Purple Emperor underside. Fermyn Woods, Northamptonshire

Central England. Extremely localized but can usually be seen reliably at the complex of woodlands, including **Fermyn Wood** and **Lady Wood** in Northamptonshire. One can park at SP 960 857 and search the main ride to the south or at SP 965 859 and follow the ride south and south-east until reaching the southern edge of Fermyn Wood. Continuing along the track across the open fields for approximately 1km will lead to Lady Wood, and the ride to the south-east is considered by local enthusiasts to be very reliable. The stand of poplar trees along its northern edge is a prime spot. At all three of these localities the butterflies regularly visit the ground.

South-east England. The species is at its most widespread in this region and may well be present in most of the larger woodlands. Among the best places to visit is **Broxbourne Woods** in Hertfordshire. After parking at TL 328 070 one should follow the ride north to the first cross-track. Shortly afterwards the ride crosses a stream and it is between these two features that the butterflies are regularly seen coming to ground. Rather conveniently there is a seat placed here for the weary emperor-

Purple Emperor

spotter. **Alice Holt Forest** in North Hampshire has a strong population and the butterflies are often seen along the eastern edge of **Bentley Station Meadow** at SU 793 428. Access is from Bentley railway station itself. The rides to the west of **Alice Holt Lodge** (SU 802 428) are also worth exploring. Across the county border into Surrey is **Oaken Wood** (SU 995 338). The Purple Emperor is seen here regularly and may be encountered along any of the rides but traditionally the place to try first is at the southernmost of the two triangular clearings, some 1km to the west of the car park. The ride leading north-west towards **Botany Bay Wood** can also be productive. **Bernwood Forest** in Buckinghamshire was at one time a premier site and it still holds the species in small numbers. From the main car park at SP 611 116 one should explore the rides leading south-east and south through Oakley Wood, York's Wood and Hell Coppice. At the latter locality, the species was once common but a recent visit by the author revealed far less willow along the rides than existed some 20 years ago and herein probably lies the problem. The nearby **Whitecross Green Wood** in neighbouring Oxfordshire (SP 600 150) also holds small numbers of Purple Emperors, though, being only about 2km away from Bernwood Forest, it is feasible that the butterflies originate from here as the adults are quite mobile and doubtless travel between nearby woodland habitats. It must be stressed that visitors to this site should not trample the rideside vegetation as this will damage the breeding areas of the Wood White. Also in Buckinghamshire, the Purple Emperor can be seen in reasonable numbers at **Finemere Wood** (park at SP 721 210 and follow the track for 500m to the wood).

South-west England. The species is extremely localized in this region and is usually only present in low numbers. Most sites are therefore not suitable for publication in this book. However, one of the most popular localities for those trying to see a Purple Emperor is here. **Bentley Wood** in South Wiltshire is visited by many people each year, and the car park at SU 258 292 is often filled at the weekends during the flight period. The butterflies regularly frequent the trees surrounding the car park and it is a common sight to find banana skins adorning the public notice board at its entrance. Indeed these are often tempting to Purple Emperors and sometimes they will even alight on parked cars. On one memorable occasion someone came close to driving off with 'His Majesty' inadvertently imprisoned in the back of his vehicle.

Wales and Ireland. Absent.

Painted Lady

The Vanessids
(Nymphalidae, subfamily Nymphalinae)

Red Admiral
Vanessa atalanta (Linnaeus)

Fig. 165 Red Admiral upperside.
Holkham, West Norfolk

Fig. 166 Red Admiral underside.
Holkham, West Norfolk

General distribution and status
Summer visitor. The Red Admiral is a common immigrant species found throughout the British Isles in varying annual numbers. The first spring arrivals originate from northern Africa and southern Europe and there are further immigrations from southern and central Europe during the course of each year.

Flight period
This species has been recorded during every month of the year, although winter survival is rare. Specimens are occasionally seen in numbers in February, but the usual presence of other migratory species, including birds, suggests that these individuals are of continental origin. The first major arrival usually occurs during May and June, and their offspring are usually supplemented by further large immigrations during August and September. Very large numbers of Red Admirals may be present in the British Isles by October and they are a familiar and spectacular sight at Ivy blossom. A return southward migration begins by the end of August, and Red Admirals can sometimes be witnessed flying over high ground or 'outward bound' over the south coast. That these movements also take place at night is supported by the fact that specimens are sometimes caught in moth traps. The optimum time to see the adults in perfect physical condition is throughout September.

Red Admiral / Painted Lady

Larval foodplants
Common Nettle is the usual foodplant but Hop, Small Nettle and Pellitory-of-the-Wall are also used.

Habitat requirements
This highly mobile species may be seen in almost any habitat from coastal sand dunes to mountain tops. It is a familiar visitor to gardens and is commonly seen feeding from the flowers of cultivated plants such as Buddleia and Ice Plant.

Identification characters, variation and similar species
Average wingspan 68mm. The Red Admiral varies little, though specimens are sometimes seen which possess a bright white spot in the red band of the forewing and these are known as form *bialbata* Cabeau. In appearance, the Red Admiral is unlike any other species found in the British Isles.

Field tips
The first males to arrive in May are very territorial and habitually patrol a beat which may be, for example, a sunny patch along a woodland ride. When so engaged, they are extremely difficult to approach and will take off at the slightest disturbance. Those wishing to photograph the species are therefore advised to wait until the late summer months. Then the butterflies are more approachable as they feed from garden flowers and Hemp Agrimony along woodland rides or Ivy blossom along country lanes and hedgerows. They are also attracted to rotting fruit; such 'bait' may prove very successful if placed on a garden bird table.

Regional prime sites
During the summer, the Red Admiral is likely to occur anywhere in the British Isles, from the Channel Isles in the south to the Shetlands in the north.

Painted Lady
Vanessa cardui (Linnaeus)

General distribution and status
Summer visitor. The Painted Lady is an immigrant species for which there is little evidence of wintering survival. It has been recorded throughout the British Isles, although annual numbers vary considerably. There are occasional years of great abundance, the last being in 1996 when many millions of individuals were estimated to be present. Conversely, there are years when the species is relatively uncommon such as 1967 when there were only about 100 records. The first spring arrivals originate from northern Africa and their offspring are supplemented throughout the year by further arrivals from mainland Europe.

Flight period
The Painted Lady has been recorded during every month of the year but the first arrivals are usually seen in late March

Painted Lady

and early April. Larger numbers appear in late May and June. If the weather is warm these may give rise to several generations, the numbers of which are boosted by further immigration. Peak numbers are reached in August, and there appears to be an occasional return southerly migration in September and October.

Larval foodplants
The most common foodplants are Spear Thistle, Creeping Thistle and Marsh Thistle. Common Nettle, Mallow and Viper's Bugloss are also used.

Habitat requirements
This highly mobile species may be encountered in any habitat, though open ground with an abundance of thistles is favoured. These are not only foodplants for the larvae but also an important source of nectar for the adults. Painted Ladies are a common sight in gardens where they feed from the flowers of many cultivated plants, particularly Buddleia and Ice Plant.

Identification characters, variation and similar species
Average wingspan 64mm. The sexes are similar and variation is rare. There is no other breeding British or Irish butterfly that resembles this species, but it is similar to the very scarce vagrant American Painted Lady. The identification features are discussed under that species (p. 201).

Field tips
The Painted Lady should be sought during August in gardens, on rough ground with abundant thistles or along woodland rides where Hemp Agrimony grows. During years when the species is common, finding it should present few problems. In the early spring it should be looked for at the flowers of willows.

Regional prime sites
This species may be encountered anywhere in the British Isles during the summer months.

Fig. 167 Painted Lady upperside.
Holkham, West Norfolk

Fig. 168 Painted Lady underside.
Holkham, West Norfolk

Small Tortoiseshell

Fig. 171 Small Tortoiseshell upperside.
Holkham, West Norfolk

Fig. 172 Small Tortoiseshell underside.
Holkham, West Norfolk

Scotland there is one generation flying from mid-July onwards, although numbers here are usually supplemented by migrants from southern Britain; the optimum time to see the butterfly in peak condition is during August.

Larval foodplants
Common Nettle and Small Nettle are the only foodplants.

Habitat requirements
The Small Tortoiseshell may be seen in most habitat types. It is a common visitor to gardens where it feeds from cultivated flowers, particularly Buddleia and Ice Plant.

Identification characters, variation and similar species
Average wingspan 55mm; the female is slightly larger than the male. Variation is usually restricted to the depth of orange and the extent and boldness of the black markings on the upperside. The only species with which confusion might arise is the very rare Large Tortoiseshell. The diagnostic features are discussed under that species (p. 203).

Field tips and regional prime sites
The Small Tortoiseshell may be encountered commonly anywhere in the British Isles. It is often found in sheds and outhouses during hibernation and is sometimes even seen inside houses over the winter. During early spring it is often the first butterfly species on the wing and it is attracted to the catkins of willows. The insects are most active during the morning when they feed and bask. In the afternoons, the males set up territories which they defend vigorously from rival males. Pre-hibernating adults spend the majority of their time feeding.

Large Tortoiseshell
Aglais (=Nymphalis) polychloros (Linnaeus)

Status

Extinct resident; scarce immigrant; protected from sale (GB). During the 19th century the Large Tortoiseshell was known to be common around London and in Essex, East Suffolk, Sussex, the New Forest and as far west as Devon, though entomologists of the day were aware of great annual fluctuations in numbers. During the first years of the 20th century it was still very common in parts of Essex and Suffolk but from 1905 it went into decline and, until 1945, it appears to have been a very scarce butterfly. The following four years saw resurgence in its fortunes but this was short-lived and, from 1949 onwards, the species went into what ultimately became a fall to extinction as a breeding British insect.

Distribution of records

The species is still recorded as a casual immigrant but monitoring its numbers is difficult. It is popular amongst butterfly breeders, and many adults either escape or are deliberately and unadvisedly released. It is also often mistaken for the Small Tortoiseshell with which it has close superficial similarities. Apparently genuine immigrants rarely number more than one per year and the most recent of these are summarized as follows (after Salmon, 2000 and B. Skinner, pers. comm.): Woburn, Bedfordshire and St Leonards, East Sussex, 1991; Bathpool, East Cornwall, 1993; Bradwell, North Essex, 1994; Worthing, West Sussex and Bradwell, North Essex, 1995; St Leonard's, East Sussex, 1997; Brightlingsea, North Essex, 1999; Throp, Dorset and Lewes, East Sussex, 2000; Farnborough, North Hampshire and Felixstowe, East Suffolk, 2001; Mistley, North Essex, 2002; Three Oaks, East Sussex, 2005 and Ashcombe Bottom, East Sussex and Lydd-on-Sea, East Kent, 2006. The majority of historical records come from south-eastern England, though they range as far widely as northern England and Wales. It was, at least until the middle of the last century, probably resident in Scotland. It

Fig. 173 Large Tortoiseshell upperside.
Spain

Fig. 174 Large Tortoiseshell underside.
Spain

Large Tortoiseshell / Camberwell Beauty

has never been recorded from Ireland or the Isle of Man. It is believed to have been resident in the Channel Isles until about 1940 but there have been only infrequent sightings since, probably of genuine immigrants.

Flight period
There is one generation a year flying from mid-July to mid-August and again after hibernation from March to May.

Larval foodplants
Wych Elm is the favoured foodplant, though other elm species may be used as well as willows, poplars and birch.

Habitat requirements
In Britain, the Large Tortoiseshell was traditionally found along tall hedgerows and avenues containing elms. In mainland Europe, it is also associated with woodland edges and clearings. Willow catkins are an important source of nectar after hibernation and these are invariably present where the butterfly breeds.

Identification characters, variation and similar species
Average wingspan 72mm; the female is usually slightly larger than the male. This species may be mistaken for the Small Tortoiseshell from which it differs in the following ways:

1. Significantly larger (Small Tortoiseshell wingspan 55mm).
2. Forewing upperside with pale spot near apex yellow rather than white; hind corner of orange area with extra large black spot; metallic blue spots in dark margin absent or inconspicuous.
3. Hindwing upperside with dark inner half reduced to large distinct spot near leading edge.
4. Forewing underside more uniform, lacking conspicuous pale plain central area and bold dark markings.
5. Hindwing underside with conspicuous pale central dot; border between inner dark half and paler outer half distinctly straighter and less indented.

Field tips
The appearance of this species as an immigrant is unpredictable and rare. If there are reports during a particular summer, it may be worth searching willow blossom the following spring for post-hibernation butterflies.

Camberwell Beauty
Aglais (=Nymphalis) antiopa (Linnaeus)

Status
Scarce immigrant. The Camberwell Beauty is a scarce, though usually annual, visitor to the British Isles. It is reared commonly in captivity and often released in misguided attempts to introduce it as a breeding species. This makes interpretation of the records

Camberwell Beauty

Fig. 175 Camberwell Beauty upperside.
France (R. Thompson)

Fig. 176 Camberwell Beauty underside.
Holkham, West Norfolk

extremely difficult and should therefore be discouraged. Perhaps the most notable exploit of this sort was undertaken by L.H. Newman who released some 500 marked individuals in Kent and Hertfordshire between 1956 and 1961. The fact that none of these was re-recorded (Emmet & Heath, 1989) illustrates well the futility of such an exercise. Few adults that arrive here naturally in the late summer survive our winters and, as mating takes place only after hibernation, the chances of natural establishment are therefore slim. The immature stages have never been found in the wild in Britain or Ireland. Abroad, it is resident in northern Spain and Portugal, eastwards through central and eastern Europe, including southern and eastern Norway and central and eastern Sweden and Finland. In western Norway, western Sweden, Denmark and The Netherlands it is known only as a migrant.

Distribution of records

The species has been recorded widely throughout the British Isles, including the Isles of Orkney and Shetland, the Isle of Man and the Channel Isles. It is only rarely seen in Ireland and most of Scotland. Most annual totals are of single individuals, but there are occasional years of abundance and these can be summarized as follows: between 1850 and 1939, approximately 930 butterflies were seen with almost half of these recorded in 1872. During the 1940s, a period well-known for many immigrant species, over 180 were noted with large numbers arriving in 1945 and 1947. The relative abundance of these records in the southern half of England suggests that the butterflies originated in central or southern Europe rather than Fennoscandia. However, the next major 'invasion' in 1976, when there were approximately 300 sightings, appears to be more focussed on the eastern part of Britain, suggesting the reverse to be the

Camberwell Beauty

case. Subsequent meteorological analyses, including 'backtracking' weather movements, support this view. In 1983, ten individuals were noted and, in 1984, there were 12 records. The last great '*antiopa* years' were in 1995 and 2006 when several hundred butterflies were seen. Other recent years when there were more than 10 individuals recorded are 1996 and 2002. There have been several recent records for the Shetland Islands, which support Scandinavian origins for these particular butterflies, but the species has not been seen during the last twenty years in the other Scottish islands, the Isle of Man or the Channel Isles.

Flight period
Single brooded. The adults emerge from hibernation in March and can be seen until May. In southern Europe, the offspring then fly in June and July, whereas in Scandinavia the butterfly is on the wing during August and September. In the British Isles, it has been recorded in every month of the year, but the peaks are during April and again in August and September.

Larval foodplants
The immature stages have never been found in Britain or Ireland. In mainland Europe, a wide variety of trees are used including willows, poplars, elms and birch.

Habitat requirements
This species usually inhabits woodlands. Immigrants to the British Isles are often seen in gardens taking nectar from cultivated flowers such as Buddleia or the juices of over-ripe fruit and, after hibernation, have been seen feeding from the blossom of willows in and around woods and scrubland.

Identification characters, variation and similar species
Average wingspan 82mm. The female is larger than the male but otherwise very similar. There is variation in the shade of the pale borders; in some individuals these are yellowish cream and in others may be almost white. Early collectors believed that only the latter proved the specimen to be 'truly British', and forgeries were made by dealers who painted white the yellow borders of continental specimens. The large size and distinctive markings preclude confusion with other species.

Field tips
During August and September, the weather arriving on the coasts of eastern England and Scotland should be monitored carefully as easterly, or north-easterly, winds passing over Scandinavia, combined with occasional weather fronts, may herald the arrival of the Camberwell Beauty. An area of low pressure to the north-west of Scotland and a low with an associated warm front to the south-east of England or a high to the north of Scotland and a low with an associated warm front over southern England would provide very encouraging conditions. Flower-rich gardens and woodlands containing Hemp Agrimony, Common Fleabane or Michaelmas Daisy should then be searched. In areas where summer

Camberwell Beauty / Peacock

Fig. 177 Wild Cherry. Holkham, West Norfolk

immigrants have been recorded, the following April should be spent watching willow blossoms in woodlands or stands of Wild Cherry, the flowers of which are highly attractive to Vanessid butterflies emerging from hibernation (Fig. 177).

Peacock
Inachis io (Linnaeus)

General distribution and status
Resident. The Peacock is widely distributed and common throughout England, Wales and Ireland, including the Isle of Man and the Channel Isles. In Scotland, it is a common resident south of a line approximately between Argyll Main in the west and Angus in the east. There are scattered records from elsewhere as far north as the Shetlands but these are thought to represent vagrant individuals, resulting from northward migration during the early summer. The species is very

Peacock

Fig. 178 Peacock upperside. Holkham, West Norfolk

Fig. 179 Peacock underside. Holkham, West Norfolk

mobile and the northernmost limit of its distribution is likely to change from year to year.

Flight period
Usually single brooded, flying from mid-July until early September and again after hibernation from the beginning of March until mid-June. Many individuals enter hibernation as early as mid-August, though these will sometimes take to the wing again in warm years and can be seen until mid-October. In exceptionally hot years there may be a small partial second emergence in September, but this is a very rare event. The best time to see adults in perfect condition is during the first three weeks of August.

Larval foodplants
Usually Common Nettle, but Hop and Small Nettle are used occasionally.

Habitat requirements and field tips
A wide variety of habitats are suitable and the Peacock may be encountered anywhere except on the highest ground; even here there is a chance of seeing an occasional nomadic individual. It is most commonly seen in gardens feeding from Buddleia blossom, along open woodland rides and clearings where Hemp Agrimony grows and on waste ground where nettles thrive.

Identification characters, variation and similar species
Average wingspan 70mm; the females being larger than the males. Apart from size there is little variation and the spectacular markings of the Peacock make confusion with other species very unlikely.

Regional prime sites
Scotland. As the species is very mobile, migrating north in early summer and south towards the end of its season, the

northerly limit of its range is difficult to predict. However, it is now known to be resident in the counties of Argyll Main, Renfrewshire, Stirlingshire, West Perthshire, Fifeshire and West and East Inverness-shire. Further north, its frequency is unpredictable and those from the far north of Scotland wishing to see the species should concentrate their efforts in the aforementioned counties.

Other regions. Widespread and common.

Comma
Polygonia c-album (Linnaeus)

General distribution and status
Resident. Over the last 200 years this species has undergone remarkable changes in distribution. In the early 1800s it was widespread over most of England and Wales and was even present in parts of southern Scotland. By the middle of that century a severe decline began and, by 1913, it was more or less restricted to the counties along the border between England and Wales and in parts of south-east England (Emmet & Heath, 1989). Even here it was considered scarce. Since that time, especially since the 1960s, a remarkable expansion has occurred that continues to this day. At the species' former peak of distribution the literature of the time usually cited Hop as the main foodplant and Comma larvae were found commonly in hop gardens. Its decline coincided with that of the hop industry and the species only hung on where the plant continued to be farmed on a large scale. Over the last century the principal foodplant has been Common Nettle and

Fig. 180 Comma upperside. Holkham, West Norfolk

Fig. 181 Comma underside. Bentley Woods, South Wiltshire

Comma

this apparent change from one 'preferred' plant to another, possibly genetic in origin, may have been a major contributor to the species' subsequent success. For a detailed account of the species' fluctuations in distribution and abundance see Pratt (1986; 1987). At the present time the Comma is widespread throughout England as far north as the border with Scotland and in Wales it is found frequently in all but upland areas. It has been recorded recently in Scotland and Ireland but some of these are thought to be vagrants or releases. In the Isle of Man, the Comma has been seen during most years since 1999 and is now thought to be resident there. It is found throughout most of the Channel Isles.

Flight period
After emerging from hibernation in March, the butterflies pair and lay eggs, and some 40 per cent of the resulting larvae develop rapidly and produce adults in late June and July of the pale form *hutchinsoni* Robson (see Hutchinson's Comma, p. 211). These then produce a second generation of the typical form that flies during late August and September. Those larvae which develop more slowly in the spring emerge as adults in late July or early August and do not contribute to the second generation but enter hibernation unmated. These are also of the typical form. The peak times to see the species in good condition are during the first and second weeks of July and between the third week of August and the first week of September.

Larval foodplants
Common Nettle is the most widely used foodplant. Others include Hop, currants, elms and willows.

Habitat requirements
Individuals of the first generation are sedentary and are usually found in open woodlands and along woodland edges and hedgerows. Those of the second brood are more mobile and are often seen in gardens and orchards where they feed on nectar from cultivated plants and on the juices of rotting fruit.

Identification characters, variation and similar species
Average wingspan 56mm. Apart from the form known as Hutchinson's Comma (p. 211) major variation is rare. At distance on the wing, the Comma may be confused with a small fritillary species or a Small Tortoiseshell, but even casual observation reveals the scalloped wing edges diagnostic of this species. The presence of the curious white comma-shaped mark on the underside will put any identification concerns beyond doubt.

Field tips
In its appropriate habitats this species should not be difficult to find as it is usually fairly common, especially in the spring when in woodlands it regularly visits the blossoms of willows and Wild Cherry. In the late summer it is a regular visitor to gardens, and a few overripe apples or pears placed on a bird table and allowed to rot may well

Comma / Hutchinson's Comma

attract this and other butterflies, such as the Red Admiral. Visits to old orchards where windfall fruit is found on the ground should also prove successful.

Regional prime sites
Scotland. The continued northward expansion of this species' range has resulted in it gaining a patchy foothold centred around the counties of Roxburghshire, Berwickshire and Midlothian.

Northern England. Less common than further south, but the Comma can be seen at the northerly edge of its range at **Whitbarrow Scar** in Westmorland (access from SD 458 867).

Central, eastern, south-east and south-west England and Wales. Widespread and generally common on all but high ground.

Western Ireland. Absent.

Eastern Ireland. Absent as a breeding species but there are several recent records from the counties of Down, Wexford, Kilkenny, Dublin and West.

Hutchinson's Comma
Polygonia c-album form *hutchinsoni* Robson

Notes
Although Hutchinson's Comma is not a subspecies, its form, colour and flight period are so distinct from the typical Comma that its inclusion here is considered to be of interest. All individuals flying in June and the first half of July are usually of this form and it is believed to result from larvae that develop exclusively during the early summer period of increasing daylength. Those which grow more slowly, with at least part of their development taking place during decreasing daylength, produce individuals of the typical form that fly from late July or early August. The form was first discovered by the great lepidopterist

Fig. 182 Hutchinson's Comma upperside.
Holkham, West Norfolk

Mrs Emma Hutchinson who, during the latter half of the 19th century, bred Comma butterflies each year in large

Hutchinson's Comma

Fig. 183 Hutchinson's Comma underside. Holkham, West Norfolk

numbers at her home in Herefordshire – one of the species' last strongholds during its decline. She is known to have sent hundreds of larvae and pupae to various parts of Britain in an attempt to halt its fall in numbers. She was also aware that the then new practice of burning hop bines during the autumn led to the destruction of many thousands of larvae and pupae and so '...bribed...' those working in the hop fields to collect '...every larva and pupa they could find...' and so preserve '...this lovely butterfly...' (Salmon, 2000).

General distribution and status
Resident. Found as the summer form throughout the range of the typical Comma.

Flight period
Late June and July with the optimum time during the first and second weeks of July.

Larval foodplants
As for the typical dark form of the Comma (p. 209).

Hutchinson's Comma / European Map

Habitat requirements
More sedentary than the late summer typical form and found mainly in open woodlands and along woodland edges and hedgerows.

Identification characters
Differs from the typical Comma in the following ways:

1. Upperside ground colour paler and more ochreous.
2. Wing margins less scalloped and with shorter projections.
3. Underside ground colour much paler ochreous; markings lighter brown; overall appearance much more marbled.

Field tips and regional prime sites
As for the Comma (p. 209).

European Map
Araschnia levana (Linnaeus)

Status
Introduction; possible vagrant. The status of this species must be regarded as uncertain. Several attempts at introduction have been made and the species' popularity amongst butterfly breeders, and its subsequent release into the wild, inevitably cast doubt on the validity of suspected natural immigrants. Discussion in much of the recent literature regards the European Map as a scarce vagrant to these shores (e. g. Asher *et al.*, 2001; Salmon, 2000) and this, along with its fascinating history in Britain, justifies its inclusion here.

Distribution of records
In 1912, the species was introduced at an unknown locality on the borders of Herefordshire, Gloucestershire and

Fig. 184 European Map (spring). France (W. Powell)

Fig. 185 European Map (summer). France (W. Powell)

European Map

Monmouthshire. Two colonies established themselves, one at Symonds Yat, Herefordshire, the other near Ganarew, some 2 km to the west in the same county. In May 1913, a specimen was caught in the Monmouthshire part of the Forest of Dean. In 1914, two were reported at Symonds Yat and nearly a dozen were collected '...several miles away...'. A further 13 specimens were collected that year in various parts of the forest and, in 1915, it was reported to have been '...taken in numbers...'. Clearly, the species was doing well as the populations appeared to be growing and successful overwintering and breeding seems to have occurred. However, a respected entomologist of the time, A.B. Farn, took exception to the idea of introducing an alien species to the British fauna and allegedly set about killing as many of the butterflies as he could find. There was no further record of the species in the area after 1915.

There was a further introduction attempt in the Forest of Dean, probably in the 1920s, though there are few details. In 1922, it was seen in the New Forest, South Hampshire, but again details are scant. In 1942, it was known to have survived at least one winter following an introduction at Kingsteignton, South Devon, and there were further unsuccessful attempts to establish the species in Worcestershire in the late 1960s and Cheshire in the early 1970s.

The most recent records are from Surrey in 1982, East Kent in 1995 and South Essex in 2001 and these are regarded by some authorities to be genuine immigrants. The Surrey specimen appeared amidst a large influx of Red Admirals and other migratory species. For a detailed account of the rather chequered history of this butterfly in Britain see Salmon (2000). Over the last 25 years, the species' range in mainland Europe has expanded extensively and it is now established in northern France and parts of Fennoscandia. With the advent of climate warming it will be interesting to see if the European Map is able to establish itself naturally in the British Isles at some time in the future.

Flight period
There are two broods flying from late April to early June and again from late July to early September.

Larval foodplants
Common Nettle and Small Nettle.

Habitat requirements
There are many suitable habitats including woodland clearings and rides, sheltered hedgerows, scrubland and meadows.

Identification characters, variation and similar species
Average wingspan 30mm (male) and 45mm (female). As can be seen from Figs. 184 and 185, the spring and summer generations are very different in appearance, the former (form *levana* Linn.) resembling a small fritillary and the latter (form *prorsa* Linn.) a miniature

European Map

White Admiral. However, examination of the underside of spring individuals will reveal the absence of silver spots present in the fritillaries and the small size of the summer specimens precludes confusion with the White Admiral.

Field tips and regional prime sites
Perhaps the best chance of finding this extremely scarce vagrant would be during weather conditions suitable for bringing large influxes of immigrants from northern France into south-eastern England or from Scandinavia to eastern counties (see Field tips for Camberwell Beauty, p. 206).

Fig. 186 European Map underside. France (W. Powell)

Dark Green Fritillary

The Fritillaries
(Nymphalidae, subfamily Argynninae)

Small Pearl-bordered Fritillary
Boloria selene subspecies *selene* ([Denis & Schiffermüller])

General distribution and status
Resident. The Small Pearl-bordered Fritillary has declined to the point of extinction in most of central and eastern England, with few colonies remaining, but is widespread and locally common throughout much of Scotland, Wales and north-western and south-western England. In north-western Scotland, the species is represented by the Northern Small Pearl-bordered Fritillary (p. 221). It is absent from Ireland, the Outer Hebrides and the northern isles of Scotland, the Isle of Man and the Channel Isles.

Flight period
In southern England, this species usually flies from mid-May to the end of June, but further north the flight period becomes progressively later and, in northern Scotland, it is on the wing during late June and July. In southern localities the optimum time to see the butterfly is during the first two weeks of June and in the extreme north it is during the first two weeks of July. In the far south-west it may appear as early as late April in some years and when this happens there can be a partial second emergence in August.

Larval foodplants
Common Dog Violet and Marsh Violet, the latter being favoured in northern localities.

Fig. 187 Small Pearl-bordered Fritillary **male upperside.** Bentley Woods, South Wiltshire

Fig. 188 Small Pearl-bordered Fritillary **female upperside.** Bentley Woods, South Wiltshire

Small Pearl-bordered Fritillary

Habitat requirements
Depending on the region, this species occupies four main habitat types which may be summarized broadly as follows:

1. Woodland glades, wide rides and clearings (southern England) (Fig. 12).
2. Damp grassland and moorland (parts of northern England and Scotland) (Fig. 20).
3. Woodland edges and tracks and wet meadows (Scotland) (Fig. 3).
4. Grassland with bracken and scrub, dune slacks and coastal cliffs (Wales and south-western, central and parts of northern England) (Fig. 18).

In all habitat types it breeds in damp localities where the foodplants grow in sheltered lush vegetation.

Identification characters, variation and similar species
Average wingspan 39mm. Variation is limited mainly to extension or reduction of the black upperside markings. It is similar in size to the Heath Fritillary (p. 250), Marsh Fritillary (p. 244) and Glanville Fritillary (p. 247), but all of these species lack the prominent silver spots on their undersides. Confusion often arises with the Pearl-bordered Fritillary (p. 222) from which it differs in the following ways:

1. Emerges later and is therefore often comparatively fresher in appearance when seen flying together.
2. Hindwing underside with marginal row of silver spots edged with black, rather than brown, chevrons; row of spots in outer third black rather than brown; central area with at least three large black-edged silver spots rather than only one; prominent dark spot near base, large and black rather than small and brown. The two species cannot reliably be separated in flight or by the upperside markings alone.

Field tips
This species roosts overnight and during dull weather on the stems and flower-heads of tall vegetation such as sedges, Jointed Rush and Bracken. Visits to known localities early in the morning should prove successful in finding the butterflies and have the advantage of providing opportunities to photograph the undersides of correctly identified individuals. As the temperature rises through the day, such chances are limited as flight activity and basking with the wings open increases. The adults regularly visit flowers of Bugle, Ragged Robin, Tormentil, Common Bird's-foot Trefoil and buttercups.

Regional prime sites
Scotland. Widespread and locally common throughout most of Scotland, though absent from the south-east, the extreme north-east, the Outer Hebrides and the Islands of Orkney and Shetland. It is represented in the north-west, the Western Isles and their adjacent mainland by the Northern Small Pearl-bordered Fritillary (p. 221). Elsewhere the species can be seen in good numbers in the south-west of the country at

Small Pearl-bordered Fritillary

Feoch Meadows, Ayrshire, by searching the damp meadows to the north and north-east of the access point at NX 263 816. In Wigtownshire, it can be found at **Wood of Cree** along the track leading north-east from NX 832 709 and, in Kirkcudbrightshire, it is present in the area just north-east of **Lochaber Loch** (NX 924 704). In East Inverness-shire, it occurs at **Craigellachie** (NH 894 119), in Stirlingshire at **Inversnaid** (access from NN 337 088) and in Mid Perthshire it is present in good numbers at **Craigower Hill** (NN 937 593) and **Tyndrum Wood** (NN 343 292). In the east, a reliable site is **Glen Doll Forest** in Angus (NO 285 761).

Northern England. It is absent from most areas, including the Isle of Man, but widespread in the north-east of the region, and there are a few colonies present in North-east Yorkshire. Here it can be found at **May Beck** (NZ 899 014) by searching along the track leading south-east through the wood in the area known locally as 'John Bond's Sheep House'. In the north-west, the easiest places to see the species are in Westmorland at **Arnside Knott** (common in the scrubby areas near the main car park at SD 432 325) and **Whitbarrow Scar** (access from SD 458 867).

Fig. 189 Small Pearl-bordered Fritillary underside. Bentley Woods, South Wiltshire

Small Pearl-bordered Fritillary

Central England. Absent from most of the region but still fairly widespread in the west and can be seen in Shropshire on the limestone grasslands at **Llanymynech** (access from SJ 266 221), sheltered parts of the moorlands of **The Stiperstones** (track north from SO 365 976) and in the **Wyre Forest** (tracks south-west, including the Dowles Brook area, from SO 762 777 and the area known as 'The Pipeline' just north-east of the Earnwood Copse car park at SO 744 783).

South-east England. Very localized and usually scarce throughout. At **Oaken Wood**, Surrey, it persists in small numbers at the second clearing south-east along the main track from the access point at SU 981 349. In East Sussex, it is found in the area around **Park Corner Heath** (west from TQ 515 147).

South-west England. The species is widespread in this region and remains in good numbers in the east along the wider rides and clearings at **Bentley Wood**, South Wiltshire (SU 258 292), **Nagshead**, West Gloucestershire (SO 606 085) and on the scrubland at **Ubley Warren** in North Somerset (ST 505 557). In the centre of the region it is fairly common on the scrubby grasslands at **Little Breach** in South Devon (track north-east from the access point at ST 105 155). Further west it is present in the bracken-dominated grasslands near the coast at **Marsland Valley** in North Devon (from SS 215 175) and along the coastal paths between **Start Point** and **Prawle Point** in South Devon (east or west from SX 802 372). In the extreme west it is common along the coastal paths around **Porthgwarra** in West Cornwall (access from the car park at SW 371 217).

Wales. In the north-west, it inhabits the coastal footpaths in the area south of **South Stack** in Anglesey (car park at SH 205 823) and, in the east, it is common on the south-facing scrubby hillsides at **Eyarth Rocks** in Denbighshire (e.g. SJ 121 540 with access from SJ 128 543). In central Wales, it is present in good numbers along the woodland trails at the RSPB reserve at **Lake Vyrnwy**, Montgomeryshire (SJ 016 190) and, in the west, it is present at **Ynis-hir** in Cardiganshire (SN 678 963) where local information can be obtained from the RSPB's reception centre. In the south-west, the butterflies live along the coastal footpaths to the south of the western end of the B4583 around **St David's Head**, Pembrokeshire (SM 734 771) and, in the south, is fairly common on the damp heathland and marshland at **Welsh Moor** (SS 520 927), Glamorgan.

Western and eastern Ireland. Absent.

Northern Small Pearl-bordered Fritillary
Boloria selene subspecies *insularum* (Harrison)

Fig. 190 Northern Small Pearl-bordered Fritillary upperside. Glasdrum Wood, West Inverness-shire

Fig. 191 Northern Small Pearl-bordered Fritillary underside. Glasdrum Wood, West Inverness-shire

Subspecies type locality and authority
Specimens from the Isle of Scalpay in the North Ebudes, Scotland, were first described as a distinct subspecies by Harrison (1937).

General distribution and status
Resident. The subspecific status of the Northern Small Pearl-bordered Fritillary is questioned by some authorities who believe it to be merely a regional form at the north-western end of a geographical cline. But populations of individuals conforming to the original description, especially those on islands, are sufficiently genetically isolated from those of the typical subspecies that their status as a subspecies is hereby maintained. It is found in several of the islands of the South, Mid and North Ebudes, their adjacent mainland and parts of north-western Scotland.

Flight period
Usually flies during June and July with the best time to see this subspecies in good condition during the last two weeks of June.

Larval foodplants
Most commonly Marsh Violet but also Common Dog Violet.

Habitat requirements
Damp localities on meadows or moorland (Fig. 20), young conifer plantations and woodland clearings and tracks (Fig. 3).

Identification characters, variation and similar species.
Very similar in size and general appearance to the nominate subspecies from which it differs in the following ways:

Northern Small Pearl-bordered amd Pearl-bordered Fritillary

1. Forewing and hindwing upperside ground colour brighter with more contrasting black markings.
2. Hindwing underside ground colour paler with markings much bolder and brighter.

Field tips
As for the Small Pearl-bordered Fritillary (p. 217).

Regional prime sites
Scotland. On the mainland, this subspecies can be seen commonly in woodland clearings, edges and tracks in West Inverness-shire at **Allt Mhuic** (NN 121 912) and **Glasdrum** (NM 998 453). At the latter site it also flies along the roadsides and at quite high altitudes in open damp meadows. Also in West Inverness-shire, it can be found along **Glen Gour** (track north from NM 979 628) on the Ardnamurchan Peninsula.

Perhaps the best examples are to be found in the western islands of Rhum, Soay, Scalpay, Mull and southern parts of Skye where specimens may be particularly brightly marked. In Rhum, North Ebudes, it is present on the moorlands of **Kinloch Glen** along the track leading west from the village of Kinloch (NM 400 002) where it ranges widely but prefers damper localities. In Skye, also in the North Ebudes, it is found on the moorlands and woodland edges to the north of **Aird of Sleat** (NG 595 015). On the more northerly mainland, it can be seen in West Ross along the minor road heading north-west from Drumrunie as it follows the northern shore of **Loch Lurgainn** (e.g. NC 139 068 and NC 127 088). There are many opportunities to pull safely off the road; there is an official car park at NC 108 095.

Other regions. Absent.

Pearl-bordered Fritillary
Boloria euphrosyne (Linnaeus)

General distribution and status
Resident; protected from sale (GB). This once locally common species has declined severely over the past 50 years, mainly through the cessation of traditional coppicing and grazing regimes. In England and Wales, it is now restricted to widely scattered, often isolated, localities south-west of a line approximately between Denbighshire in the north-west and East Kent in the south-east. Outside this area there are strong colonies in Westmorland and West Lancashire but elsewhere it appears to be on the verge of extinction. In Scotland, it is very localized in the south and absent in the north but in central and western parts is widespread and sometimes locally common. In Ireland, it is restricted to the Burren limestone districts of Clare and South-east Galway. It is absent

Pearl-bordered Fritillary

from the western and northern isles of Scotland, the Isle of Man and the Channel Isles.

Flight period

Usually late April to early June in the south, getting progressively later further north where it flies from mid-May to the end of June. In southern England, the best time to see the species is during the first three weeks of May with sometimes a partial second emergence during August. In northern England, the peak is during the last week of May and the first week of June and, in Scotland, it should be sought during the first two weeks of June.

Larval foodplants

In the south, Common Dog Violet is most frequently used, whilst in the north there is a preference for Marsh Violet. Heath Dog Violet has also been recorded.

Habitat requirements

As with the previous species the Pearl-bordered Fritillary utilizes specific habitats depending upon the region in which it is found. These can be summarized broadly as follows:

1. Broad woodland rides and clearings and plantations usually younger than 10 years of age (southern central England, south-east England and eastern south-west England) (Fig. 12).
2. Grassland with bracken and scrub (Wales, northern central England, northern England, western south-west England and western Ireland) (Fig. 18).
3. Broad woodland tracks and edges of open sheep- or deer-grazed woodland meadows with bracken (Scotland) (Fig. 3).

In all habitats short vegetation with abundant dead dry plant material, such as bracken fronds, is required as the eggs are laid here.

Fig. 192 Pearl-bordered Fritillary upperside. New Forest, South Hampshire

Fig. 193 Pearl-bordered Fritillary underside. New Forest, South Hampshire

Pearl-bordered Fritillary

Identification characters, variation and similar species
Average wingspan 43mm. Major variation in the wing markings is rare. The most likely species with which it can be confused is the Small Pearl-bordered Fritillary. Distinguishing features are discussed under that species (p. 217).

Field tips
In all habitats this species is a frequent visitor to flowers, particularly in the early morning and evening, and it appears to have a preference for purple and yellow blossoms such as those of Bugle and buttercups, respectively. If these can be located at a known site the butterflies will probably not be far away. In Scotland, it should be sought along the south-facing edges of open woodland where this meets bracken growing in grazed pasture. Areas that have been trampled by stock are preferred. Again there should be an abundance of low-growing flowers. Roosting butterflies are easy to find during dull weather as they perch openly on sedges and bracken.

Regional prime sites
Scotland. The species is fairly widely distributed in central Scotland and can be found in good numbers in the west at **Allt Mhuic**, West Inverness-shire (NN 121 912), where local information can be obtained at the Visitor Centre. It can also be seen in the same county, but in smaller numbers, at **Glasdrum** (NM 998 453). Here the clearings and the track created below the power lines are the best places to search. In the north, it is seen at **Slattadale Forest**, West Ross. Here it is found in the more open areas of the forest along the marked trails east and south-east of the official car park at NG 891 713. In the east, is present at **Linn of Tummel** (NN 913 610) in East Perthshire and **Cambus O' May** (NO 422 973) and **Clais Fearnaig** (NO 066 932) in South Aberdeenshire. Further south, it is restricted to the counties of Dumfriesshire and Kirkcudbrightshire. Here it can be found on the north-western side of **Lochaber Loch** (NX 924 704) and in other open areas and woodland edges in **Mabie Forest** (access from NX 950 711).

Northern England. In the east of the region, the species may be on the verge of extinction as few strong colonies remain, and it is therefore not appropriate to publish their whereabouts here. However, in the west it can be seen reliably in scrubby areas at **Whitbarrow Scar** (access from SD 458 867), **Arnside Knott**, Westmorland (access from SD 453 774) and **Leighton Moss**, West Lancashire (SD 478 751).

Central England. Very localized in this region and generally found in small numbers. Two well-known sites are in Shropshire at **Llanymynech**, (SJ 266 221) where it inhabits the south-facing slopes, and the **Wyre Forest** (main access from SO 767 777) where it can be seen along the wider woodland rides and

Pearl-bordered Fritillary

clearings, particularly in the Dowles Brook area at approximately SO 745 764 and the section known as 'The Pipeline' just north-east of the **Earnwood Copse** car park at SO 744 783. In Herefordshire it flies in **Haugh Wood** (SO 595 366).

Eastern England. Absent.

South-east England. It is absent or in severe decline throughout most of the region. At **Oaken Wood**, Surrey (SU 995 338) it is still present in small numbers but perhaps the best place to see the species in this region is the **New Forest**, South Hampshire, where it can usually be seen along the broader rides such as those at **Standing Hat**, near Brockenhurst (e.g. near the track junction at SU 318 052).

South-west England. In the east of the region, it occurs in good numbers at **Bentley Woods**, South Wiltshire, along the rides and in clearings near the car park (SU 258 292). Further west, it is fairly widespread in the counties of North and South Devon where it tends to occupy more open habitats such as scrubby grasslands where bracken grows. In North Devon, it resides in such localities near the coast at **Marsland Valley** (SS 215 175) and, in South Devon, it should be looked for along the tracks west from the access point to **Kiddens Plantation** (SX 842 847). At the western edge of its range, it is found at **Bunny's Hill** (west from the reserve entrance at SX 117 675 to approximately SX 120 680) and along the **Millendreath/Seaton undercliffs** beneath the monkey sanctuary (SX 269 541) in East Cornwall. In the north of the region, it is present at **Hailey Wood** in East Gloucestershire (SO 965 016).

Wales. The species is extremely localized in Wales and more or less restricted to a few sites in the north-east and the south-west. In the north-east, it is present at **Allt Dolanog**, Montgomeryshire (south-facing slopes at approximately SJ 063 133), and **Eyarth Rocks**, Denbighshire, where it is most commonly seen at **Craig-adwy-wynt Ridge** (SJ 121 540). In the south-west, it can be found at **Cwm Soden** in Cardiganshire by following the footpath north-west for about 1km from the village of Nanternis (SN 366 579).

Western Ireland. Found only in the limestone district of the Burren in Counties Clare and South-east Galway. Here it is usually seen only in small numbers and inhabits limestone pavement interspersed with scrub. It may be sought in the areas centred on **Carran** (R 279 990) and **Mullagh More** (R 330 960) and the hinterland of **Black Head** (close to M 150 115). Great care should be taken when pursuing this swift butterfly, as running on limestone pavement is likely to result in injury.

Eastern Ireland. Absent.

Queen of Spain Fritillary
Issoria lathonia (Linnaeus)

Status

Scarce immigrant. The Queen of Spain Fritillary is a very rare visitor, although there have been periods of relative abundance and occasional instances of breeding and the establishment of short-lived colonies.

Distribution of records

In England, this highly migratory butterfly has been recorded from most of the counties south of North Somerset in the west and East Suffolk in the east. Elsewhere there are records from Buckinghamshire, Hertfordshire and Worcestershire. In Scotland, there is a single record from Roxburghshire (*c.*1868) and, in Ireland, there are two records (1864 and 1960). In the Channel Isles it is seen regularly and has been known to breed.

The butterfly was first recorded in the early 18th century and at that time was considered to be resident at Gamlingay in Cambridgeshire (Salmon, 2000). However, several non-British species, including Niobe Fritillary (*Argynnis niobe* (Linnaeus)) and the Scarce Swallowtail (*Iphiclides podalirius* (Linnaeus)), were also regularly reported from the same locality. Great scepticism therefore surrounded their credentials as unscrupulous dealers were

Fig. 194 Queen of Spain Fritillary upperside. Switzerland (R. Harrington)

Queen of Spain Fritillary

thought to be responsible for selling continental specimens as genuine British examples. The 'Cambridgeshire' records aside, it was regarded as a rare insect of erratic occurrence. The first period of relative abundance was between 1818 and 1872 when, during the latter year, no less than 50 specimens were recorded. There then appears to have been a period of great scarcity and the species was rarely noted until 1892. From then until 1939 it was seen, on average, once a year and the next notable influx was not until 1945 when 45 individuals were noted. Over the next 45 years it was again very scarce and the more recent records, all of singletons, can be summarized as follows: Surrey, South Hampshire and South Devon (1976), North Hampshire (1978), East Kent (1979 and 1987), Hertfordshire (1982), Dorset (1983) and South Hampshire (1988). The 1990s saw another period of increased sightings with several notable instances. In 1991, five were seen at the same locality in the Channel Isles whilst in 1993, several were seen together at Spurn Head in South-east Yorkshire. Between 1995 and 1998 a total of 15 individuals were recorded during consecutive years at Minsmere in East Suffolk. This prompted justifiable speculation that the species had bred at the site, but none of the immature stages was found. During this period there were several other records from East Suffolk and neighbouring North Essex. The most recent records are of single individuals seen in Dorset, Cambridgeshire and Staffordshire in 2003 and in 2006 two were seen in the Isles of Scilly.

Fig. 195 Queen of Spain Fritillary underside. Switzerland (R. Harrington)

The species is established in the Mediterranean region, coastal areas of The Netherlands and parts of Sweden and Finland. Increasing reports of the butterfly in other parts of The Netherlands and in Belgium, northern France and Finland suggest its range is expanding into north-west Europe.

Flight period
In mainland Europe, there are two or three broods between March and October. In Britain, the species has been seen from June onwards but the majority of records are from September and October.

Larval foodplants
Many species of violets and pansies have been recorded, but Wild Pansy and Field Pansy appear to be favoured at northerly

Queen of Spain Fritillary / High Brown Fritillary

latitudes such as those of the British Isles.

Habitat requirements
In northern Europe, it is usually found in well-drained habitats such as coastal dunes and heathland. Elsewhere its requirements are less specific and it can be found in most habitat types.

Identification characters, variation and similar species
Average wingspan 48mm; the female is larger than the male. There is little variation in the wing markings. It superficially resembles several other fritillary species but can be identified immediately by the very angular, pointed outline to both fore- and hindwings. The large prominent silver spots on the underside of the hindwings are conspicuous and diagnostic.

Field tips and regional prime sites
The chances of finding this scarce butterfly are very slim. Perhaps the best prospects would be amongst dune systems on the south-east or east coast of England in September and early October. Weather conditions similar to those described under field tips for the Camberwell Beauty (p. 206) may prove fruitful. Areas of the coast where the Dark Green Fritillary is common could be a good starting point as their presence suggests an abundance of violets (the shared foodplant) that may be of interest to a visiting 'Queen of Spain'.

High Brown Fritillary
Argynnis adippe ([Denis & Schiffermüller]) subspecies *vulgoadippe* Verity

Subspecies type locality and authority
Specimens from the New Forest in South Hampshire, England, were first given subspecific status by Verity in 1929. The nominate subspecies is widespread in continental Europe but does not occur in the British Isles.

General distribution and status
Resident; fully protected (GB). Since the 1950s, when traditional woodland coppicing was greatly reduced, this species has undergone one of the most severe declines of any British butterfly. Until that time most of the older authors stated that it was widespread and common in most of the larger woodlands in southern, central and north-west England and parts of Wales. Today it is absent from much of its former range and is more or less restricted to the Morecambe Bay area of north-west England, several localities around Dartmoor and Exmoor in South Somerset, North and South Devon and a few scattered sites in Wales. As a result of extensive research into its ecological

High Brown Fritillary

requirements and subsequent habitat management it now appears to be holding its own and the decline has been slowed. In some areas the butterfly is once more fairly common. There appear to be no historical records from Scotland, Ireland, the Isle of Man or the Channel Isles.

Flight period
Single brooded, flying from mid-June to mid-August, although at sites in north-west England it is on the wing about two weeks later. The best time to see the butterfly is during the first two weeks of July in Wales and southern England and the last two weeks of July in north-west England.

Larval foodplants
Several species of violet are used, the more frequent being Common Dog Violet and Hairy Violet.

Habitat requirements
Two main types of habitat are used and these can be summarized as follows:

1. Grassland and bracken mosaics where trampling by stock, especially ponies and/or cattle break up the dead bracken litter thus allowing the continuing presence of the larval foodplants and providing the necessary warm microclimate for the developing larvae (Fig. 18).
2. Cleared areas of woodland on rocky limestone outcrops and their adjacent broad rides and scallops (Fig. 198).

In all habitat types controlled growth of bracken and an abundance of nectar sources such as bramble, thistles and Ragwort are essential. For detailed accounts of habitat management for this butterfly see Warren (1994; 1995) and Warren & Oates (1995).

Identification characters, variation and similar species
Average wingspan 62mm; the female is slightly larger than the male. Major variation in the wing markings is rare. On the wing this species may resemble

Fig. 196 High Brown Fritillary upperside.
Gait Barrows, West Lancashire

Fig. 197 High Brown Fritillary underside.
Gait Barrows, West Lancashire

High Brown Fritillary

a large individual of the Comma (particularly form *hutchinsoni*), but careful examination, even through binoculars, reveals the distinctive scalloped wing edges of that species when the butterfly soars or glides. The most likely source of confusion, however, is with the Dark Green Fritillary, especially as the two can often be seen flying together. Even at close quarters it is extremely unwise to attempt identification on the wing, but when settled the High Brown Fritillary can be distinguished in the following ways:

1. Hindwing upperside with central row of black squared spots often, but not always, larger and bolder.
2. Hindwing underside with a row of white-centred brown spots in outer third; inner two thirds ground colour basically brown rather than green; edges of outer row of silver spots marked with brown chevrons rather than green.
3. Forewing underside with dark spots near the tip brown rather than green and often white-centred.

Field tips

On the wing this striking and powerful butterfly is hard to miss but getting close enough to examine and photograph it is a different matter. However, it is a

Fig. 198 Habitat of the High Brown Fritillary at Gait Barrows, West Lancashire

High Brown Fritillary

regular visitor to the blossoms of brambles, thistles and Ragwort and when engaged in feeding it can be remarkably obliging. The best tactic is therefore to find such flowers at a known locality and simply await its arrival. During the earlier part of the morning, fine views of the uppersides can be obtained, but to see the undersides the afternoons are probably best as the butterflies then tend to feed more with their wings closed in an attempt to regulate their body temperature. Views of the underside are essential for accurate identification.

Regional prime sites

Scotland. Absent.

Northern England. The species is known from several localities around the Morecambe Bay area of Westmorland and West Lancashire and recommended places to visit are **Arnside Knot** where it is fairly common and under the protection of efficient wardening (open scrubby areas that are passed on the way to the car park SD 450 775) and **Whitbarrow Scar** (access from SD 458 867). It is also present in good numbers at **Gait Barrows,** West Lancashire (SD 482 777) but a permit must be obtained before visiting the site (see Appendix II under Gait Barrows).

Central England. Extinct at most of its former strongholds and now only found in numbers at one private site in Herefordshire. Publication of the details is thus not appropriate.

Eastern and south-east England. Probably extinct.

South-west England. At **Bentley Woods** in South Wiltshire (SU 258 292), the species is recorded occasionally but its status there is uncertain. Concentrated attempts to find the butterfly at this popular site are to be encouraged and findings, along with a contact telephone number, should be entered in the log book situated at the official car park. In South Somerset, it was found formerly on the south- and west-facing slopes of **Bossington Hill** (access from SS 911 477) but it may now be extinct there. In North Devon, it is present on the bracken and grass slopes near the coast at **Marsland Valley** (SS 215 175) and near the coast at Heddon's Mouth (track north to the bay from the car park near the Hunters Inn at SS 655 482). In South Devon, the species maintains a stronghold on parts of Dartmoor; here it can be seen in good numbers on the south-west facing slopes of **Aish Tor**, approximately 4km north-west of Buckfastleigh (SX 703 707).

Wales. The species has a very scattered distribution in this region but can be seen near the village of Dolanog, Montgomeryshire, adjacent to the B4382 on the south-west facing slopes of **Allt Dolanog** (SJ 063 133). In the south, it occurs at **Old Castle Down**, Glamorgan (follow the concessionary footpath across the down north-east of the access point at SS 896 754).

Western and eastern Ireland. Absent.

Dark Green Fritillary
Argynnis aglaja subspecies *aglaja* (Linnaeus)

General distribution and status
Resident. This is the most widespread of the fritillaries and is found, sometimes commonly, in suitable habitats throughout much of the British Isles. It is absent from large areas of central and eastern England and in Ireland its distribution is mainly coastal. It is present in many of the Scottish Islands as far north as Orkney. It is also found on the Isle of Man and Sark in the Channel Isles. In Scotland, Ireland and the Isle of Man it is represented by the Scottish Dark Green Fritillary (p. 236). The status of this butterfly appears generally to be stable, although the number of individuals present at any given site may vary greatly from year to year.

Flight period
There is a single generation flying between early June and early September. The optimum time to see the species is during the second and third weeks of July but in the far north it is during the last week of July and the first week of August.

Larval foodplants
The usual foodplants are Common Dog Violet, Hairy Violet and Marsh Violet, the latter being preferred in the north.

Habitat requirements
The four preferred main habitats can be summarized as follows:

1. Flower-rich calcareous grassland, usually with areas of scrub or scattered bushes (Fig. 8).
2. Acid grassland with bracken (Fig. 18).
3. Flushes, river valleys and other wet areas on moorland (Fig. 20).
4. Coastal grasslands and dune systems (Fig. 6).

It can also be seen occasionally along wide woodland rides or clearings where these occur close to those habitats mentioned above.

Identification characters, variation and similar species
Average wingspan 63mm; the female is

Fig. 199 Dark Green Fritillary male upperside. Holkham, West Norfolk

Fig. 200 Dark Green Fritillary female upperside. Holkham, West Norfolk

Dark Green Fritillary

slightly larger than the male. Major variation is rare and appears to occur most frequently during hot summers. Pale forms, in which the orange ground colour is replaced with grey or cream, are referable to form *albescens* Verity, and very dark individuals, where the black markings are extended to cover most of the wings, reach their extreme in form *wimani* Holgren (Fig. 203). When flying, or when only the upperside is in view, this species can easily be confused with the High Brown Fritillary. The identification features are discussed under that species (p. 228). However, on moorlands or coastal grasslands any large fritillary encountered is likely to be this species. In woodlands, confusion is possible in flight with the Silver-washed Fritillary (p. 239) but in that species the forewings are far more pointed, and examination of a specimen at rest will reveal characteristically dissimilar markings, particularly on the undersides. In moorland areas, great care must be taken not to confuse this species with fast-flying diurnal males of the Oak Eggar moth, *Lasiocampa quercus* (Linnaeus) (Lasiocampidae) as they may look remarkably similar and, at a distance, can deceive even the most experienced lepidopterist.

Field tips

During the early morning and evening, adults often congregate at favoured feeding areas and can then be seen and photographed in good numbers. On grasslands, such areas are often at the top or the base of a slope and the butterflies have a definite preference for purple flowers such as knapweeds, thistles and willowherbs. In moorland areas, roadsides and flushes containing thistles are often used. The males spend the majority of their time patrolling low over the vegetation in search of females. They then fly conspicuously but rapidly, and feeding visits to flowers are often brief, thus making photographic opportunities scarce. Female behaviour is somewhat different and they are generally far less conspicuous. Their flights are often brief

Fig. 201 Dark Green Fritillary male underside. Sharpenhoe, Bedfordshire

Fig. 202 Dark Green Fritillary female underside. Holkham, West Norfolk

Dark Green Fritillary

and interspersed with long periods of basking and crawling amongst the vegetation in search of egg-laying sites. Casual observation of a colony may reveal many flying males but apparently few, if any, females. The best method of finding the females during the main part of the day is to patiently watch the males as, when they locate a potential mate, they immediately drop to the ground and courtship can there be observed and photographed with ease. The undersides are often difficult to see as the butterflies usually hold their wings open flat whilst feeding and basking. As the temperature rises during the day, they can sometimes be found feeding with their wings closed. Mid-afternoon is perhaps the best time to see such behaviour.

Regional prime sites

Scotland. Represented here mainly by the Scottish Dark Green Fritillary (p. 236) but in southern localities, most individuals conform to the nominate subspecies. Suggested sites are the open moorlands of **Mabie Forest**, Kirkcudbrightshire (e.g. NX 950 708) and **Whiteadder Reservoir** (NT 666 633) and **St Abb's Head** (NT 912 775) in Berwickshire.

Northern England. There are large areas of this region where this species

Fig. 203 Dark Green Fritillary form *wimani*. Sharpenhoe, Bedfordshire (K. Earp)

Dark Green Fritillary

was present in former times but is now apparently absent. However, it is widespread on the grasslands of the north-west and can be seen reliably in Westmorland at **Smardale Gill** (NY 740 082), **Whitbarrow Scar** (access from SD 458 867) and **Arnside Knott** (access from the car park at SD 450 775). At the latter two sites it can be very common and flies in company with the High Brown Fritillary. In the south-west it is present on the dunes at **Ainsdale Hills** (SD 300 115) in South Lancashire (follow the public footpaths south from the holiday camp at Ainsdale-on-Sea (SD 310 129)). In the east of the region it is very localized but can be seen in good numbers on grasslands in North-east Yorkshire at **Deepdale** (SE 911 910), **Fen Bog** (south-west of access point at SE 857 982) and **Pexton Banks** (SE 852 860). On the **Isle of Man**, it is represented by the Scottish Dark Green Fritillary (p. 236).

Central England. Absent from most of the region but widespread in the Derbyshire moorlands, for example at **Lathkill Dale** (SK 203 664). In the west, on the border with Wales, the species can be seen on moorlands in Shropshire such as the **Long Mynd** to the west of Church Stretton (access from the many car parks e.g. SO 425 945). At both of these moorland sites, the most favoured areas are in the vicinity of wet areas such as flushes. In the east of the region, it is very localized with apparently no reliable site.

Eastern England. Extremely localized in this region but, where it occurs, it can occur in large numbers. In the south-east of the region, it is common along the coast of West Norfolk at **Holkham Dunes** (west from TF 890 450 to **Gun Hill** at TF 850 457). In East Norfolk, it is very common on the dunes at **Horsey Gap** (TG 465 242). In the south-west of the region, it is can be abundant on the chalk grasslands at **Sharpenhoe Clappers** in Bedfordshire (steep slopes to the north-east of the car park at TL 065 295).

South-east England. In this region the Dark Green Fritillary is largely an insect of calcareous grasslands. In such habitats it is seen at **Stony Green Hill**, Buckinghamshire (SU 866 991) and, in the neighbouring county of Surrey, at **Box Hill** (e.g. the area known as 'Juniper Valley' at TQ 182 523). In the east, it is present at **Troseley Country Park**, West Kent (TQ 633 611) and, in the south-east, on the stretch of downland just east of **Birling Gap**, East Sussex (TV 554 960). In the south of the region, it is found on the coastal grasslands at **Compton Down** on the Isle of Wight at SZ 372 848 and, in the south-west, is common on the flower-rich meadows of **Martin Down** (SU 058 192) and **Pitt Down** (SU 418 293), South Hampshire.

South-west England. Widely distributed throughout the region where it may be expected to be seen, although sparingly, on many of the moorlands of Devon

Dark Green Fritillary / Scottish Dark Green Fritillary

and Cornwall. Away from coastal localities, its appearance can be rather unpredictable but the following sites are recommended. In the north, it is found on the grasslands of **Prestbury Hill**, East Gloucestershire (SO 993 248) and at **Stoke Camp**, North Somerset (park at ST 486 513 and walk 300m east to the reserve entrance at ST 489 512). In the south-east, it is fairly common on the coastal downlands of Dorset such as those at **Ballard Down** (from just north of the lay-by at SZ 022 808 walk east along the south-facing slope). Further west in the region, it is present in good numbers in coastal moorland areas of the **Marsland Valley** in North Devon (access from SS 215 175) and, in South Devon, at **Bolt Head** (coastal path south of the car park at SX 713 376). In the south-west, it abounds at **Penhale Sands**, West Cornwall (from the footpaths through the dunes south of the car park at SW 767 587 the butterflies can be seen at approximately SW 767 570).

Wales. Mainly coastal in the south-west but otherwise widely distributed throughout. In the north, in the island of Anglesey, it flies along coastal paths such as those leading south of the RSPB reserve at **South Stack** (access from SH 205 823). Travelling south along the coast it is found at **Benar Dunes**, Merionethshire (south-east of the car park at SH 573 227) and at **Ynys-hir**, Cardiganshire (SN 678 963). Inland, in Denbighshire, it is present in good numbers on the limestone grasslands at **Eyarth Rocks** (access at SJ 128 543 and walk west to SJ 121 540) and at **Allt Dolanog** (SJ 065 129) in Montgomeryshire. It is found along most of the south coast, and visits are recommended to **St Govan's Head**, Pembrokeshire (coastal path south-east of the car park at SR 967 930), **Whiteford Burrows**, Glamorgan (north-east of SS 440 935) and **Old Castle Down**, Glamorgan (concessionary paths north-east across the common from SS 896 754).

Western and eastern Ireland. Represented here by the Scottish Dark Green Fritillary (see below).

Scottish Dark Green Fritillary
Argynnis aglaja subspecies *scotica* Watkins

Subspecies type locality and authority
Specimens from Lochinver in West Sutherland, Scotland, were first described as a subspecies by Watkins (1923).

General distribution and status
Resident. This subspecies is found throughout Scotland (with the exception of the Shetland Islands and the isles of Lewis, Col and Tiree), Ireland (where it

Scottish Dark Green Fritillary

is mainly coastal in distribution) and the Isle of Man. However its characteristic features are expressed most strongly in individuals from the Western Isles of Scotland and their adjacent mainland. Elsewhere, many specimens appear superficially similar to the typical subspecies and, in southern Scotland, their appearance may be indeterminate.

Flight period
Usually from mid-June to late August, peaking during the last two weeks of July.

Larval foodplants
As for the Dark Green Fritillary (p. 232), although Marsh Violet is preferred in the north.

Habitat requirements
See Dark Green Fritillary (p. 232).

Identification characters and similar species
Differs from the typical subspecies in the following ways:

1. Male hindwing underside with silver spots more conspicuously edged with black.
2. Female forewing with costa and apex more rounded, giving a more ample overall appearance.
3. Female upperside ground colour with pinkish tinge and more strongly suffused with bluish-black scales; pale marginal spots contrastingly paler than ground colour, often almost white.
4. Female forewing underside with ground colour tinged deep pinkish.
5. Female hindwing underside with green suffusion darker and more extensively tinged with brown; silver spots more strongly edged with black.

Field tips
As for the Dark Green Fritillary (p. 232). In flight, the females of the Scottish Dark Green Fritillary often appear very dark and tinged with purple. They can be surprisingly dissimilar to their southern counterparts.

Fig. 204 Scottish Dark Green Fritillary male upperside. Ardnamurchan, West Inverness-shire

Fig. 205 Scottish Dark Green Fritillary female upperside. Arisaig, West Inverness-shire

Scottish Dark Green Fritillary

Fig. 206 Scottish Dark Green Fritillary male underside. Ardnamurchan, West Inverness-shire

Fig. 207 Scottish Dark Green Fritillary female underside. Arisaig, West Inverness-shire

Regional prime sites
Scotland. In north-eastern, central and eastern Scotland many individuals are superficially very similar to those of the nominate subspecies. Close examination should reveal at least some of the distinguishing features described above and, in most cases, individuals from the north-east are slightly larger and brighter than their English counterparts. In the east, it can be seen on the coastal dunes at **Forvie Sands**, North Aberdeenshire (NK 020 265), **Balkello Common Wood**, Angus (along the east-west track centred on NO 366 391) and at **Tentsmuir**, Fifeshire (tracks north from the car park at NO 499 242). In central Scotland, it is found in good numbers in the damper areas of moorland and in the vicinity of flushes at **Ben Lawers**, Mid Perthshire (follow the nature trails from the visitor centre at NN 609 379). In the west, one is more likely to encounter the true Scottish Dark Green Fritillary and at **Allt Mhuic**, West Inverness-shire (NN 121 912), many of the females are conspicuously dark. However, it is on the west coast that the most spectacular examples are found and these reach their extremes in the western islands, the darkest forms being seen most often on the Atlantic coastlines, such as that at **Kilninian** on the Isle of Mull, Mid Ebudes (NM 394 454). On the mainland, in West Inverness-shire, reliable areas to search are **Glen Gour** (the main track north from NM 979 628), the roadside moorlands and damp woodland edges along the B8007 between **Strontian** and **Ardnamurchan Point** (ending at NM 416 675), and the roadsides and damp meadows along the minor road south-west of Arisaig leading to **Rubh' Arisaig** (ending at NM 625 850).

Western Ireland. Widespread and fairly common throughout the Burren limestone district of Clare and South-east Galway (e.g. near **Caherconnell**

at R 240 970). In the north, it is found at **Sheskinmore**, West Donegal (G 961 953) and, in the south, is present along much of the south coast of Co. Cork where it can be seen reliably at **Castlefreke**, West Cork (south-east of the car park at W 335 345).

Eastern Ireland. In the south a reliable site to visit is at **Ballyteigue Burrow**, Wexford (S 899 076). Further north it occurs at **Lullymore**, Kildare (N 695 264) and at **Bloody Bridge**, Down (J 388 270).

Other regions. Absent.

Silver-washed Fritillary
Argynnis paphia (Linnaeus)

General distribution and status
Resident. Restricted to woodlands south-west of a line approximately between Montgomeryshire in the west and East Kent in the east. Outside this area there are outlying colonies in Westmorland and West Lancashire and also at other scattered sites, many of which may be the results of introductions. It is widely distributed throughout Ireland but is absent from Scotland, the Isle of Man and the Channel Isles. Following a general decline during the 1950s and 1960s, there has been a slight increase in range but it is difficult to assess the degree of its significance against a backdrop of introductions, both documented and unauthorized, that have taken place in recent years. In its strongholds this large and conspicuous butterfly is often common.

Flight period
Single brooded, flying between mid-June and late August. The optimum

Fig. 208 Silver-washed Fritillary male upperside. Farley Mount, South Hampshire

Fig. 209 Silver-washed Fritillary female upperside. Bentley Woods, South Wiltshire

Silver-washed Fritillary

time to see the species is during the second and third weeks of July.

Larval foodplants
Common Dog Violet is most frequently used.

Habitat requirements
The Silver-washed Fritillary is a true denizen of broad-leaved woodlands (Fig. 12), where it is usually seen in glades and open sunny rides, although the females require more shaded areas for egg-laying. Woodland with about 50 per cent shade is said to be ideal (Emmet & Heath, 1989). It is also able to utilize mixed coniferous and deciduous woodlands in the south-west of its range where it can also be found along sheltered country lanes, especially where these are adjacent to woods.

Identification characters, variation and similar species
Average wingspan 75mm; the female is slightly larger than the male. Males differ from the females in having conspicuous horizontal black bars of scent scales on the forewings. Major variation is very rare, although a proportion of the females in certain populations constitute the form *valesina* Esper in which the usual orange ground colour is replaced with bronze-green (see Greenish Silver-washed Fritillary, p. 242). Within its woodland habitat there is little chance of mis-identifying this butterfly. Although the Dark Green and High Brown Fritillary may sometimes be seen with the present species, both lack the diagnostic pointed forewings and both possess well-defined silver spots on the undersides.

Field tips
The large size and bright orange colouration of this species make it easy to detect where it occurs. Although the butterflies are often very active as they swoop in elegant fashion along woodland rides, both sexes are regular visitors to flowers such as brambles, thistles and Common Ragwort and can then be approached with ease. The males are attracted to orange objects and will come readily to flashing indicator lights on motor cars. Old-time collectors devised an ingenious, if frivolous, piece of equipment to attract the butterfly. It was known as a 'mobile' and consisted of a motor that rotated a long arm at the end of which was fixed either an unwanted dead male specimen or a piece of orange paper. Once set in motion this contraption would invariably attract the desired visitors. More complicated designs replaced the 'bait' specimen or paper with a rotating orange and black cylinder and this was said to work equally well.

Regional prime sites
Scotland. Not recorded since the 19th century.

Northern England. Well established at several sites in the Morecambe Bay area of West Lancashire and Westmorland where it can be seen easily at **Whitbarrow Scar**,

Silver-washed Fritillary

Westmorland (access from SD 458 867). Outside this area, there are a few scattered colonies where the insect is usually uncommon and publication of their whereabouts is hence inappropriate.

Central England. Absent or very scarce in the north-eastern half of the region but elsewhere it is widespread and often locally common. Suggested sites to visit are the **Wyre Forest**, Shropshire, where the butterfly can sometimes be very common (follow the forest walks from the car park at SO 762 777) and **Monk Wood**, Worcestershire (SO 804 607).

Eastern England. There are several small colonies in the south-west of the region that are probably the results of introductions and, because of their vulnerability, are not suitable for publication here.

South-east England. Generally widespread in this region, although scarcer in the east. In Surrey, it can be seen at **Norbury Park** (TQ 152 550) and, in East Sussex, it is present in good numbers at **Rowland Wood** (access from TQ 515 147). In the south-west, it is fairly common in parts of the **New Forest**, South Hampshire (e.g. **Denny Wood** (SZ 335 070), **Pondhead Inclosure** (SU 308 070), **Standing Hat** (SU 315 037)) and in **Alice Holt Forest**, North Hampshire (SU 801 432). In the north, it is present at **Wendover Woods**, Buckinghamshire (SU 892 074).

Fig. 210 Silver-washed Fritillary underside.
Bentley Woods, South Wiltshire

South-west England. Widespread and generally common in suitable habitats throughout the region. Some suggested sites to visit are: **Nagshead**, West Gloucestershire (SO 606 085), **Bentley Woods**, South Wiltshire (SU 258 292), **Lydlinch Common**, Dorset (south-west to **Brickles Wood** from ST 737 137), **Little Breach** (ST 105 155) and **Plymbridge Wood** (SX 523 586) in South Devon and **Bunny's Hill**, East Cornwall (access from SX 117 675 with the butterflies at approximately SX 120 680).

Wales. Absent from much of the north of the country and from the higher ground but widespread and sometimes common elsewhere. In northern central Wales, it is fairly common at the RSPB reserve at **Lake Vyrnwy** (SJ 016 190) and at **Allt Dolanog** (SJ 063 133), Montgomeryshire. Further south, it can be seen in Cardiganshire at **Ynis-hir** (SN 678 963) and at **Pembrey**

Silver-washed Fritillary / Greenish Silver-washed Fritillary

Country Park, Carmarthenshire (SS 405 005).

Western Ireland. Widespread, very localized and rarely common. The most reliable sites to visit are **Coole Park**, South-east Galway (M 430 030) and **Dromore Wood**, Clare (R 365 870).

Eastern Ireland. Widespread but very localized and usually only found in small numbers. Visits to **King's Bog**, Kildare (N 715 091) and **Ballykeeffe Wood**, Kilkenny (S 410 510) should be successful. In the north, it can be seen at the Ulster Wildlife Trust reserve at **Glenarm Forest**, Antrim (D 304 111).

Greenish Silver-washed Fritillary
Argynnis paphia form *valesina* Esper

General distribution and status
Resident. The Greenish Silver-washed Fritillary is not a subspecies of the Silver-washed Fritillary but is merely a form found only in the females of certain populations. At some sites it

Fig. 211 Greenish Silver-washed Fritillary. Farley Mount, South Hampshire

Greenish Silver-washed Fritillary

may constitute up to 40 per cent of the individuals present, although it is usually found at much lower proportions (see Ford, 1945). The excitement evoked amongst butterfly-watchers by its scarcity and spectacular appearance justifies its treatment here as a 'specific' taxon. It is seen mainly in Dorset, South Wiltshire and South Hampshire but may occur rarely elsewhere.

Flight period, habitat requirements and larval foodplants
As for Silver-washed Fritillary (p. 239), although one should remember that female Silver-washed Fritillaries emerge a week or so later than the males.

Identification characters, variation and similar species
Average wingspan 77mm. This form differs from the typical Silver-washed Fritillary in having the usual orange ground colour completely replaced with a deep bronze-green. Its large size and distinctive colouration sets it apart from other species and hence makes confusion with them very unlikely.

Field tips
Very few sites produce this form in good numbers, and anyone wishing to see it is advised to visit one of the prime sites listed below and simply wait at a patch of flowering bramble for feeding Silver-washed Fritillaries. Some specimens of the typical female have a bronze tinge to their wings but care should be taken not to confuse these with the true *valesina* in which there is absolutely no trace of orange or brown.

Regional prime sites
At one time the Greenish Silver-washed Fritillary was considered to be extremely scarce outside the New Forest in South Hampshire, but a general decline of the species as a whole in that area precludes its continued relative abundance there. Although it may occur in small numbers elsewhere its strongholds remain in central southern England where it can regularly be seen at the following sites.

South-east England. **Farley Mount Country Park** (especially Crab Wood), South Hampshire (SU 433 293).

South-west England. **Bentley Woods** in South Wiltshire (SU 258 292) and **Piddles Wood** (access from ST 792 127) and **Eastcombe Wood** (SY 827 098) in Dorset.

Other regions. Absent or scarce.

Fig. 212 Greenish Silver-washed Fritillary underside. Farley Mount, South Hampshire

Marsh Fritillary
Euphydryas aurinia (Rottemburg)

Fig. 213 Marsh Fritillary upperside. Bentley Woods, South Wiltshire

Fig. 214 Marsh Fritillary underside. Lydlinch Common, Dorset

General distribution and status
Resident; fully protected (GB and NI). The Marsh Fritillary is a species of great conservation concern throughout Europe. In many countries a decline of 50 per cent has been estimated and the species has recently become extinct in The Netherlands (Asher *et al.*, 2001). In the British Isles, it was once widespread over much of England and Wales as well as parts of southern and eastern Scotland. Today it has disappeared from all of eastern Britain; its range is now limited to south-west England, south-west and parts of north-west Wales, the islands of south-western Scotland and their adjacent mainland and Ireland, where it remains locally widespread. There is a handful of colonies in north-west England but these appear to be on the verge of extinction. In eastern England there is one colony that is the result of an unauthorized introduction. It has never been recorded in the Isle of Man or the Channel Isles.

The butterfly is prone to spectacular fluctuations in population size. In some years at known colonies its numbers may be below the observation threshold, and therefore be presumed to have become extinct, only to 'reappear' several years later. At the other extreme, Frohawk (1886) describes an event in Shropshire in 1884 where so many 'countless thousands' of larvae were seen that the ground was 'blackened by the swarm'. The species is now extinct in that county.

Flight period
Mid-May to early July in a single generation, peaking during the first two weeks of June. In Scotland the optimum time of appearance is during the second and third weeks of June.

Larval foodplants
The usual foodplant is Devil's-bit Scabious, although Small Scabious and Field Scabious are used occasionally (Asher *et al.*, 2001).

Marsh Fritillary

Habitat requirements

The Marsh Fritillary requires open sunny habitats where the requisite amount of direct warm sunshine allows rapid development of the larvae. In such circumstances colonies may be found on various types of grassland such as wet meadows containing tussock-forming grasses (Fig. 19), heaths, moorlands, calcareous hillsides (usually south- or west-facing) and large woodland clearings. The latter habitat may often be temporary as natural vegetative encroachment usually leads to a degree of over-shading that prevents the species' continued presence. Colonies are compact, discrete and prone to local extinction through adverse weather conditions and mortalities caused by the parasitoid wasp *Apanteles bignellii* Marshall. These natural processes are usually countered by the formation of 'metapopulations'. These comprise several loosely-linked colonies that are in close enough proximity to each other to allow recolonization should a nearby habitat patch become available through the extinction of a neighbouring population. The adult butterflies are often reluctant to cross natural barriers such as hedgerows or expanses of water. However, some females may travel several kilometres to colonize new sites and, when so doing, may be encountered some distance from their usual habitats.

Identification characters, variation and similar species

Average wingspan 40mm; the female is slightly larger than the male. The distinctive markings of this species are unlike those of any other butterfly found in the British Isles and misidentification is therefore unlikely. Variation within the basic pattern is considerable and several geographic forms have been named. The typical form found in England and Wales is referred to as form *anglicana* Fruhstorfer. In Scotland, individuals may have more contrast between the orange ground colour and the cream markings and these are referable to as form *scotica* Robson. In Ireland this contrast may be even greater; such specimens are known as form *hibernica* Birchall. Although subspecific status was at one time proposed for the Irish form, it is now considered unjustified as such variation is often the result of climatic conditions and population size rather than purely geographical factors. Ford & Ford (1930) provide detailed further reading on this subject. Adults that have been flying for two or three days lose many of the scales from their wings and appear translucent or glossy (Fig. 215) and this gave rise to the popular name of 'Greasy Fritillary' used by lepidopterists of the 19th century.

Field tips

At a known locality this species is very easy to locate. The males establish small territories and will actively investigate any other butterfly that strays too close. Much of their short lives, usually only three or four days, is spent patrolling in search of females and they are easy to see as they fly low over the vegetation. Both sexes feed regularly from a variety of

Marsh Fritillary

flowers and both spend long periods basking, especially in the mornings and evenings.

Regional prime sites
Scotland. Restricted mainly to the islands of Islay, Jura and Mull, Mid Ebudes, and their adjacent mainland. There are numerous sites in **Islay**, and information regarding the species there should be obtained from the Islay Natural History Trust (see Appendix II). Elsewhere it can be seen reliably at **Taynish** National Nature Reserve in Kintyre (NR 732 845) and, in small numbers, at **Glasdrum Wood**, West Inverness-shire (beneath the power lines at NM 998 453).

Northern England. There are three known colonies in Cumberland and all are extremely vulnerable. Publication of their whereabouts is therefore not appropriate.

Central England. Extremely scarce and restricted to perhaps one remaining vulnerable colony. Publication of this site is hence not appropriate.

Eastern England. There is a thriving colony at **Chambers Farm Wood**, North Lincolnshire (park at the Visitor Centre at TF 149 739 and go to the area known as Little Scrubs Meadow at TF 145 744). This population is the result of an unauthorized introduction.

South-east England. Very scarce in this region but can be seen in small numbers along Bockerley Ditch at **Martin Down**, South Hampshire (park at SU 037 201 and follow the ditch to the south and south-east). Site maps are available at the car park.

South-west England. The species is widely distributed in this region. In Dorset it can be found in good numbers at **Hod Hill** (ST 852 112), **Lankham Bottom** (ST 610 003) and **Lydlinch Common** (meadow east of the gate on the A3030 approximately 1km south-west of the junction with the A357 at ST 729 130). Further west, in South Somerset, it is present sparingly at **Buckland Wood** (ST 185 175) and, in North Devon, occurs at **Dunsdon** National Nature Reserve (SS 295 078). In East Cornwall, it can reliably be seen at **Breney Common** (SX 054 610).

Wales. Well distributed in the western half of the country with strong colonies in parts of the north-west and south-west. In the north, it can be seen in

Fig. 215 'Greasy' Fritillary. Lydlinch Common, Dorset

Marsh Fritillary / Glanville Fritillary

Merionethshire at **Morfa Harlech** (SH 559 340) (permit required prior to visiting from Countryside Council for Wales (see Appendix II)) and **Tir Stent** (SH 754 164). In the south, it is present in Glamorgan at **Caeau Ffos Fach** (SN 576 120), **Welsh Moor** (SS 520 917) and **Pengwern Common** (SS 531 916).

Western Ireland. Widely scattered but very localized. It occurs in fair numbers at **Ballydoogan Bog**, South-east Galway (north-east off the N65 on track along the western edge of the bog at M 674 180) and at **Bunduff Lough**, Sligo (G 712 553).

Eastern Ireland. Widespread but also very localized. It is present in good numbers at **Lullymore**, Kildare (N 693 260) and, in Down, on the National Trust's reserve at **Murlough** (J 405 345).

Glanville Fritillary
Melitaea cinxia (Linnaeus)

General distribution and status
Resident; protected from sale (GB). The Glanville Fritillary was formerly found in many localities in south-eastern England as far north as Lincolnshire from where it was first described in 1703. The specimens were collected by Lady Eleanor Glanville, a highly respected entomologist of the day, and were originally given the name of 'Lincolnshire Fritillary'. Of passing interest, Lady Glanville's will was contested via an 'Acts of Lunacy' ruling as the relatives involved claimed that '…none but those who were deprived of their Senses [sic], would go in pursuit of butterflies.' The judge at the trial found in

Fig. 216 Glanville Fritillary upperside.
Hordle Cliffs, South Hampshire

Fig. 217 Glanville Fritillary underside.
Hordle Cliffs, South Hampshire

Glanville Fritillary

Lady Glanville's favour after testimony from other leading contemporary entomologists. Today, the species is generally restricted to a few localities along the southern coast of the Isle of Wight and in Guernsey and Alderney in the Channel Isles. There is a single vulnerable colony on the mainland of South Hampshire and a recently rediscovered population, of unauthorized introduction, in North Somerset. Where it occurs it can often be the commonest butterfly on the wing. However, numbers can fluctuate greatly from year to year and, as may be the case in the Somerset colony, sometimes fall below the observation threshold and the species is then presumed extinct. There seem to be few threats to the butterfly's future in the British Isles at the present time. Amongst those that are a threat, coastal defence work may interfere with the natural processes of undercliff slippage on which the species relies for the creation of suitable habitat, and severe storms such as those in Jersey in 1988 which appear to have rendered the island's colonies extinct.

Flight period
Single brooded, flying from late May until the beginning of July with a peak during the first three weeks of June. Following an unusually warm spring there may be a partial second emergence in early August.

Larval foodplants
This species feeds almost exclusively on Ribwort Plantain, though fully-grown larvae have been found on Buck's-horn Plantain where the usual foodplant has become short in supply due to voracious feeding.

Habitat requirements
The main habitat in Britain comprises coastal grassland on undercliffs where slippage and erosion cause the ongoing formation of bare areas of soil. Here the foodplant can grow and colonize in abundance and the microclimate is warm (Fig. 14). The south-facing coastal chalk downs and the deeply incised coastal valleys, known locally as 'chines', of the Isle of Wight provide ideal conditions for the butterfly. Large colonies may sometimes be established on chalk grassland further inland, although these are usually transient. During the 18th century it was known to occur in sheltered areas of open woodlands in Lincolnshire, but no British colonies are known in such habitats today. Like the Marsh Fritillary, it forms metapopulations which undergo periodic extinction and recolonization and are apt to suffer from inbreeding depression (Saccheri *et al.*, 1998).

Identification characters, variation and similar species
Average wingspan 45mm; the female is slightly larger than the male. The only species with which this could be confused is the Heath Fritillary (p. 250). However, as each is very localized in its distribution with no overlap, there is little chance of misidentification. A diagnostic feature of the Glanville

Glanville Fritillary

Fritillary is the presence of black spots within the row of orange submarginal patches on the hindwing upperside. These are absent in the Heath Fritillary. The Pearl-bordered and Small Pearl-bordered Fritillaries are both similar in size, but both of these species have more ample, rounded forewings and possess large conspicuous silver spots on their undersides. Major variation in the Glanville Fritillary is rare.

Field tips

On calm sunny days this butterfly is easy to locate along cliff edges and undercliffs where it flies with rapid wingbeats interspersed with graceful glides, feeding regularly from cliff-top flowers such as Thrift. It is usually only active in warm conditions, although during windy periods it can still be found in sheltered hollows beneath the cliffs. It must be stressed, though, that the ground in such places is often unstable and searching for the butterfly under poor weather conditions is potentially extremely dangerous and is not to be recommended. Following heavy rain, the undercliffs should quite definitely be avoided.

Regional prime sites

South-east England. The British stronghold for the species is along the southern coast of the Isle of Wight. Here it can best be seen in good numbers in the area around **Compton Chine** (SZ 372 848). Taking the car ferry from Lymington (leaving at half-hourly intervals) can be an expensive business, but travelling as a foot passenger is relatively cheap. A public bus service leaves Yarmouth ferry port four times a day and drops off passengers at Compton Farm. A short walk south after crossing a stile leads directly to the coastal path where the butterflies are found. The ferry crossing from Lymington to Yarmouth and the bus journey from Yarmouth to Compton Farm each take about half an hour. Further east along the coast, the butterfly is common near Ventnor at **Wheeler's Bay** (SZ 776 570) where, from the promenade at the base of the undercliff, as many as 100 Glanville Fritillaries have been seen on a single visit in recent years. On the mainland, in South Hampshire, there is a small colony at **Hordle Cliffs**, although numbers here can be very low. For example in 2004, the author saw no more than three individuals on each of three visits. From the 'Pay and Display' car park at SZ 263 926 take the path south and then east along the coast to search the flower-rich undercliffs at approximately SZ 268 921. Whilst this mainland site may appear convenient for seeing the Glanville Fritillary, success is not guaranteed and time should be allowed to make the ferry journey to the species' strongholds on the Isle of Wight.

South-west England. A colony of presumed unauthorized introduction was discovered during the early 1980s at **Sand Point**, North Somerset (track from the National Trust car park to the trigonometric point, then south to the scrub-cleared slope close to ST 327 660).

Glanville Fritillary / Heath Fritillary

Specimens were seen here until at least 2000, but by 2004 the insect was assumed to have died out. However, in 2005 several individuals were again seen. There is speculation as to whether the butterfly recovered from almost perilously low numbers under its own powers or was the subject of fresh introductions. The latter seems most likely and, although local entomologists must delight in seeing such an 'alien' animal in their district, its origin should be formally acknowledged.

Other regions. Absent.

Heath Fritillary
Melitaea athalia (Rottemburg)

General distribution and status
Resident; fully protected (GB). In the British Isles, the Heath Fritillary is found only in two areas of England: Somerset, Cornwall and Devon in the south-west and Essex and Kent in the south-east. There are historical records from other parts of central, eastern and southern England, although it has never been reported from the Channel Isles. It is regarded as a species in decline, but several reintroduction schemes and active habitat management have revived its long-term prospects (see Warren, 1991). Even so, one formerly thriving colony in East Cornwall has disappeared within the last three years.

Flight period
Single brooded. In Cornwall, the adults fly between the last week of May and the first week of July but at other south-western sites and those in the south-east, the flight period is from the second week

Fig. 218 Heath Fritillary male upperside.
Hadleigh Great Wood, South Essex

Fig. 219 Heath Fritillary female upperside.
Hadleigh Great Wood, South Essex

Heath Fritillary

in June to the first week in August. At south-eastern localities, an occasional second emergence has been recorded during late August and early September. This is unusual and only occurs in exceptionally hot summers when development from the first generation is accelerated. The optimum time to see the species is during the last week of June and first week of July. In Cornwall, it should be sought during the last two weeks of June.

Larval foodplants

In the south-east, Common Cow-wheat is utilised exclusively. In the south-west, Common Cow-wheat is used on heathland habitats, but in grassland localities Ribwort Plantain and Germander Speedwell are the usual foodplants. Other plants have been recorded on occasions but those listed are favoured.

Habitat requirements

In south-eastern sites, the Heath Fritillary inhabits broad woodland rides with sunny openings and clearings where coppicing or felling has taken place (Fig. 13). Such areas encourage the growth of Common Cow-wheat on which the eggs are laid. If clearings and rides are not maintained the plant, and therefore the butterfly, cannot survive. In the south-west, this species inhabits sheltered, Bilberry-dominated valleys on Exmoor where Common Cow-wheat occurs and, in Devon and Cornwall, open unimproved grassland where Ribwort Plantain and/or Germander Speedwell grow (Fig. 18).

Identification characters and similar species

Average wingspan 42mm; the female is slightly larger than the male. The Glanville Fritillary is the only species which could cause confusion as it is superficially similar. However, as mentioned under that species, it is restricted to the Isle of Wight, one site on the coast of South Hampshire and at an introduction site in North Somerset. The two species are therefore very unlikely to occur at the same locality. Small Pearl-bordered and Pearl-bordered Fritillaries are similar in size but both have more ample, rounded forewings and possess large silver spots on the hindwing undersides.

Field tips

At woodland sites, such as those in the south-east, one should look for broad rides and tracks with scalloped edges where trees have been removed. The larval foodplant, Common Cow-wheat, is in bloom at the time when the butterflies are on the wing, and areas where the

Fig. 220 Heath Fritillary underside.
Hadleigh Great Wood, South Essex

Heath Fritillary

conspicuous yellow flowers carpet the ground are those most likely to attract Heath Fritillaries (Fig. 221). Both sexes fly throughout the day when the temperature rises above around 17°C, provided there is at least some sunshine. During the early morning, they are lethargic and spend a great deal of time basking conspicuously on sunlit vegetation and can then be spotted from some distance. At this time, ideal photographic opportunities present themselves as the butterflies are very approachable and will even crawl onto one's hand. During the rest of the day, they fly actively and feed from the flowers of brambles and buttercups. At more open sites, such as those in the south-west, Tormentil is often visited.

Regional prime sites
Scotland, northern, central and eastern England. Absent.

South-east England. The reintroduction site at **Hadleigh Great Wood**, South Essex, is an excellent place in the south-east to see the Heath Fritillary. From junction 30 of the M25, follow the A13 for Southend-on-Sea until the junction with the A129(N) and the B1014(SW). After the roundabout take the second left-hand turning onto New Road, left onto Rectory Road and then straight on to Poors Lane. Park at the end of the housing estate at TQ 818 878 and follow the woodland tracks north-east for about 250m to Dodd's Grove and Hadleigh Great Wood. During a sunny day in late June dozens of individuals can be seen here.

The large complex of woodlands to the north and west of Canterbury, East Kent, is home to many strong colonies of this species. Favoured areas to visit are **Church Wood**, just west of Hoath (TR 122 595) and **East Blean Wood**, just west of Maypole (TR 194 644).

South-west England. In East Cornwall, the species was reintroduced in 2006 to **Greenscombe Wood**, approximately 1km south of Luckett (SX 391 723). Elsewhere in the south-west there are several colonies centred on the South Somerset section of Exmoor, including **Haddon Hill** (track north from just west of the lay-by at SS 979 285 for 100m and then east for approximately 200m to the moorland containing abundant Common Cow-wheat adjacent to the woods), **Alcombe Common** (park in the village at Manor Road just before 'access only' sign and walk south for some 500m to the

Fig. 221 Common Cow-wheat. Hadleigh Great Wood, South Essex

Heath Fritillary

Aldersmead stables and then east for about 200m to the bracken-dominated moorland and search the area containing Common Cow-wheat immediately to the south) and **Dunkery Hill** (park at SS 895 406 and take the track east for about 800m to the area of Common Cow-wheat and bracken-dominated scrub beyond the eastern side of the line of woodland on the south-facing slopes of Bin Combe (SS 910 410). Continuing east from here, a further colony is present about 200m along the track close to SS 910 410). At many of the sites in Somerset the numbers of Heath Fritillary encountered vary, sometimes dramatically, over time. In recent years numbers seem to have declined somewhat at Dunkery Hill. The once-thriving colony at nearby **Crawter Hill** may even have declined almost to the point of extinction, but extensive work has taken place in recent times to revive the habitat; the site is thus well worth a visit. Crawter Hill is on the west side of Horner Wood, just south of Porlock, at SS 893 459. Parking is available on the hill. From there follow the main track until the favoured area is reached about halfway up the slope where the track bends sharply as it crosses a stream near an isolated group of pine trees.

Wales and western and eastern Ireland. Absent.

Meadow Brown

The Browns
(Nymphalidae, subfamily Satyrinae)

Speckled Wood
Pararge aegeria (Linnaeus) subspecies *tircis* (Godart)

Subspecies type locality and authority
Specimens from Germany were first described as a subspecies by Godart (1821), but no specific locality is cited. Individuals superficially similar to the nominate subspecies are widespread in southern Europe and North Africa.

General distribution and status
Resident. Since the early part of the 20th century, when it was restricted to south-western England, Wales and parts of south-eastern Scotland, the Speckled Wood has undergone a dramatic range expansion that continues to the present day. This may be related to climate amelioration but the exact causes are still not known (see Hill *et al.*, 1999). It is now widespread and common in suitable habitats in England south of a line approximately between Westmorland in the west and South-east Yorkshire in the east, although there are a few scattered colonies further north. It is common in the Channel Isles but absent from the Isle of Man. In the Isles of Scilly, it is represented by the Isles of Scilly Speckled Wood (p. 258). In Wales and Ireland, it is common throughout with the exception of exposed high ground. In Scotland it is now represented solely by the Scottish Speckled Wood (p. 257).

Flight period
Between late March and early October in three overlapping broods. These appear to peak around the first two

Fig. 222 Speckled Wood upperside. Kelling, East Norfolk

Fig. 223 Speckled Wood underside. Holkham, West Norfolk

Speckled Wood

weeks of May, the last two weeks of July and the first two weeks of September, although the timing varies considerably from year to year depending on spring temperatures and concomitant larval development.

Larval foodplants
Many species of grass are used, the most commonly recorded being Cock's-foot, Yorkshire Fog and False Brome.

Habitat requirements
Throughout most of its range this is a species of woodland rides and glades, although in some southern localities it can also be found along hedgerows, roadsides and in parks and gardens. Damp localities within the general range are usually preferred.

Identification characters, variation and similar species
Average wingspan 51mm; the female is slightly larger than the male. The male possesses a conspicuous bar of greyish brown scent scales on the forewings which is absent in the female. Variation is considerable. Individuals of the first generation generally have larger pale spots on the upperside than those of later broods. The eye-spots on the hindwings (usually four) can be reduced in number and some may lack the white pupils. The colour of the pale upperside markings may vary between white (as in the Scottish Speckled Wood, p. 257) and tawny orange (as in the Isles of Scilly Speckled Wood, p. 258). Specimens are found occasionally where these markings are fulvous-orange (as in the nominate subspecies of southern Europe). Despite the extent of variability, confusion with any other species is unlikely.

Field tips
Both sexes feed from aphid honeydew in the canopy and can often be seen flying high amongst the trees. However, the males are very conspicuous at lower elevations as they defend territories that are usually centred on small patches of sunlit vegetation. Intruding males are engaged with vigour, often taking the dispute – a spiral 'dance' – high into the trees. Whilst so occupied they are difficult to photograph as they are very aware of nearby movement. Males also actively patrol in search of females and are then also very easy to find. In the early mornings both sexes bask conspicuously and at this time can be approached easily. Although their preferred diet is honeydew, the butterflies will also feed from flowers such as ragworts and brambles.

Regional prime sites
Scotland. Formerly present in the south-western border region, East and West Lothian, Midlothian, East Perthshire, Fifeshire and South Aberdeenshire but not recorded there since the 1930s. In the North-west Highlands, the Grampian Highlands, the Clyde Isles and the South and North Ebudes, the species is represented by the Scottish Speckled Wood (p. 257).

Speckled Wood / Scottish Speckled Wood

Northern England. Widespread and locally common in lowland areas. At the northern edge of its range, it can be seen in the west at **Arnside Knott**, Westmorland (SD 450 775) and in the east at **Owston Wood**, South-west Yorkshire (SE 565 105).

Central, eastern and south-east England. Widespread and common throughout.

South-west England. Widespread and common throughout, but in the Isles of Scilly it is represented by the Isles of Scilly Speckled Wood (p. 258).

Wales. Widespread and common, though absent from the higher ground.

Western and eastern Ireland. Widespread and generally common.

Scottish Speckled Wood
Pararge aegeria subspecies *oblita* Harrison

Subspecies type locality and authority

Specimens from Loch Scresort in the Isle of Rhum, North Ebudes, Scotland, were first described as a subspecies by Harrison (1949).

General distribution and status

Resident. Restricted to western and north-western Scotland and its neighbouring islands; East Sutherland, East Ross, East Inverness-shire, Moray, Banffshire and North Aberdeenshire. It is absent from the Outer Hebrides, Coll, Tiree and the Islands of Orkney and Shetland. Throughout its range it is generally common in suitable habitats.

Fig. 224 Scottish Speckled Wood upperside.
Loch Creran, West Inverness-shire

Fig. 225 Scottish Speckled Wood underside.
Loch Creran, West Inverness-shire

Scottish and Isles of Scilly Speckled Wood

Flight period
There are usually two broods flying from late April to mid-June, with a peak during the second and third weeks of May, and mid-July to mid-September, peaking during the last three weeks of August. During some years, the first generation is present in relatively small numbers. In warm seasons there may be a partial third emergence in late September.

Larval foodplants
As for the Speckled Wood (p. 255).

Habitat requirements
Woodland tracks and openings, usually preferring damp, partially shaded areas.

Identification characters, variation and similar species
Differs from the nominate Speckled Wood in the following ways:

1. Upperside ground colour much darker, often approaching black.
2. Upperside and underside pale markings larger and whitish rather than cream.
3. Hindwing underside with marginal band usually tinged purple; row of pale spots whitish and more conspicuous.

Individuals of the partial third generation are usually generally darker with smaller pale markings.

Field tips
As for the Speckled Wood (p. 255). Because spring-generation individuals have the larger, more attractive pale spots on the upperside it is perhaps these, during the second and third weeks of May, that would give most satisfaction to those wishing to see and photograph this subspecies.

Regional prime sites
Scotland. In the west of its range, it can be seen in the woodlands of **Knock Craggie**, East Ross (NC 328 051), **Glen Affric**, East Inverness-shire (NH 277 281) and **Glasdrum**, West Inverness-shire (NM 998 453). Further east, it is found at **Blackfold**, East Inverness-shire (NH 592 407) and, near the eastern limit of its range, it is present at **Fochabers Woods** in Banffshire (NJ 343 575).

Other regions. Absent.

Isles of Scilly Speckled Wood
Pararge aegeria subspecies *insula* Howarth

Subspecies type locality and authority
Specimens from the Isles of Scilly, England, were first described as a subspecies by Howarth (1971a).

General distribution and status
Resident. This subspecies is found exclusively in the Isles of Scilly where it is widespread and common.

Isles of Scilly Speckled Wood

Flight period and larval foodplants
As for the Speckled Wood (p. 255).

Habitat requirements
In the Isles of Scilly it is not necessarily restricted to woodlands and can be found in more open habitats such as hedgerows, enclosed meadows and scrubland. Slightly sheltered localities are usually preferred.

Identification characters, variation and similar species
Differs from the nominate Speckled Wood in the following ways:

1. Upperside with pale patches tawny orange rather than cream and often larger.
2. Forewing underside with central pale patches being pale orange rather than cream.
3. Hindwing underside with marginal band tinged purple.

Seasonal variation is similar to that of the Speckled Wood, although usually expressed to a lesser degree. Confusion with other species is unlikely.

Field tips
As for the Speckled Wood (p. 255).

Regional prime sites
South-west England. The Isles of Scilly Speckled Wood is widespread and common throughout the islands and may be expected to be seen with ease in **St Mary's** and **Tresco** to where the established travel services by sea or helicopter operate (see Appendix II: Isles of Scilly). Departing from Penzance, West Cornwall, day return fares are available via both modes of transport, and enough time should be available on either for this endemic subspecies to be found almost immediately on arrival. For example it can be seen along hedgerows within a few minutes of the airfield at St Mary's.

Other regions. Absent.

Fig. 226 Isles of Scilly Speckled Wood upperside. St Mary's, Isles of Scilly

Isles of Scilly Speckled Wood underside. St Mary's, Isles of Scilly

Wall
Lasiommata megera (Linnaeus)

General distribution and status
Resident. This species has undergone major fluctuations in its range over the last 150 years and at present it is generally in steep decline (see Fox *et al.*, 2006). In much of central, south-eastern and eastern England, it has disappeared from its former sites, and over much of its national range its strongholds are now on the coasts. In Scotland, it is restricted to the extreme south-west and, in England and Wales, is absent from mountainous areas. It remains widespread and locally frequent on the Isle of Man and in the Channel Isles and there was a report from the Isles of Scilly, West Cornwall, in 2005. Even at established sites it is rarely seen in numbers.

Flight period
Usually two broods flying from early May to late June and from late July to mid-September. The peak periods are during the last week of May and the first week of June and the second and third weeks of August. In northern England and southern Scotland, the flight periods may be delayed by approximately two weeks, and the optimum times for seeing the species should be adjusted accordingly. In southern mainland England, the Channel Isles and parts of southern Ireland there may be a partial third emergence in favourable years during October.

Larval foodplants
A wide variety of grasses, most commonly Cock's-foot, Yorkshire Fog, Common Bent, False Brome, Black Bent, Tor-grass and Wavy Hair-grass.

Habitat requirements
The Wall is found on open sunny grasslands that are interspersed with exposed areas of soil or rocks. On the coast it inhabits dune systems, undercliffs and foreshores. Inland, it prefers unimproved grassland, where trampling stock creates bare patches of earth, wasteland or other disturbed ground, roadside verges, open

Fig. 228 Wall male upperside. Stiffkey, West Norfolk

Fig. 229 Wall female upperside. Holkham, West Norfolk

Wall

woodland rides and abandoned quarries. Females are very particular when choosing egg-laying sites and invariably select sunny sheltered spots on the edges of grass stands. These may be within recesses in the stands themselves, on the edges of animal-made holes and footprints or the sides of banks and rock faces, or grasses at the bases of hedges and isolated bushes.

Identification characters, variation and similar species

Average wingspan 49mm; the female is slightly larger than the male. The latter possesses a conspicuous bar of dark scent scales on the forewings that is absent in the female. Variation is uncommon and is usually restricted to the number of eye-spots on the hindwing and the occasional presence of two white 'pupils' in those of the forewing. In flight, the Wall may resemble one of the small fritillaries but examination of the butterfly at rest will reveal the characteristic eye-spot on the forewing upper- and underside. This is absent in all the fritillary species.

Field tips

At a known locality, the Wall should be sought where grasses grow amongst areas of bare ground. Here the butterflies may spend long periods basking with their wings outspread. Perches are usually chosen on sunlit patches of bare earth, rocks and walls, and males will sometimes congregate in such places from where they often patrol in search of females. Females are most often found in the vicinity of the foodplants but they

Fig. 230 Wall underside. Holkham, West Norfolk

also spend periods basking between egg-laying sorties. During the heat of the day both sexes are conspicuously active and difficult to approach. However, during the mornings and evenings, when the ambient temperature is relatively low, they are reluctant to fly and can then be examined closely and photographed with ease.

Regional prime sites

Scotland. Found only in the south-west, this species can most reliably be seen in Kirkcudbrightshire on the coastal path at **Castlehill Point** (access from NX 854 523) and at **Wood of Cree** (NX 382 709).

Northern England. Absent from the higher ground. Widespread in the west and east of the region, although most often associated with coastal localities. Towards the northern limits of its range it can be seen in Westmorland at **Arnside Knott** (SD 450 775) and **Whitbarrow**

Wall / Small Mountain Ringlet

Scar (access from SD 458 867) in the west and at **Tyne Riverside Country Park**, South Northumberland (north of Prudhoe at NZ 086 633) in the east.

Central England. Widespread and frequent throughout with the exception of the higher ground and in parts of the south-west, where it is apparently less common.

Eastern England. Widespread and frequent throughout, though usually most common in coastal localities.

South-east England. Apparently absent from many central parts of its former range but widespread and frequent elsewhere, particularly along the coasts.

South-west England. Widespread and frequent throughout.

Western Ireland. Widespread but seemingly very localized, although under-recording may be a factor. In the north, it can be seen at **Carrickfin**, West Donegal (B 783 229) and further south along the southern shores of **Lough George**, Clare (R 375 924).

Eastern Ireland. Absent from much of the north, although found frequently along the southern half of the east coast. In the south, it is widespread but localized. Here it can be seen reliably at **Howth Head**, Dublin (O 269 372) and **Ballyscanlan**, Waterford (S 540 029).

The Small Mountain Ringlet group
Erebia epiphron (Knoch)

Introductory notes
This species is now represented in the British Isles by two subspecies (English and Scottish Small Mountain Ringlets), both of which are endemic. A third taxon is thought to have been present in Ireland until at least the end of the 19th century and it is possible that it may still be extant. Only four Irish specimens still exist (Nash & Samson, 1990) and their subspecific status will now probably never be known, as the sample is simply too small for confident attribution. However, some authorities (e.g. Ford, 1945; Baynes, 1964) suggest they may be referable to subspecies *aetheria* (Esper). Baynes also speculates on the species' continued existence in the Irish county of West Mayo; the prospect of rediscovering this 'lost' butterfly is indeed exciting. In order to open the door to further research it is thought desirable to treat this enigmatic, and possibly extant, insect as a distinct subspecies: the Irish Mountain Ringlet *Erebia epiphron* (Knoch) ssp. *aetheria* (Esper).

English Small Mountain Ringlet
Erebia epiphron (Knoch) subspecies *mnemon* (Haworth)

Fig. 231 English Small Mountain Ringlet **upperside.** Fleetwith, Cumberland

Fig. 232 English Small Mountain Ringlet **underside.** Fleetwith, Cumberland

Subspecies type locality and authority
Specimens from Red Screes in Cumberland, England, were first described as a subspecies by Haworth (1812). The nominate subspecies does not occur in the British Isles.

General distribution and status
Resident; protected from sale (GB). Restricted to high mountainous areas in the English Lake District of Cumberland and Westmorland. Its status appears to be stable, but accurate monitoring is made difficult by the inhospitable terrain and unpredictable weather that dominates the areas where it lives. The cessation of traditional sheep grazing, resulting in a rank sward, and reforestation may pose a threat to the species' future. It is also possible that global warming will be detrimental to this sedentary and ecologically-specialized high altitude butterfly.

Flight period
Single brooded, flying for approximately three weeks between mid-June and late July. The peak time varies considerably from year to year according to the weather, but the first two weeks of July are usually reliable.

Larval foodplants
The sole foodplant is Mat-grass.

Habitat requirements
The Small Mountain Ringlet is the only truly montane species resident in the British Isles. It inhabits open Mat-grass dominated grassland at high altitude (Fig. 20), the English subspecies usually being found between an altitude of around 500m and 700m. It prefers wet areas, such as flushes and boggy hollows and there appears to be little preference for aspect, some colonies, unlike those of the Scottish subspecies, occurring even on north-facing slopes.

English Small Mountain Ringlet

Identification characters, variation and similar species

Average wingspan 32mm. Variation is considerable and can affect the size and shape of the orange patches and the prominence, or even presence, of the black spots therein. Confusion with other species is highly unlikely as no other similar species occurs in the same habitat.

Field tips

The Small Mountain Ringlet can prove one of the most difficult of British butterflies to find. Its colonies are usually situated far from established trails and often involve a long, and sometimes arduous, climb over rough terrain.
The weather in mountainous areas is notoriously unpredictable and can change almost without warning. These factors can combine to produce a potentially dangerous situation and careful planning and appropriate clothing are required. Thus strong walking boots are a necessity, along with a hat and good quality waterproof overgarments. A warm jacket and/or pullover should always be taken along. Always remember: layers of clothing can easily be removed if one is too hot but they cannot be added if they are not in one's rucksack. An apparently simple rule, but one that is often overlooked by those inexperienced in mountain trekking. It is also wise to take a compass, a map, cold and hot drinks and some food. The inexperienced should never climb alone and another person, not involved in the expedition, should always be told of one's plans together with an estimated time of return. Make sure that your mobile telephone is fully charged before departure.

The butterflies are associated with Mat-grass-dominated slopes or plateaus and here they should be sought in wet areas, particularly along flushes and in boggy patches. They usually fly only in bright sunshine and when the sun is obscured by clouds they quickly drop to the ground, reappearing in numbers as soon as the sun reappears. However, if the ambient temperature is above approximately 17°C, a few individuals may be seen in dull weather and may also be disturbed into flight from low vegetation. The males are conspicuously active as they patrol in erratic manner low over the grasses in search of potential mates, investigating any brown objects they encounter. Both sexes feed from whatever flowers may be available, most commonly those of Tormentil. However, such nutrition is not actually essential as the adults emerge from the pupae carrying large deposits of body fat that are utilised in the absence of nectar. The best method of photographing the butterflies is to note where they land as a cloud passes over as then, for a few moments, they may remain openly in view before crawling into shelter. Watching the same spot as the sun re-emerges will usually result in similar opportunities.

Regional prime sites

Scotland. Represented by the Scottish Small Mountain Ringlet (p. 265).

English and Scottish Small Mountain Ringlet

Northern England. Perhaps the most accessible site is **Fleetwith**, Cumberland (SD 215 135). Park near Seatoller Fell (SD 225 136) and climb the well-made trail to the plateau about 1km to the west. The butterflies can be seen most often in the boggier areas and in smaller numbers over the drier grasslands. **Cold Pike** (SD 264 034), also in Cumberland, is another reliable site. Park at Three Shires Stone (SD 275 028) and walk approximately 1.5km north-west to the summit. From here search the south-west facing slopes and pay particular attention to the flushes.

Western Ireland. See Irish Small Mountain Ringlet (p. 266).

Other regions. Absent.

Scottish Small Mountain Ringlet
Erebia epiphron subspecies *scotica* Cooke

Subspecies type locality and authority
Specimens from Loch Rannoch in Perthshire, Scotland, were first described as a subspecies by Cooke (1943).

General distribution and status
Resident; protected from sale (GB). Restricted to western central Scotland based around the counties of Argyll Main, West Inverness-shire and Mid Perthshire, with a few outlying colonies elsewhere in the general area. Populations appear to be stable but monitoring is difficult in the harsh, isolated and unpredictable locations in which the butterfly lives.

Flight period
Usually later than its English counterpart,

Fig. 233 Scottish Small Mountain Ringlet upperside. Creag Meagaidh, West Inverness-shire

Fig. 234 Scottish Small Mountain Ringlet underside. Creag Meagaidh, West Inverness-shire

Scottish and Irish Small Mountain Ringlet

flying from the end of June until the beginning of August. The best time to see the species in Scotland is during the second and third weeks of July, though this will vary according to weather conditions.

Larval foodplants
Mat-grass and possibly other grasses.

Habitat requirements
Similar to those of the English Small Mountain Ringlet but found between an altitude of 350m and 900m and usually restricted to south-facing slopes (Fig. 20).

Identification characters, variation and similar species
Average wingspan 37mm. The Scottish subspecies is consistently larger than the English one and is also often brighter with more conspicuous orange patches. Wing pattern variation is similar to that found in the English Small Mountain Ringlet. Confusion with other species is highly unlikely.

Field tips
Same as for the English Small Mountain Ringlet (p. 263), although the Scottish populations are predominantly to be found on south-facing aspects.

Regional prime sites
Scotland. The most popular place to visit is **Ben Lawers**, Mid Perthshire (NN 609 379) where there is an information centre and a marked nature trail along which the butterfly can be seen at elevations above 500m. Another good site is at **Creag Meagaidh**, West Inverness-shire (from the official car park on the north side of the A86 (NN 479 870) take the track leading north-west past the white warden's cottage for about 3km and search the flush around the stand of birches on the west side of the valley at NN 460 894).

Other regions. Absent.

Irish Small Mountain Ringlet
Erebia epiphron subspecies *aetheria* (Esper)

Subspecies type locality and authority
The type locality is unknown, but Tolman & Lewington (2004) suggest it was probably in Austria. The first specimen caught in the British Isles was from Croagh Patrick in West Mayo, Ireland (Baynes, 1964).

Status
Uncertain; possibly extinct resident. There are a few 19th century records of the Small Mountain Ringlet from Ireland, from which only four specimens survive. It has not been recorded since 1918 (Nash & Samson, 1990). The taxonomic status of such a

Irish Small Mountain Ringlet

small sample of specimens is difficult to assess, but Ford (1945) ascribes them to the dark form *nelamus* Boisduval that occurs commonly and consistently within populations of subspecies *aetheria* (Esper) from high elevations in the southern Alps of mainland Europe. He, and others, suggests that they belong to this subspecies (although the spelling is '*aetherius*'). Beirne (1952) goes on to describe the history and establishment of the species in the British Isles as 'fairly typical of Alpine species'. He states categorically that in Britain it is represented by two subspecies, one in England and Scotland (now in fact regarded as two subspecies) and one in the mountains of western Ireland. He speculates that the species arrived in southern England via the loess steppe during a glacial phase and, as the ice retreated, became isolated at high altitude. A subsequent glacial advance then divided the population into two; one in England and another in Ireland which '...developed into the Irish subspecies'. A further glacial advance is then

Fig. 235 An individual of form *nelamus* Boisduval photographed in Switzerland (R. Harrington) that is similar in appearance to museum specimens of the Irish Small Mountain Ringlet.

Irish Small Mountain Ringlet

thought to have isolated what are now regarded as the English and Scottish subspecies. Such a hypothesis would certainly satisfy the criteria needed for genetic isolation and, therefore, the conditions for subspeciation. Baynes (1964) continues the intrigue by suggesting areas where searches should be undertaken to try to rediscover the species in Ireland. He describes the localities where the butterfly may still live as 'wild' and 'mountainous'. This, along with the notoriously inclement climate of western Ireland, certainly presents a challenge to anyone wishing to uncover the continued existence of the Irish Small Mountain Ringlet.

Distribution of records

Only four specimens remain, three of which are in the National Museum of Ireland. These were caught at Croagh Patrick, West Mayo, in 1854; Lough Gill, Sligo, in 1895; and Nephin, West Mayo, in 1897. A fourth specimen, discovered as recently as 1990, now resides at the Ulster Museum. Its label reads 'Irish 30.6.18' but no locality is given (Nash & Samson, 1990).

Flight period

In the high Alps of mainland Europe, this subspecies flies during July and August. The Croagh Patrick specimen was caught in June, as was the 1918 specimen, but no detailed information is available for the other two individuals.

Larval foodplants and habitat requirements

Not known but probably as for English Small Mountain Ringlet (p. 263).

Identification characters and similar species

Differs from the English and Scottish Small Mountain Ringlet in having the orange patches much reduced, giving an overall darker appearance.

Field tips and regional prime sites

Western Ireland. Baynes (1964) suggests the likeliest place to rediscover this butterfly is the Nephin Beg area of West Mayo. There are several peaks in excess of 500m in this region that may warrant attention and, at the risk of being speculative, these are listed below with their grid references. It would probably be wise to concentrate mainly on slopes with a southerly aspect as these are known to be suitable for both of the British subspecies.

1. Corslieve (719m) F 914 141
2. Nephin Beg (627m) F 931 104
3. Glennamong (627m) F 913 095 and peaks to the south-west (711m) F 902 031
4. Bengorm (580m) F 929 015
5. Buckoogh (587m) F 993 016
6. Birrencorragh (697m) G 014 051
7. Nephin (806m) G 102 080

Other regions. Individuals of form *nemalus* occur occasionally in English and Scottish populations.

The Scotch Argus group
Erebia aethiops (Esper)

Introductory notes
According to the current nomenclature this species is represented in Britain by two subspecies, the Scotch Argus (see below) and the Western Scotch Argus (p. 271). However, in Scotland, where both subspecies occur, they appear to be sympatric along the borders of their distributions and there are no quantifiable data regarding the occurrence or frequency of interbreeding or gradation in appearance of the adults of the two taxa. Further research is needed to establish whether or not subspecific status is valid in this case as the two described forms may merely be those found at either end of an east-west cline. In order to conform to established views they are here still treated as separate subspecies but the observer keen to see both would be wise to visit sites at the extreme eastern and western ends of their distributions in Scotland. The two populations in north-west England appear to contain a mixture of individuals that conform to both taxa but the majority are the Scotch Argus *sensu stricto*.

Scotch Argus
Erebia aethiops subspecies *aethiops* (Esper)

General distribution and status
Resident. Widespread and common in the north-eastern quarter of Scotland. In England, it was formerly locally widespread in the north but is now present only at two sites in Westmorland.

Flight period
There is a single generation flying between late July and early September with a peak during the second and third weeks of August.

Fig. 236 Scotch Argus upperside. Smardale, Westmorland

Fig. 237 Scotch Argus underside. Smardale, Westmorland

Scotch Argus

Larval foodplants
In Scotland, the usual foodplant is Purple Moor-grass whilst in England the larvae feed on Blue Moor-grass. Other species of grass may sometimes be used.

Habitat requirements
In Scotland, the butterfly inhabits acid or neutral grasslands that are either lightly grazed or ungrazed. It can be very common in meadows, woodland clearings and sheltered bogs and along river valleys and roadsides (Fig. 3). In mountainous areas it is found up to an altitude of around 500m. The two remaining colonies in England are on limestone grassland containing scrub and open areas of woodland.

Identification characters, variation and similar species
Average wingspan 45mm; the female is slightly larger than the male. The female also differs in having a slightly paler ground colour, the orange markings are usually brighter and broader and the eye spots therein are often more prominent. The markings on the underside of the hindwing are brighter and more contrasting. In approximately 50 per cent of females, the pale bluish-grey areas of the hindwing underside are replaced with ochre. This form is known as *ochracea* Mosley. In flight, it may be overlooked as a Meadow Brown, but the pale orange forewing undersides of that species are usually visible as the wings are held closed briefly in mid-beat. At rest, the orange bands and rows of conspicuous eye-spots on both forewing and hindwing are usually diagnostic. However, the possibly resident Arran Brown is similar and the comparative identification features are discussed under that species (p. 272).

Field tips
Where it occurs this species is often common, conspicuous and easy to find. The males spend most of their time patrolling just above the grasses in search of potential mates and can then be seen from some distance, even from the window of a moving car. The females are usually less visible but are easily found as they bask openly for long periods. When the sun shines, activity levels are high but, on days of intermittent sun, a passing cloud will see the butterflies drop immediately into the grass. These conditions often provide the best photographic opportunities. On sunny east-facing slopes the butterflies become active very early in the morning and will take to the wing as soon as the ambient temperature rises above about 15°C (Emmet & Heath, 1989). Above such temperatures they are easily disturbed into flight on dull days and even during light rain.

Regional prime sites
Scotland. Widespread and common in the following regions: East Ross, East Inverness-shire, East Perthshire, Banffshire, Moray and North and South Aberdeenshire. To see typical examples of this subspecies one should visit the latter four (eastern) counties as those in the west may contain many individuals similar

to subspecies *caledonia* or intergrades. A visit to the **Glen More Forest Park**, East Inverness-shire (parking at the RSPB reserve at Loch Garten at NH 979 185), may well prove fruitful as the Scotch Argus is abundant throughout the area.

Northern England. Restricted to two colonies in Westmorland: **Arnside Knott** (car park at SD 450 775) and **Smardale Gill** (park at Smardale Village (NY 740 082) and follow the dismantled railway west/south-west for approximately 1km to the cleared areas).

Other Regions. Absent.

Western Scotch Argus
Erebia aethiops subspecies *caledonia* Verity

Subspecies type locality and authority
Specimens from Galashiels on the borders of Selkirkshire and Roxburghshire, Scotland, were first described as a subspecies by Verity (1911).

General distribution and status
Resident. Widespread and common throughout most of western and south-western Scotland, although scarce in the extreme north and absent from much of the Central Lowlands. It is absent from the Islands of Orkney and Shetland and from many of the Western Isles including the Outer Hebrides.

Flight period
As for the Scotch Argus (p. 269).

Larval foodplants
Purple Moor-grass and possibly other grasses.

Fig. 238 Western Scotch Argus upperside.
Ardnamurchan, West Inverness-shire

Fig. 239 Western Scotch Argus underside.
Ardnamurchan, West Inverness-shire

Western Scotch Argus / Arran Brown

Habitat requirements
Neutral and acid grasslands (see Scotch Argus, p. 269 and Fig. 3).

Identification characters, variation and similar species
Average wingspan 40mm; apart from its smaller size, it differs from the typical subspecies in the following ways:

1. Forewing more elongated and pointed.
2. Forewing upperside often with orange band constricted centrally and rarely containing more than three pupilled eye-spots (often four in the nominate Scotch Argus).
3. Hindwing underside with less contrasting markings.

Field tips
As for Scotch Argus (p. 269).

Regional prime sites
Scotland. The Western Scotch Argus is usually very common throughout its range but, due to the uncertainty of its taxonomic status, individuals conforming most closely to the subspecific description should be sought in the west and south-west of the country.

Other regions. Absent.

Notes
It is possible to see both of the Scotch Argus subspecies in a single day. From the subspecies *aethiops* colonies in Westmorland a visit could be made to Dumfries-shire where several populations of subspecies *caledonia* occur near the border with England. **Hightae Mill Loch** is accessed from Mossgrove (NY 082 798). From here walk past the house along the track leading to the woodland strip on the edge of the loch where the butterflies may be seen at NY 083 802. Nearby there is some rough grassland adjacent to the minor road between **Hightae** and **Blackrig** where the butterfly flies in the vicinity of NY 076 800 and NY 073 805.

Arran Brown
Erebia ligea (Linnaeus)

Status
Uncertain; possible resident. There have been several records of this species in Britain and, since it first appeared in the entomological literature in 1804, controversy has surrounded its continued presence on the British list. Several leading authorities of the past (e.g. South, 1941) appear not to regard the specimens as being of genuine British origin. But considering the remoteness of some of its alleged Scottish haunts, its superficial similarity to the Scotch Argus and the apparently *bona fide* circumstances under which the records came to light, this author is of the belief (perhaps romantic) that the Arran Brown did fly – and may still do – in some

Arran Brown

Fig. 240 Arran Brown upperside.
Switzerland (R. Harrington)

Fig. 241 Arran Brown underside.
Switzerland (R. Harrington)

remote Scottish glen. Right or wrong, the facts are outlined below for further scrutiny. If ever there was a chance of glory for an enterprising lepidopterist then surely it lies in the 'rediscovery' of this enigmatic butterfly – assuming it does indeed reside in Scotland.

Distribution of records

In 1804, the species was first recorded by Sir Patrick Walker. He caught it in the Isle of Arran, Clyde Isles, along with specimens of the Scotch Argus and at the time both were regarded as new to the British fauna. Three specimens were discovered in 1944 in the G. H. Simpson-Hayward collection labelled '1860' and '1860 and 62' from the Isle of Mull, Mid Ebudes. A further individual was discovered in a small collection compiled by A.B. and J.W. Gillespie during the latter part of the 19th century. It was amongst specimens of the Scotch Argus and a loose label found in the box stated '*Erebia Blandiana* [=*E. aethiops* (Scotch Argus)]/ taken on Bute (North End) July 1871'. Pelham-Clinton (1964) discusses these records in depth, along with a final one supposedly from Galashiels in Selkirkshire, the genuineness of which he doubts, and the reader is referred to his article for further details. He concludes by expressing his belief that the species possibly still occurs in damp woods in the south of Scotland. A specimen allegedly caught at Margate, East Kent, in 1875 is almost certainly the result of the activities of a fraudulent dealer. Finally, a specimen was exhibited at the British Entomological and Natural History Society in 1977 by T. J. Daley. It was with specimens of the Scotch Argus and the captor assumed it was merely an aberrant form of that species. It was caught, with others that he had not set, on 5th August 1969 in a remote part of the western side of Rannoch Moor, Argyll Main. At the time, Daley was a young schoolboy and had never collected abroad in countries where this particular form of the Arran Brown is

Arran Brown / Marbled White

found. So it may indeed occur at Rannoch Moor in low numbers.

Flight period
Single brooded, flying from the end of June to the end of August.

Larval foodplants
Unknown in Britain but in mainland Europe it feeds on grasses including finger-grasses and Wood Millet.

Habitat requirements
Grasslands, often in light damp woodlands.

Identification characters
Average wingspan 49mm; the female is slightly larger than the male. Superficially similar to the Scotch Argus (p. 269) and Western Scotch Argus (p. 271) from which it differs in the following ways:

1. Fringes of all wings chequered black and white.
2. Hindwing undersides with conspicuous white streak that is broader in the female, often forming a whitish band.

Field tips and regional prime sites
Scotland. Considering the entomological attention received by the Isle of Arran since this butterfly was first recorded, it seems unlikely that it will be seen there again. The only advice that can here be offered is to examine all large *Erebia* individuals encountered, particularly in western Scotland, and hope for good fortune. Rannoch Moor, where Daley apparently found his specimens, seems a good place to begin.

Other regions. Unlikely to occur.

Marbled White
Melanargia galathea (Linnaeus) subspecies *serena* Verity

Subspecies type locality and authority
Specimens from Abbots Ripton in Cambridgeshire and Abbots Wood in East Sussex, England, were first described as this subspecies by Verity (1913). The nominate subspecies does not occur in the British Isles but is widespread in western and central Europe.

General distribution and status
Resident. Widespread and locally common or abundant in England and parts of Wales south-east of a line between Glamorgan in the west and North-east Yorkshire in the east. However, it is absent from much of eastern England and scarce in most of the south-east. It is not found in Scotland, Ireland or the Isle of Man. There is a single record from Jersey in the Channel Isles. Since the 1980s, there appears to have been a northward and eastward expansion of the species' range.

Marbled White

In suitable habitats, particularly on calcareous downland, colonies may contain thousands of individuals.

Flight period
There is a single generation flying between mid-June and late August with a peak during the second and third weeks of July.

Larval foodplants
Red Fescue and Sheep's Fescue are the usual foodplants, although other closely related grass species have been recorded.

Habitat requirements
This is very much a species of grasslands, particularly unimproved grassland on chalk or limestone (Fig. 8). It is found on downland and coastal clifftops, along roadsides, woodland rides and clearings and railway embankments and cuttings, and on waste ground and set-aside fields. It requires a tall sward that is subjected to little or no grazing.

Identification characters, variation and similar species
Average wingspan 56mm; the female is slightly larger than the male. The underside of the female hindwing has the darker areas tinged more conspicuously greenish cream. Variation is rare and is usually limited to either expansion or reduction of the black markings. There is

Fig. 242 Marbled White male underside (left) and female. Sharpenhoe, Bedfordshire

Marbled White

Fig. 243 Marbled White female underside.
Collard Hill, South Somerset

no other resident species with which the Marbled White can be confused.

Field tips
Where it occurs this conspicuous butterfly simply cannot be overlooked. When feeding, they appear to have a preference for purple flowers, particularly knapweeds and thistles. The wings are usually held closed during this activity, although in the early morning, evening and during dull periods, they often rest and feed with their wings held open. These are therefore the best times to obtain photographs of the uppersides.

Regional prime sites
Scotland. Absent.

Northern England. Restricted to a few colonies in the south-east. In South-east Yorkshire, it can be seen reliably on the grasslands to the south-east of **Fridaythorpe** (SE 878 581) and at **Thixendale** (SE 838 612).

Central England. Widely distributed but very localized. In Northamptonshire, it is common at **Barnack Hills** (TF 074 048). In Warwickshire, it occurs at **Ufton Fields** (park on the minor road approximately 1km south of Ufton and explore the disused quarry workings to the east at SP 378 615) and, in Worcestershire, it is present at **Windmill Hill** on the south side of the B4510 between Evesham and Cleeve Prior (SP 072 477). In Shropshire, it has recently become established in the Willow Bank area of the **Wyre Forest** (SO 745 733).

Eastern England. There is a thriving introduced colony at **Chambers Farm Wood** in North Lincolnshire (car park and visitor centre at TF 145 744. Go to the area known as Little Scrubs Meadow). Elsewhere it is restricted to the south-west of the region where it is common on the chalk downlands of Bedfordshire such as those at **Totternhoe Knowles** (SP 986 217) and **Whipsnade Downs** (SP 998 186).

South-east England. Common and widespread in the west of the region and in East Kent. In the east, it is found at **Lydden Down**, East Kent (TR 277 453) and, a little further west, it can be seen at **Malling Down** in East Sussex (TQ 423 107). In the west, it is common at **Magdalen Hill Down** in North Hampshire (SU 505 292) and, further north, at **Stony Green Hill** (SU 866 991) and **Bernwood Forest** (SP 611 117) in Buckinghamshire.

South-west England. The Marbled White is widespread and common apart from in West Cornwall. A few suggested sites are: **Prestbury Hill**, East Gloucestershire (SO 993 248), **Bentley Woods**, South Wiltshire (the north clearing at SU 258 292), **Ballard Down** (from just north of the lay-by at SZ 022 808 walk east along the south-facing slope) and **Hod Hill**, Dorset (ST 852 112), **Collard Hill**, South Somerset (ST 489 341), **Little Breach**, South Devon (ST 105 155), and **Greenscombe Wood**, East Cornwall (SX 391 723).

Wales. Absent from most of the country except for a few colonies in the south and south-east. In Glamorgan, it is abundant at **Whiteford Burrows** (SS 440 935) and, in Carmarthenshire, at **Pembrey Country Park** (SN 405 005). Elsewhere populations are scattered and too vulnerable for publication of their whereabouts.

Western and eastern Ireland. Absent.

The Grayling group
Hipparchia semele (Linnaeus)

Introductory notes

In Britain and Ireland there are six recognized subspecies of the Grayling. In each case, the majority of the respective population's individuals conform to the type description. However, such is the degree of variability within the species as a whole, that many specimens may not do so, and hence care must be taken to know exactly what one is looking for at each site visited. The text descriptions and photographs must be studied thoroughly if one is to enjoy these remarkable geographical forms to the full.

Grayling
Hipparchia semele subspecies *semele* (Linnaeus)

General distribution and status

Resident. The Grayling is widespread and common in suitable habitats. The nominate subspecies is found around the coasts of much of England and Wales, the Isle of Man and the Channel Isles, but is absent in such habitats in much of south-eastern and north-eastern England. Even though mainly coastal in distribution, large inland populations are found on some of the heaths and well-drained hillsides of southern and eastern England and occasionally elsewhere.

In the islands of western Scotland and their adjacent mainland, the species is

Grayling

represented by the Atlantic Grayling (p. 284) and in the rest of Scotland by the Scottish Grayling (p. 282). On the Great Orme in Caernarvonshire lives the Great Orme Grayling (p. 281) and in Ireland there are two subspecies: the Burren Grayling in the limestone district of Clare and South-east Galway (p. 286) and the Irish Grayling elsewhere (p. 287).

Flight period
Single brooded; flying from early July to mid-September with a peak during the last week of July and the first two weeks of August. (Note that the flight period is significantly different for the Great Orme Grayling, p. 281).

Larval foodplants
A wide variety of grasses: the most commonly-recorded are Sheep's Fescue, Red Fescue, Bristle Bent, Early Hair-grass and Tufted Hair-grass.

Habitat requirements
In coastal localities, the Grayling inhabits grasslands such as dune systems, shingle expanses, salt marshes and those found amongst rocky outcrops (Figs. 6 and 17). The largest inland colonies are usually associated with heaths, calcareous grassland and downs (Figs. 10 and 16), but can also be found in open areas of light woodland and along open forest tracks and fire breaks where there are

Fig. 244 Grayling. Cley, East Norfolk

Grayling

areas of exposed soil. Smaller colonies are occasionally found in disused quarries (Fig. 9) and other abandoned industrial sites such as spoil heaps. All the habitats are characteristically well-drained and contain areas of exposed ground or rock in sunny situations.

Identification characters, variation and similar species

Average wingspan 56mm; the female is usually larger than the male. Apart from the larger size, the female has large pale cream or pale orange patches on the upperside of both the fore- and hindwings. However, apart from in flight during gliding, these are rarely seen as this species almost always settles with its wings tightly closed. The undersides of the sexes are similar, although the female often has larger eye-spots on the forewings. The ground colour and markings on the underside of the hindwings, critical for subspecific identification, are very variable, even within a given population. Therefore, as aforementioned, the text descriptions and photographs provided for each subspecies should be studied thoroughly prior to observations if one is to appreciate the geographical forms of the Grayling to their full. The characteristic bounding flight, interspersed by glides with the wings held in an acute 'V', makes this species distinct from any other in its favoured habitats.

Field tips

The Grayling (and all its subspecies) is incredibly well camouflaged when it settles. The markings on the underside of the hindwings make it very difficult indeed to spot unless the exact place of landing has been identified. During the early morning and evening, the butterfly will present the whole of the hindwing surface to the sun but, at other times, will lean into the sun and therefore cast no shadow, thus making its concealment that more effective. The males can sometimes be seen contesting territories or pursuing females, but flights are often short and easily missed. The best way to find the species at a known locality is simply to walk through or alongside areas of exposed earth or rock and hope to disturb individuals into flight. Having done so, the place of landing should be noted with care and a stealthy approach made. This butterfly is extremely alert and any sudden movement will often result in the forewings being quickly raised to reveal the eye-spots followed by another short flight. The casting of a shadow anywhere near the insect should always be avoided as this will cause the same reaction. During very warm weather they can be seen feeding at flowers of Ragwort, heather or bramble and can then easily be approached. Generally, though, the best photographic opportunities are available in the early morning.

Regional prime sites

Scotland. See Scottish Grayling (p. 282) and Atlantic Grayling (p. 284).

Northern England. Common in suitable habitats along the entire western coast with a few inland colonies. Suggested

Grayling

sites are: **Whitbarrow Scar** (access from SD 458 867) and **Arnside Knott** (SD 450 775), Westmorland, **Warton Crag**, West Lancashire (SD 492 724) and **Ainsdale Hills**, South Lancashire (SD 300 115). In the north-east, it is present at **Ross Links** (NU 143 374) and, just east of Bamburgh, on the dunes at **Red Barns** (NU 195 345) in North Northumberland. In the south-east of the region, it is extremely localized and known from only one site in South-east Yorkshire. Publication of its locality is hence considered inappropriate.

Central England. Found only in the west of the region where it is widespread and common in Shropshire on the rocky outcrops and old lead mining sites of the **Stiperstones** (track north from the car park at SO 365 976) and the limestone quarries of **Llanymynech** (SJ 266 221). Further north, in Cheshire, it can be seen at **Red Rocks Marsh** (SJ 205 875).

Eastern England. Common on the dunes of the coasts of West and East Norfolk, where it can be seen at **Holkham Dunes** (parking at TF 891 448) and **Horsey Gap** (TG 465 242), respectively. It flourishes also on the shingle sea defences at **Cley**, East Norfolk (TG 059 449). On the coast of East Suffolk it is present at **Westleton Heath** (TM 453 695). Inland sites are scarce and in the north of the region, it is known only from **Risby Warren** in North Lincolnshire (track west and then south-east from the access point at SE 929 144). It is fairly widespread in the Brecklands of East Anglia but can be difficult to find. Perhaps the most reliable site here is **Cavenham Heath**, West Suffolk (TL 757 727 via the village of Tuddenham), where it frequents the main sandy track through the heathland section of the reserve.

South-east England. Mainly restricted to the heathlands of the south-west of the region. In its heartlands it is common at **Chobham Common** (SU 975 646) and **Thursley Common** (SU 900 417) in Surrey and throughout the heathlands of the **New Forest** (SU 20/30) in South Hampshire.

South-west England. Widespread and common along much of the coast with a few strong inland colonies. Suggested sites to visit are: **Arne** (SY 972 878) and **Studland Heath** (SZ 034 835), Dorset, **Bolt Head**, South Devon (south to the coast from SX 713 376), **Gwennap Head**, West Cornwall (access from SW 371 218 and butterflies at SW 365 218), **Braunton Burrows**, North Devon (SS 463 351), **Crook Peak** hilltop viewing point, North Somerset (north-west of the parking area at ST 392 550) and **Prestbury Hill**, East Gloucestershire (access from SO 993 248).

Wales. Widespread and common around much of the coast. Suggested sites to visit are: **Holy Island** (coastal path from SH 205 823), **Benar Dunes**, Merionethshire (SH 573 227), **St Govan's Head**, Pembrokeshire

Grayling / Great Orme Grayling

(coastal path from SR 967 930), and **Oxwich Point** (access from SS 502 865) and **Port-Eynon Point** (SS 467 848) in Glamorgan. In the south-east of the country there are interesting inland sites in Monmouthshire where the species inhabits regenerating coal tips and other former industrial locations on the western side of the Blorenge Mountain (park at **Pen-ffordd-goch Pond** (SO 255 107) and walk south towards Blaenavon). On the **Great Orme**, Caernarvonshire, it is represented by the Great Orme Grayling (see below).

Western Ireland. See Irish Grayling (p. 287) and Burren Grayling (p. 286).

Eastern Ireland. See Irish Grayling (p. 287).

Great Orme Grayling
Hipparchia semele subspecies *thyone* (Thompson)

Fig. 245 Great Orme Grayling. Great Orme, Caernarvonshire

Great Orme Grayling / Scottish Grayling

Subspecies type locality and authority
Specimens from the Creuddyn Peninsula (Great Ormes Head) in Caernarvonshire, Wales, were first described as a subspecies by Thompson (1944).

General distribution and status
Resident. Restricted to the Great Orme in Caernarvonshire where it is common.

Flight period
Significantly earlier and shorter-lived than the other Grayling subspecies, flying between early June and mid-July with a peak during the last two weeks of June and the first week of July.

Larval foodplants
As for the Grayling (p. 277).

Habitat requirements
The Great Orme Grayling inhabits rocky areas on grassy slopes and disused quarries (Fig. 9).

Identification characters, variation and similar species
Considerably smaller than the typical subspecies with an average wingspan of 50mm. It also differs in the following ways:

1. Upperside generally paler, although this is rarely seen in living individuals.
2. Hindwing underside paler and more uniform with patterns less contrasting; pale areas are tinged ochreous.

Variation is not as extensive as that of the typical subspecies. There is no similar species.

Field tips
As for the Grayling (p. 277).

Regional prime sites
Wales. Widespread and common over much of the western part of the **Great Orme**, Caernarvonshire (parking at SH 766 833), although most reliably seen near rocky outcrops and disused quarries such as those at Great Orme Mine (Fig. 9).

Other regions. Absent.

Scottish Grayling
Hipparchia semele subspecies *scota* (Verity)

Subspecies type locality and authority
Specimens from northern Scotland were first described as a subspecies by Verity (1911), although no specific locality is given.

General distribution and status
Resident. Found commonly in coastal localities throughout Scotland. It is absent from the islands of Lewis, North Uist and Benbecula and the Isles of Orkney and Shetland. Inland populations

Scottish Grayling

Fig. 246 Scottish Grayling. Castlehill Point, Kirkcudbrightshire

are very scarce. In the Western Isles and their adjacent mainland its place is taken by the Atlantic Grayling (p. 284).

Flight period and larval foodplants
As for the Grayling (p. 277). Although the flight period is generally shorter, the optimum time for observation is the same.

Larval foodplants
As for the Grayling (p. 277).

Habitat requirements
The Scottish Grayling usually inhabits rocky coastlines (Fig. 17) and dune systems (e.g. Fig. 6).

Identification characters, variation and similar species
Apart from its slightly smaller size it differs from the typical Grayling in the following ways:

1. Upperside with pale markings paler and more extensive, although these are rarely seen in living specimens.
2. Forewing underside with pale ground colour paler yellow.
3. Hindwing underside marked densely with black, rather than dark brown, flecks on a white, rather than cream,

Scottish Grayling / Atlantic Grayling

ground colour; central pale band usually well-defined and white.

Variation is extensive and similar to the Grayling in degree. There is no similar species.

Field tips
As for the Grayling (p. 277).

Regional prime sites
Scotland. In the western islands and their adjacent mainland, the species is represented by the Atlantic Grayling (see below). Elsewhere the Scottish Grayling is common on rocky headlands and coastal dunes throughout with the exception of the far north where it is scarce or absent. In the north-east, it is common in the dunes area of the Scottish Wildlife reserve at **Ferry Links**, East Sutherland (take the track north-east of the car park at NH 805 957) and at **Findhorn Dunes**, East Inverness-shire (park at NJ 042 648 and walk to approximately NJ 405 647). On the east coast, it can be seen at **Forvie Sands**, North Aberdeenshire (NK 020 265) and, in the south-east, at **St Abb's Head**, Berwickshire (NT 910 680). In the south-west, there is a strong colony on the rocky coastal path at **Castlehill Point,** Kirkcudbrightshire (south of the car park at NX 852 536).

Other regions. Absent.

Atlantic Grayling
Hipparchia semele subspecies *atlantica* **(Harrison)**

Subspecies type locality and authority
Specimens from the island of Vatersay in the Outer Hebrides, Scotland, were first described as a subspecies by Harrison (1946).

General distribution and status
Resident. Common on rocky coastlines in most of the western islands of Scotland and their adjacent mainland, although absent from Lewis, Benbecula and North Uist.

Flight period and larval foodplants
As for the Scottish Grayling (p. 282).

Habitat requirements
The Atlantic Grayling inhabits rocky headlands and outcrops on the coast (Fig. 17) and, where present, their adjacent heathland.

Identification characters, variation and similar species
Average wingspan similar to that of the nominate subspecies from which it differs in the following ways:

1. Upperside markings more contrasting and brighter, although these are rarely seen in the wild.

2. Forewing underside with pale

Atlantic Grayling

markings paler.
3. Hindwing underside generally brighter with pale areas often tinged orange; dark flecks numerous, bold and jet black rather than dark brown; central pale band usually well-defined, white and bold.

Variation is extensive and similar to the Grayling in degree. There is no similar species.

Field tips
As for the Grayling (p. 277).

Regional prime sites
Scotland. This spectacular subspecies is common on rocky coastal headlands throughout its range but with an apparent preference for sites with a south-westerly aspect. In the Outer Hebrides, it is present on the islands of **Pabbay**, **Sandray** and **Vatersay**. The latter can be reached via a causeway that connects it to the larger island of Barra which, in turn, is serviced by a regular car ferry (see Appendix II: Caledonian MacBrayne) between Oban and the island's main town of Castlebay. In the Inner Hebrides, it is common along the coasts of all the islands of the South, Mid and North Ebudes, e.g. **Treshnish Point** (NM 340 487), Isle of Mull, Mid Ebudes. For some of these islands there

Fig. 247 Atlantic Grayling. Ardnamurchan Point, West Inverness-shire

Atlantic Grayling / Burren Grayling

are few recent records but this is almost certainly due to under-recording. The subspecies' distribution on the westernmost mainland is not accurately known but it is present on the rocky headlands of **Ardnamurchan Point**, West Inverness-shire (NM 416 675).

Further research in this area would be extremely valuable. Further north, in West Sutherland, it is present on the coastal trail around **Achmelvich Bay** (north from the car park in Achmelvich at NC 057 248).

Other regions. Absent.

Burren Grayling
Hipparchia semele subspecies *clarensis* de Lattin

Subspecies type locality and authority
Specimens from Co. Clare, Ireland, were first described as a subspecies by de Lattin (1952), though no specific locality is given.

General distribution and status
Resident. Widespread in the Burren limestone district of Clare and South-east Galway where it is often the most common species on the wing.

Flight period and larval foodplants
As for the Grayling (p. 277).

Habitat requirements
The Burren Grayling occupies the limestone pavement where grasses grow amongst exposed rock (Fig. 10).

Identification characters, variation and similar species
Average wingspan slightly smaller than the nominate subspecies from which it also differs in the following ways:

1. Upperside ground colour generally much lighter with pale markings – cream in the male and pale ochre in the female. Although these markings are rarely seen in detail in living specimens, the overall pale impression is very noticeable in flight.
2. Forewing underside with pale area around eye-spot light ochreous-cream.
3. Hindwing underside ground colour very pale and tinged greyish; dark flecks considerably less numerous; pale central band bold and chalky white.

Variation is less extensive than that of the nominate subspecies. There is no similar species.

Field tips
As for the Grayling (p 277).

Regional prime sites
Western Ireland. This subspecies is restricted to the limestone pavement of the Burren where it flourishes locally. It may be seen throughout the area but tends to be more numerous near the

Burren Grayling / Irish Grayling

Fig. 248 Burren Grayling. Craggagh, Co. Clare

coast and the first-time visitor is recommended to explore the strip of land adjacent to the sea immediately north-west of the R477 road between **Ballynahown** and **Black Head** (e.g. M 12 06).

Other regions. Absent.

Irish Grayling
Hipparchia semele subspecies *hibernica* Howarth

Subspecies type locality and authority
Specimens from Killarney in North Kerry, Ireland, were first described as a subspecies by Howarth (1971b).

General distribution and status
Resident. Widespread and locally common around most of the Irish coastline. Inland, populations are scarce.

Irish Grayling

Fig. 249 Irish Grayling. Dingle, Co. Kerry

Flight period and larval foodplants
As for the Grayling (p. 277).

Habitat requirements
The Irish Grayling inhabits rocky coastlines (e.g. Fig. 17) and dune systems (e.g. Fig. 6). Inland it is found occasionally in dry areas and open tracks on the edges of bogs.

Identification characters, variation and similar species
Average wingspan as in the nominate subspecies from which it differs in the following ways:

1. Upperside ground colour more richly brown with pale markings tinged conspicuously rufous. Although these marking are rarely seen in live individuals, the overall impression in flight is of a much warmer-coloured butterfly that appears very different to the typical Grayling.
2. Forewing underside with pale areas more orange-tinged.
3. Hindwing underside generally warmer in tone with rich chocolate-brown markings; basal area notably darker.

Variation is extensive and similar to that of the Grayling in degree. There is no similar species.

Irish Grayling / Gatekeeper

Field tips
As for the Grayling (p. 277).

Regional prime sites
Western Ireland. In the north, it is widespread and common along much of the coast of East Donegal but scarce from there south to West Mayo. Perhaps the best site to visit in the north is at **Kildoney Point** in East Donegal (approximately G 820 640). In the south-west, it is again widespread and common on the coast and can be seen reliably in South Kerry at **Dunquin** (about 0.5km west of the town on the sparsely-vegetated moorland leading to the sea immediately south of the R559 road at Q 320 010) and at **Castlegregory** (Q 608 152 and adjacent dunes).

Eastern Ireland. Widespread and common along most of the coast but seemingly absent from Meath and Louth. In the north it occurs at **Donabate Dunes**, Dublin (O 240 470) and at **Bloody Bridge**, Down (J 388 270). Further south, in Wexford, it is present on the dunes at the **Raven National Nature Reserve** (T 110 250). In the south-west, on the border with western Ireland, it is common at **Knockadoon Cliffs**, East Cork (X 089 694).

Other regions. Absent.

Gatekeeper (Hedge Brown)
Pyronia tithonus (Linnaeus) subspecies *britanniae* (Verity)

Subspecies type locality and authority
Specimens from Bude in East Cornwall and Benfleet in South Essex, England, were first described as this subspecies by Verity (1915). The nominate subspecies does not occur in the British Isles but is widespread in much of central and southern Europe.

General distribution and status
Resident. Widespread and very common throughout England and Wales on all but high ground south of a line approximately between Westmorland in the west and South-east Yorkshire in the east. There has been a recent northward expansion into Cumberland in the west and North-east Yorkshire in the east, but colonies in both areas are usually relatively small and mainly coastal in distribution. It is absent from the Isle of Man and from Scotland, and in Ireland is restricted to coastal areas of the southern and south-eastern counties. It is common in the Channel Isles.

Flight period
Single brooded, flying between mid-July and late August, with a peak during the first two weeks of August.

Gatekeeper (Hedge Brown)

Fig. 250 Gatekeeper male upperside.
Holkham, West Norfolk

Fig. 251 Gatekeeper female upperside.
Holkham, West Norfolk

Larval foodplants
A wide variety of fine grasses is used, including Sheep's Fescue, Common Bent and Annual Meadow-grass.

Habitat requirements
This is typically a butterfly of hedgerows, woodland rides and scrubland where tall grasses occur. In parts of its range it also occupies downland, coastal undercliffs and heathland containing patches of scrub. Bramble is an important nectar source and habitats where it grows are favoured.

Identification characters, variation and similar species
Average wingspan 43mm; the female is slightly larger than the male. The male also differs from the female in having a bold dark brown bar of scent scales across each forewing. Variation is uncommon, although extra eye-spots may occasionally be present on both the upper- and underside. Confusion with other species is unlikely, but the inexperienced observer may mistake a large female for a particularly brightly-marked female Meadow Brown. It differs from that species in the following ways:

1. Hindwing upperside with small but conspicuous white-pupilled eye-spot.
2. Hindwing underside with well-defined row of small dark patches containing conspicuous white dots.

Field tips
This familiar butterfly is easy to find and photograph as it spends long periods basking, wings open, on sunlit foliage. It is a regular visitor to the flowers of bramble and other plants. A few minutes spent watching the butterflies around a bramble bush or patch of Ragwort in a suitable habitat should be all that is needed for success.

Gatekeeper (Hedge Brown)

Regional prime sites
Scotland. Absent.

Northern England. Absent from much of the north of the region and the central high ground. Toward the northern edge of its range, it can be seen at **Askham Lots**, Westmorland (SD 209 767) and **Staveley Lagoon**, Mid-west Yorkshire (access from SE 365 635).

Central, eastern, south-east and south-west England. Widespread and common throughout.

Wales. Widespread and common throughout but absent from the higher ground.

Western Ireland. Restricted to the extreme south of the region where it can be seen in West Cork at **Rinneen Forest** (W 190 320), **Rathruane Beg** (V 964 376) and **Shirkin Island** (W 013 259).

Eastern Ireland. Very localized and restricted to a few sites near the coast in the south and south-east. It can be seen reliably at the **Raven National Nature Reserve**, Wexford (T 110 250).

Fig. 252 Gatekeeper undersides. Holkham, West Norfolk

The Meadow Brown group
Maniola jurtina (Linnaeus)

Introductory notes

According to the latest authoritative nomenclature, the Meadow Brown is represented in the British Isles by four subspecies. Apart from the Irish Meadow Brown, which is genetically isolated from the others by the Irish Sea, there appear to be no clearly definable geographical dividing lines between the taxa. Some schools of thought consider the remaining three to be merely intergraded regional forms, each of which predominate in certain areas. If this view is correct, then the subspecific status for the Isles of Scilly Meadow Brown (p. 296), the Hebridean Meadow Brown (p. 298) and the British Meadow Brown (see below) is indeed questionable. (This is particularly so with the latter two as a broad north-south band of intermediate forms exists through central Scotland). However, each of these three forms is clearly different in appearance where they predominate and for this reason, and in order to conform to the current nomenclature, they continue to be here treated as subspecies. The subspecific status of populations from the Channel Isles requires further study.

British Meadow Brown
Maniola jurtina (Linnaeus) subspecies *insularis* Thomson

Subspecies type locality and authority

Specimens from the Isle of Wight, England, were first described as this subspecies by Thomson (1969). The nominate subspecies does not occur in the British Isles but is widespread across continental Europe.

General distribution and status

Resident. Widespread and abundant throughout England and Wales and in Scotland east of a line approximately between Ayrshire in the south-west and Moray in the north-east.

Flight period

Due to a protracted and variable rate of larval development this species has a long flight period and is seen between mid-June and mid-October. Throughout most of its range, the optimum time to see the species in good condition is during the last three weeks of July and the first week of August. This is slightly later in the north of Scotland where it is represented by the Hebridean Meadow Brown (p. 298).

Larval foodplants

The Meadow Brown has a preference for fine grasses such as Sheep's Fescue and Annual Meadow-grass but some coarse grasses, such as Cock's-foot and False Brome, are also used by older larvae.

Habitat requirements

Ubiquitous on most types of grassland throughout its range.

British Meadow Brown

Fig. 253 British Meadow Brown male upside. Glapthorn Cow Pasture, Northamptonshire

Fig. 254 British Meadow Brown female upside. Fakenham, West Norfolk

Identification characters, variation and similar species

Average wingspan 52mm; the female is slightly larger than the male. The female also differs from the male in having a paler brown ground colour and large bold pale orange patches on the fore- and, in many individuals, hindwings. Minor variation is common, and individuals from any given population can resemble the subspecies from another region. On the interface between Hebridean Meadow Brown and British Meadow Brown, and Isles of Scilly Meadow Brown and British Meadow Brown, many intermediate forms may be encountered. In flight, the male of this species may resemble a Ringlet but close observation will reveal a characteristic flash of orange as the Meadow Brown momentarily closes its wings in mid-beat.

Fig. 255 British Meadow Brown male underside. Holkham, West Norfolk

Fig. 256 British Meadow Brown female underside. Fakenham, West Norfolk

British Meadow Brown / Irish Meadow Brown

Field tips
This species is so common and conspicuous that hundreds may be seen flying together in suitable habitats throughout its range and it simply cannot be missed.

Regional prime sites
Scotland. Widespread and abundant throughout the eastern, southern and south-western parts of the country. In the west, north-west, north and the Orkney Islands, it is represented by the Hebridean Meadow Brown (p. 298).

Northern England. Widespread and abundant on all but the highest ground.

Central, eastern and south-east England. Widespread and abundant throughout.

South-west England. Widespread and abundant, but in the Isles of Scilly it is represented by the Isles of Scilly Meadow Brown (p. 296). Many individuals from the extreme south-western mainland also closely resemble, or are inseparable from, this subspecies.

Wales. Widespread and common throughout on all but the highest ground.

Western and eastern Ireland. See Irish Meadow Brown (see below).

Irish Meadow Brown
Maniola jurtina subspecies *iernes* Graves

Subspecies type locality and authority
Specimens from Co. Kerry, Ireland, were first described as this subspecies by Graves (1930a), though no specific locality is given.

General distribution and status
Resident. Very common or abundant throughout Ireland.

Flight period, larval foodplants and Habitat requirements
As for the British Meadow Brown (p. 292).

Identification characters, variation and similar species
Larger than the British Meadow Brown with an average wingspan of 54mm. It also differs in the following ways:

1. Male forewing upperside with distinct orange band in which is usually set a double white-pupilled eye-spot.
2. Male forewing underside with orange area clearly divided into pale outer and darker inner halves (rather than unicolorous) separated by a distinct dark brown line.
3. Male and female underside with dark flecking strongly expressed; eye-spots

Irish Meadow Brown

Fig. 257 Irish Meadow Brown male upperside. Craggagh, Co. Clare

Fig. 258 Irish Meadow Brown female upperside. Craggagh, Co. Clare

tiny or absent.
4. Female forewing upperside with orange band usually extending into central part of wing but always broken by a dark brown line.
5. Female hindwing upperside usually with a strongly expressed orange central band or patch.
6. Female forewing underside as in male but contrast greater and dividing line even more strongly expressed.
7. Female hindwing underside brightly marked with conspicuous pale buff band contrasting greatly from the ground colour.

For variation and similar species see British Meadow Brown (p. 292).

Field tips
As for the British Meadow Brown (p. 292).

Fig. 259 Irish Meadow Brown male underside. Craggagh, Co. Clare

Fig. 260 Irish Meadow Brown female underside. Craggagh, Co. Clare

Irish Meadow Brown / Isles of Scilly Meadow Brown

Regional prime sites
Western and eastern Ireland.
Individuals conforming most accurately to the type description are found in the counties of the south-west of western Ireland and their adjacent islands, although they may occur throughout both regions.

Other regions. Absent.

Isles of Scilly Meadow Brown
Maniola jurtina subspecies *cassiteridum* Graves

Subspecies type locality and authority
Specimens from the Isles of Scilly off the coast of West Cornwall, England, were first described as a subspecies by Graves (1930b).

General distribution and status
Resident. It is very common throughout the Isles of Scilly. In West Cornwall, specimens can be found that closely resemble or are inseparable from this subspecies.

Flight period, larval foodplants and habitat requirements
As for the British Meadow Brown (p. 292).

Identification characters, variation and similar species
Average wingspan is similar to that of the British Meadow Brown from which it differs in the following ways:

1. Male forewing upperside with distinct orange band in which there is often a double white-pupilled eye-spot.

Fig. 261 Isles of Scilly Meadow Brown male upperside. St Mary's, Isles of Scilly

Fig. 262 Isles of Scilly Meadow Brown female upperside. St Mary's, Isles of Scilly

Isles of Scilly Meadow Brown

Fig. 263 Isles of Scilly Meadow Brown male underside. St Mary's, Isles of Scilly

Fig. 264 Isles of Scilly Meadow Brown female underside. St Mary's, Isles of Scilly

2. Male forewing underside with orange area divided weakly into pale outer and darker inner halves separated by a distinct brown line.
3. Male hindwing underside with conspicuous dark flecking; pale band usually lighter; eye-spots more strongly developed, white-pupilled and ringed with orange.
4. Female forewing upperside with orange band extending into centre of wing but broken by a dark brown line.
5. Female forewing underside similar to the male but with more contrast between pale outer and dark inner halves; dividing brown line more strongly expressed.
6. Female hindwing underside very heavily and conspicuously flecked with dark brown; pale band lighter, more conspicuous and pale greyish buff in colour.

For variation and similar species see the British Meadow Brown (p. 292).

Field tips and regional prime sites
South-west England. The Isles of Scilly Meadow Brown is very common throughout the islands and should easily be located within a few minutes of arrival there during its flight period. Individuals conforming to this subspecies are found regularly in the south-west of the West Cornwall mainland.

Other regions. Absent.

Hebridean Meadow Brown
Maniola jurtina subspecies *splendida* White

Fig. 265 **Hebridean Meadow Brown male upside.** Ardnamurchan, West Inverness-shire

Fig. 266 **Hebridean Meadow Brown female upside.** Arisaig, West Inverness-shire

Subspecies type locality and authority
Specimens from Longa Island off the coast of West Ross, Scotland, were first described as a subspecies by White (1871).

General distribution and status
Resident. Widespread and very common west of a line approximately between the Clyde Isles in the south-west and the Orkney Islands in the north-east. This subspecies also occurs commonly throughout the Isle of Man (Chalmers-Hunt, 1970).

Flight period
It flies between the end of June and the end of August. The optimum time to see the Hebridean Meadow Brown is during the third and fourth weeks of July.

Larval foodplants and habitat requirements
As for the British Meadow Brown (p. 292).

Identification characters, variation and similar species
Average wingspan is similar to that of the British Meadow Brown from which it differs in the following ways:

1. Male upperside much darker brown, velvety and often with a greenish or bluish iridescence.
2. Male forewing upperside with eye-spot set in a much deeper reddish-orange patch; patch sometimes extending into a band but usually broken by streaks of the ground colour along the veins and heavily suffused with dark brown.
3. Male forewing underside with orange area darker and divided in half by a dark brown transverse line.
4. Male hindwing underside more uniform in colour with pale band obscure; dark flecking well developed; eye-spots tiny or absent.
5. Female forewing upperside with orange patch well developed and extending well into the centre of the

Hebridean Meadow Brown / Small Heath

Fig. 267 Hebridean Meadow Brown male underside. Ardnamurchan, West Inverness-shire

Fig. 268 Hebridean Meadow Brown female underside. Ardnamurchan, West Inverness-shire

wing but usually heavily suffused with the ground colour.
6. Female hindwing upperside with well developed pale band usually tinged pale orange.
7. Female forewing underside with orange area darker.
8. Female hindwing underside heavily flecked dark brown; pale band greyish, conspicuous and with inner edge tinged yellow.

For variation and similar species see the British Meadow Brown (p. 292).

Field tips and regional prime sites
Scotland. Individuals conforming most accurately to the type description are found in the Western Isles and their adjacent mainland, though they do occur throughout its range.

Northern England. Common throughout the Isle of Man.

Other regions. Absent.

Small Heath
Coenonympha pamphilus subspecies *pamphilus* (Linnaeus)

General distribution and status
Resident. Although there appears to have been a slight, but steady, decline in the abundance of this species since the 1970s (Asher *et al.*, 2001) the Small Heath remains a very widespread and locally common butterfly. It is scarce in the island of Lewis in the Outer Hebrides and absent from the Isles of Orkney and Shetland but otherwise is found throughout the British Isles. In the Isle of Rhum, North Ebudes, the species is represented by the Hebridean

Small Heath

Small Heath (p. 302).

Flight period
Due to the variable development rate of the larva of this species it is possible to see the Small Heath in southernmost localities at any time between late April and early September. It is double brooded over most of its range in southern and central England and in Ireland. Here the optimum times to see the species are during the last week of May and the first two weeks of June and during the first three weeks of August. In northern England and Scotland, it is single brooded, flying from mid-June to mid-August, with a peak during the first three weeks of July.

Larval foodplants
A variety of fine grasses is used, most commonly Annual Meadow-grass, Common Bent and Sheep's Fescue.

Habitat requirements
Any grassland where the sward is kept short and contains the larval foodplants can accommodate this species. It has a preference for well-drained situations such as downland, heathland and coastal dunes (Figs 6, 8 and 16). Large populations can also be present on moorlands up to an altitude of about 650m. Elsewhere it may be seen along open woodland rides and roadsides, on waste ground and in parks and large gardens. In open habitats the males require the presence of isolated trees or bushes around which to congregate in what might be compared to leks used by certain birds for display, competition and attracting females.

Identification characters, variation and similar species
Average wingspan 35mm; the female is slightly larger than the male. Apart from the size, the sexes are similar. The tone of the ground colour and the width of the dark border on the upperside may vary considerably but this is rarely seen clearly in living specimens as they always rest with their wings closed. The presence and development of the pale central marking and the small eye-spots on the hindwings are subject to considerable variation. This species could easily be confused with poorly-marked individuals of the Scottish Large Heath (p. 309) from which it differs in the following ways:

1. Usually smaller. There can be an overlap in size between large female Small Heaths and small male Large Heaths, although this is rare.
2. Upperside usually with much more clearly defined dark borders. These can often be seen in flight.
3. Forewing underside with ground colour brighter orange; eye-spot usually larger and more conspicuous.
4. Hindwing underside with central pale flash usually creamy white or off-white. (This is whiter and more conspicuous in the Large Heath.) Eye-spots, where present, usually centred white rather than black and ringed brown rather than white.

Field tips
At a known locality one may see males patrolling in search of females during hot weather. At such times they are very active

Small Heath

and difficult to photograph. During cooler periods they congregate near landmarks such as isolated bushes and can then be approached more easily, especially in the early mornings, as they perch. The females only visit these sites briefly in order to mate and are best sought in the vicinity of the foodplants. Here they can readily be disturbed from the grasses and, after landing, be approached with ease. As mentioned, both sexes invariably settle with their wings closed.

Regional prime sites

Scotland. Widespread and common in suitable habitats throughout apart from in the far north where it is more localized. It is absent from the Island of Lewis in the Outer Hebrides and Isles of Orkney and Shetland.

Western Ireland. Common in the limestone district of the Burren, Clare and South-east Galway, and locally widespread elsewhere. It is probably under-recorded in this region.

Eastern Ireland. Very common in suitable habitats in the counties of Antrim, Down, Armagh, Louth, Dublin, South Tipperary, Waterford and Wexford and locally widespread, although probably under-recorded elsewhere.

Other regions. Widespread and very common in suitable habitats throughout.

Fig. 269 Small Heath. Burnham Norton, West Norfolk

Hebridean Small Heath
Coenonympha pamphilus subspecies *rhoumensis* Harrison

Subspecies type locality and authority
Specimens from the Isle of Rhum in the North Ebudes, Scotland, were first described as a subspecies by Harrison (1948).

General distribution and status
Resident. At present this subspecies is only known from the Isle of Rhum in the North Ebudes where it appears to be widespread and locally common. It may occur in the neighbouring islands of Canna, Eigg and Muck but has not specifically been searched for there as far as is known. Its subspecific status is a matter of dispute but this cannot be resolved until more is known about the taxon's distribution and the consistency of its morphology. There are very few extant specimens in collections and, so far as the author is aware, the individual figured below is the first and only ever to be photographed alive and published. More research into this delightful and little-known butterfly is therefore warranted.

Flight period
Single brooded, flying from late May to the end of July, with a peak during the last week of June and the first week of July.

Larval foodplants
As for the Small Heath (p. 299).

Fig. 270 Hebridean Small Heath. Kinloch, Isle of Rhum

Hebridean Small Heath

Habitat requirements
In the Isle of Rhum it appears to be fairly widely distributed but, because its status as an assumed endemic subspecies has not been appreciated, little information has been gathered. It is presumed that it inhabits moorland, and the author found it on the grassy edges of meadows.

Identification characters, variation and similar species
Average wingspan and variation presumed to be similar to that of the Small Heath (p. 299) from which it differs in the following ways:

1. Forewing underside duller orange with borders more silver-grey; pale area around eye-spot smaller or absent.
2. Hindwing underside more silver-grey and less tinged olive; central pale flash greyer, less tinged cream, and narrower.
3. In flight overall appearance eye-catchingly paler and greyer.

For similar species see the Small Heath (p. 299).

Field tips and regional prime sites
Scotland. The Hebridean Small Heath is only known from the Isle of Rhum in the North Ebudes where it is regarded as being the island's commonest and most widespread species. This may well be the

Fig. 271 Habitat of the Hebridean Small Heath at Kinloch, Isle of Rhum

Hebridean Small Heath / Southern Large Heath

case but the author visited Rhum (in poor weather) on 10th June 2004 and found the butterfly difficult to locate. On a day trip to the island time is very limited and so, to enable the visitor to find it quickly, directions to a known site are hereby given. From the pier at **Kinloch** take the main road north around the bay until, after approximately 0.75km, it turns sharply west and joins a marked nature trail. Immediately on leaving the village, turn north towards the scrub-covered hillside and then search west along the path on its southern edge from NM 400 002 (Fig. 271). This site is about 30 minutes walk from the pier.

The Isle of Rhum can be reached using the passenger ferry service from Arisaig (see Appendix II under Arisaig Marine) or from Mallaig with Caledonian MacBrayne, who also offer travel from Mallaig to the nearby islands of Canna, Eigg and Muck (Appendix II, Caledonian MacBrayne).

Other regions. Absent.

The Large Heath group
Coenonympha tullia (Müller)

Introductory notes

This species is represented in the British Isles by three subspecies: the Southern Large Heath (see below) in the south of its range and the Scottish Large Heath (p. 309) in the north (both are distinct in appearance). The Northern Large Heath (p. 307), in the central part of its range, is a variable butterfly that can exhibit characters of the other two at the northern and southern limits of its distribution. This has led to much debate over the validity of subspecific status for all three, but, in order to conform to the presently accepted nomenclature, their status has here been maintained. The nominate subspecies is widespread in northern and eastern Europe but does not occur in the British Isles.

Southern Large Heath
Coenonympha tullia subspecies *davus* (Fabricius)

Subspecies type locality and authority

Specimens from Hamburg, Germany, were first given subspecies status by Fabricius (1777). No locality is given.

General distribution and status

Resident. Locally common but restricted to only a few sites in north-west and central England. As much as 90 per cent of the Large Heath's lowland peat bog

Southern Large Heath

habitat in the British Isles has been lost since the beginning of the 19th century through drainage for agricultural development, afforestation and peat extraction. Fortunately, most colonies of this particular subspecies are now on nature reserves or Sites of Special Scientific Interest and are therefore subject to a certain degree of protection.

Flight period
Single brooded, flying from mid-June to early August, with a peak during the second and third weeks of July.

Larval foodplants
Usually Hare's-tail Cottongrass; Common Cottongrass and Jointed Rush are used occasionally.

Habitat requirements
The Southern Large Heath inhabits lowland mosses and peat bogs, containing cottongrass and an abundance of Cross-leaved Heath. The latter is an important nectar source for the adult butterflies (Fig. 4).

Identification characters, variation and similar species.
Average wingspan 37mm. The ground colour of the male is considerably darker than that of the female and this is very noticeable in flight. The size and shape

Fig. 272 Southern Large Heath. Whixall Moss, Shropshire

Southern Large Heath

of the eye-spots on the underside of the hindwings vary considerably and forms where they are very large are referred to as *cockaynei* Hopkins. Occasionally they are spectacularly elliptical in shape and this form is known as *lanceolata* Arkle. In its chosen habitat there is no species with which the Southern Large Heath can be confused.

Field tips
When searching for any of the Large Heath subspecies the first thing to look for are patches of cottongrass (the larval foodplant) as these are very distinctive and conspicuous and should point to the right general area (see Fig. 4). Sunny weather is essential for seeing this butterfly as it is reluctant to fly during dull periods. However, if the ambient temperature is above about 17°C it is easy to disturb from the vegetation even in cloudy conditions. In favourable weather it is easy to spot as it patrols low, but conspicuously, with a characteristic bouncing flight. Both sexes feed regularly from the flowers of Cross-leaved Heath and can then be approached with confidence. It invariably rests with its wings closed and the upperside is therefore never seen clearly in living specimens. The habitat where this butterfly lives can be dangerous and a stumble into a deep hole amongst the heathers is likely and could easily result in injury. Rushing excitedly around a peat bog, particularly on one's own, is therefore not to be recommended. One should simply stay on the paths and wait for the butterflies to come close; this is also far more respectful to this scarce and fragile habitat. It should also be noted that venomous Adders are present at many such localities.

Regional prime sites
Northern England. In Westmorland it can be seen in good numbers at **Bellart How Moss** (area south-west of the car park at SD 458 838) and **Meathop Moss** (track west of the car park at SD 447 821). Both sites are accessed from the A590, a major road that demands great care. In West Lancashire, it is present at **Winmarleigh Moss** (SD 440 470), north of the minor road between Winmarleigh and Stake Pool.

Central England. In Shropshire, where perhaps the best examples of this subspecies are seen, a visit to **Whixall Moss** is a must (reserve car park at SJ 505 125) but, prior to arrival, it is necessary to obtain a permit from Natural England (see Appendix II under Whixall Moss).

Other regions. Absent.

Northern Large Heath
Coenonympha tullia subspecies *polydama* (Haworth)

Subspecies type locality and authority
Specimens from Yorkshire, England, were first described as a subspecies by Haworth (1803), though no specific locality is given.

General distribution and status
Resident; fully protected (NI). In Great Britain, it is locally common in parts of central and north-west Wales and in England in Cumberland, North and South Northumberland, North-east Yorkshire and North Lincolnshire. It is absent from Anglesey and the Isle of Man. In Scotland, it is widespread and locally common from the border with England northwards to a line approximately between Renfrewshire in the west to South Aberdeenshire in the east. In Ireland, it is widespread and locally common in the north but with only widely scattered small colonies elsewhere.

Flight period, larval foodplants and habitat requirements
As for the Southern Large Heath (p. 304).

Identification characters, variation and similar species
Average wingspan similar to that of the Southern Large Heath from which it differs in the following ways:

1. Ground colour of both sexes paler on

Fig. 273 Northern Large Heath. Kirkconnell Flow, Kirkcudbrightshire

Northern Large Heath

both upper- and underside.
2. Hindwing underside with eye-spots smaller and much less frequently and conspicuously white-pupilled, especially in northern populations; eye-spot in hind corner of wing rarely double.

Variation in the size and number of hindwing eye-spots is considerable and clinal. In individuals from the north they are usually very small and are sometimes absent. Such specimens closely resemble the Scottish Large Heath (p. 309). Within its favoured habitat it is unlikely to be confused with any other species.

Field tips
As for the Southern Large Heath (p. 304 and Fig. 4).

Regional prime sites
Scotland. Widespread and locally common over most of its range. In Stirlingshire, the Northern Large Heath occurs just south of Fallin at **Wester Moss** (NS 837 911). Further south, some beautiful examples can be seen commonly at **Feoch Meadows**, Ayrshire (NX 263 816) and **Kirkconnell Flow**, Kirkcudbrightshire (car park at NX 967 700 where there is a site map available; follow directions to the central peat dome). In the same county it can be seen in good numbers at **Knowetop Lochs** where access is available on the south side of the A712 approximately midway between Balmaclellan and Corsock (NX 706 786).

Northern England. Widespread in South Northumberland where it flies some 8km west of Newborough at **Muckle Moss** (path north from the car park at NY790 661) and around 20km north of Corbridge at **Hartside** (park 1km east of the A68 near the cattle grid (NY 916 822) and search the bog on the north side of the road). Further south, in North-east Yorkshire, it is fairly common about 8km north of Lockton at **Fen Bog** (park at SE 857 982 and explore the bog along the track to the south-west) and the mires to the east of the wooded area of **May Beck** (NZ 90 01; access from NZ892 024).

Eastern England. Found only at **Thorne Waste** in North Lincolnshire (SE 759 145).

Wales. Widespread and locally common in the north-west with a few small colonies elsewhere. In Merionethshire, it can be seen reliably at **Cors Goch** (SH 968 332) and, on the south side of Llyn Celyn, at **Ffridd y Fawnog** (south side of the minor road at SH 858 387).

Western Ireland. Widespread and locally common in the north where it inhabits **Rabley Hill**, East Donegal (G 715 702). Further south, it is found in West Galway in the Connemara National Park at **Letterfrack** (L 712 573) and at **Ardderry Lough** (L 988 460).

Eastern Ireland. Widespread in the north but very localized elsewhere. In

Northern Large Heath \ Scottish Large Heath

Offaly, it is present at **Clara Bog** (N 260 293) and in Kildare, at **Mound's Bog** (N 785 186).

Other regions. Absent.

Scottish Large Heath
Coenonympha tullia subspecies *scotica* Staudinger

Subspecies type locality and authority
Specimens from Scotland were first described as a subspecies by Staudinger & Rebel (1901), though no specific locality is given.

General distribution and status
Resident. Widely distributed and locally common in Scotland north of a line approximately between the Clyde Isles in the west and North Aberdeenshire in the east. It has been recorded from all of the larger islands off the west coast (with the exception of Tiree) and, in the northern Isles, it is widespread in the Orkneys but absent from the Shetlands.

Flight period
Throughout most of its range the flight

Fig. 274 Scottish Large Heath. Creag Meagaidh, West Inverness-shire

Scottish Large Heath

period is similar to that of the Southern and Northern Large Heath but at high altitude and, in the far north, it flies between early July and late August with a peak during the last two weeks of July.

Larval foodplants
As for the Southern Large Heath (p. 304).

Habitat requirements
Similar to those of the Southern Large Heath (Fig. 4) but is also found in boggy areas at altitudes of up to 800m (Thomson, 1980) such as at Creag Meagaidh, in West Inverness-shire, where it can be seen flying with the Scottish Small Mountain Ringlet (Fig. 20).

Identification characters, variation and similar species
Average wingspan is similar to that of the Southern and Northern Large Heath. Variation in the number and size of the eye-spots on the hindwing underside is less extensive than that in the other two subspecies. However, individuals from the south of its range may resemble northerly examples of the Northern Large Heath, from which it differs in the following ways:

1. Ground colour of upperside paler with pale greyish margins creating a 'ghostly' impression in flight.
2. Upperside of fore- and hindwings with eye-spots minute or absent, although this feature is rarely seen in resting or feeding living individuals as the wings are invariably held closed.
3. Male hindwing underside with eye-spots minute, usually numbering only two, and sometimes absent; all markings, including the central pale flash, less conspicuous.
4. Female hindwing underside with eye-spots usually smaller, less conspicuous, fewer in number and sometimes absent.

In its chosen habitat the Scottish Large Heath is unlike any other species.

Field tips
On seeing a Scottish Large Heath in flight for the first time one can be forgiven for being confused as it appears quite unlike the other two subspecies – especially worn examples or those from more northerly latitudes. They are very much paler and greyer and have what might be described as a 'soft' or 'ghostly' appearance.

Regional prime sites
Scotland. Widespread and locally common throughout most of its range but scarcer in the east and absent from the Shetland Isles and from Tiree in the Mid Ebudes. In the north, it is present in good numbers at **Forsinard** in Caithness (NC 890 424). In the west, it flies in West Ross at **Beinn Eighe** (visitor centre at NH 001 650) and, in West Inverness-shire, at **Allt Mhuic** (visitor centre at NN121 912). Similarly, on the Ardnamurchan peninsula, it occurs in boggy areas along the side of the B8007 between Strontian and Kilchoan such as those at **Loch Mudle** (NM 540 660) and **Lochuisge** on the

Scottish Large Heath / Ringlet

west side of the junction of the A848 and B8043 (NM 780 556). In West Inverness-shire, it is widespread and common in suitable habitats throughout the **Glen More Forest Park**. Here one can park at the RSPB reserve car park at **Loch Garten** (NH 979 185) and explore the many open boggy sites in the area such as those along the minor road leading westwards from the reserve. In the same county it is common at **Creag Meagaidh** where it flies in company with the Scottish Small Mountain Ringlet (see p. 266 for site details).

Other regions. Absent.

Ringlet
Aphantopus hyperantus (Linnaeus)

General distribution and status
Resident. Widespread and locally very common throughout most of the British Isles south of a line approximately between the South Ebudes in the west and Banffshire in the east. Presently it is absent from many western parts of northern England, north-western parts of the Midlands, the Isle of Man and the Channel Isles. In Scotland, it is missing from many of the offshore islands. In Ireland, it is widespread and locally common. During the 19th century it disappeared from large parts of its range but, since the 1930s, has rapidly expanded and recolonized its former range.

Flight period
Single brooded, flying from late June to mid-August, with a peak during the second and third weeks of July. The males emerge over a week before the females.

Fig. 275 Ringlet male upperside. Holkham, West Norfolk

Fig. 276 Ringlet female upperside. Thetford Forest, East Suffolk

Ringlet

Fig. 277 Ringlet underside. Fakenham, West Norfolk

Fig. 278 Ringlet form *arete* underside (below). Cumberland (S. Doyle)

Larval foodplants
A wide variety of grasses may be used, most commonly Tufted Hair-grass, Cock's-foot and Creeping Bent.

Habitat requirements
The Ringlet inhabits damp areas of tall, lush grassland. In northern, and some eastern, localities these may be in fairly open areas such as wet meadows but elsewhere partial shade is favoured. Here it can be found along woodland rides, hedgerows, roadside verges and river banks and in parks, gardens, scrubland and set-aside fields. Bramble and thistles provide important nectar sources and should be present in abundance.

Identification characters, variation and similar species
Average wingspan 47mm; the female is slightly larger than the male. Apart from in size, the sexes are similar, although the female often has more prominent eye-spots on the upperside than the male. Variation is common and extensive and is concerned mainly with the development of the eye-spots on the underside. The best-known forms, which can occur commonly in some populations, are *arete* Müller (commonly known as the Blind Ringlet) where the rings are reduced to tiny white dots (Fig. 278), *crassipuncta* Burkhardt where they are much enlarged, and, perhaps most spectacular of all, *lanceolata* Shipp in which they are both enlarged and pear-shaped with streaked pupils. Individuals are not infrequently found where the ground colour is that of milky coffee and these are known as *pallens* Schultz. There appears to be clinal variation with specimens in the north being slightly smaller and greyer than their counterparts from the south (Emmet & Heath, 1989).

In flight, the Ringlet may be confused with a male Meadow Brown but, when

Ringlet

fresh, the present species has clear white fringes to the wings. Further, the Meadow Brown usually shows flashes of orange from the underside of the forewings at the peak of each wingbeat. This aside, there is no other species that possesses the bold 'ringlet' markings from which this butterfly gets its name.

Field tips
This very common species can easily be located by waiting near favoured nectar sources such as brambles, thistles and Wild Privet. During the heat of the day only the underside may be exposed whilst it is resting or feeding. Early mornings provide the best opportunities to photograph the upperside as the insects bask openly whilst warming up for the day's activities.

Regional prime sites
Scotland. Widespread and common south of a line approximately between the South Ebudes in the west, where it is present in Colonsay, Jura and Islay, and Banffshire in the east. There have been occasional recent sightings from further north, which suggest the species is still expanding its range in that direction.

Northern England. Widespread and common in most of the region with the exception of large parts of South and West Lancashire, Westmorland, Cumberland and South Northumberland where it is very localized, scarce or absent. Presumably, the ongoing range expansion evident in the species should see this situation change over the coming years.

Central England. Common throughout with the exception of the north-west corner of the region and the species' recent expansion appears to be filling this gap.

Other regions. Widespread and common throughout.

Monarch

The Monarchs
(Nymphalidae, subfamily Danainae)

Monarch (Milkweed)
Danaus plexippus (Linnaeus)

Status

Scarce immigrant. Since the first record, in 1876, the numbers of Monarchs seen each year has steadily increased to the point where it is now regarded as being an annual visitor. In recent years, numbers have regularly reached double figures and occasionally several hundred have been reported. Despite this, there is little chance of the species colonizing the British Isles as its usual foodplants, milkweeds, do not grow here. Since the mid-19th century the Monarch has expanded its range from its traditional home in the Americas to include regions as far afield as Australia and New Zealand, the Atlantic islands and parts of southern Europe. In America, the species is famous for its annual migration from Canada to its wintering grounds in Mexico, a distance of some 3,600km (Urquhart & Urquhart, 1977; Brower, 1995). It is probably whilst so engaged, during the hurricane 'season' of September and October, that the vast majority of individuals recorded in the British Isles gets carried here across the Atlantic Ocean on storm fronts originating in the Gulf of Mexico. Asher *et al.* (2001) suggest that this transatlantic journey could take as little as four days. In Europe, the Monarch is now resident in southern Spain, from where it was first recorded as breeding in 1983, and in Gibraltar. It is also resident off the west coast of Africa in the Canary Islands (Asher *et al.*, 2001).

Distribution of records

First recorded in 1876 in Neath in Glamorgan, South Wales (Salmon, 2000). Between then and 1988 some 450 individuals were noted, most of which arrived in 1968 and 1981. There have been three major influxes since: in 1995 approximately 200 were recorded, in 1999 there were about 300 sightings and in 2001 large numbers were again seen. The Monarch has been recorded from most parts of the British Isles but there is a strong bias towards the south-western coasts of England, Wales and Ireland. This, and the fact that the species is often accompanied by the arrival of American birds (particularly in the Isles of Scilly and south-west Cornwall), supports the theory of its transatlantic origin. However, in 1983 and 1985 specimens were recorded at the same time as immigrant moths from south-western Europe. This suggests that, occasionally, Monarchs may arrive here from their breeding grounds in southern Spain, Gibraltar or the Canary Islands.

Monarch (Milkweed)

Flight period
Mainland European populations are continuously brooded but those in North America hibernate through the winter months. In Britain and Ireland, the great majority of records occur during September and October.

Larval foodplants
This species is restricted to milkweeds, none of which occur in the British Isles.

Habitat requirements
The Monarch usually inhabits flower-rich meadows where its foodplants grow. In Europe, it is found in coastal valleys close to cultivated areas. In the British Isles, the species has been recorded inland on several occasions but the vast majority of sightings are coastal.

Identification characters and similar species
Average wingspan 97mm. This huge butterfly, with its distinctive orange and black markings, cannot be confused with any other species found in the British Isles.

Field tips and regional prime sites
During September and October one should study the Atlantic weather charts and watch for deep depressions originating in the Gulf of Mexico and

Fig. 279 Monarch upperside. Isles of Scilly (G. Thoburn)

Monarch (Milkweed)

crossing the ocean towards the south-west coasts of Britain and Ireland. These may well be a precursor to the arrival of Monarchs. One should then check for sightings of American birds (see Appendix II under Bird reports) such as Bobolink *Dolichonyx oryzivorus* (Linnaeus), Red-eyed Vireo *Vireo olivaceous* (Linnaeus), Upland Sandpiper *Bartramia longicauda* (Bechstein) and Buff-breasted Sandpiper *Tryngites subruficollis* (Vieillot). Should any of these have been reported, a trip to south-west Cornwall or the Isles of Scilly during the first subsequent spell of warm weather may well prove rewarding. Although the services listed in Appendix II are primarily for birdwatchers, they often also report sightings of this wonderful butterfly.

Fig. 280 Monarch underside. Isles of Scilly (G. Thoburn)

Marbled White

Appendix I:
Alphabetical list of foodplants

Agrimony
Agrimonia eupatoria L.

Alder
Alnus glutinosa (L.)

Alder Buckthorn
Frangula alnus Miller

Angelica
Angelica sylvestris L.

Annual Meadow-grass
Poa annua L.

Ash
Fraxinus excelsior L.

Bell Heather
Erica cinerea L.

Bilberry
Vaccinium myrtillus L.

Birch
Betula spp.

Bitter Vetchling
Lathyrus montanus Bernh.

Black Bent
Agrostis gigantea Roth

Black Medic
Medicago lupulina L.

Blackthorn
Prunus spinosa L.

Bladder Senna
Colutea arborescens L.

Blue Moor-grass
Sesleria albicans (L.)

Bluebell
Endymion spp.

Bracken
Pteridium aquilinium (L.)

Bramble
Rubus fruticosus agg. L.

Bristle Bent
Agrostis curtsii Kerg.

Broad-leaved Dock
Rumex obtusifolius L.

Broad-leaved Everlasting Pea
Lathyrus latifolius L.

Broom
Cytisus scoparius (L.)

Buddleia
Buddleia davidii Franchet

Bugle
Ajuga reptans L.

Buck's-horn Plantain
Plantago coronopus L.

Buckthorn
Rhamnus cathartica L.

Bullace
Prunus domestica L.

Buttercup
Ranunculus spp.

Charlock
Sinapis arvensis L.

Clover
Trifolium spp.

Alphabetical list of foodplants

Cock's-foot
Dactylis glomerata L.

Common Cottongrass
Eriophorum angustifolium Honckeny

Common Bent
Agrostis tenuis Sibth.

Common Bird's-foot Trefoil
Lotus corniculatus L.

Common Cow-wheat
Melampyrum pratense L.

Common Dog Violet
Viola riviniana Reichenb.

Common Fleabane
Pulicaria dysenterica (L.)

Common Nettle
Urtica dioica L.

Common Rockrose
Helianthemum nummularium (L.)

Common Sorrel
Rumex acetosa L.

Common Stork's-bill
Erodium cicutarium (L.)

Cowslip
Primula veris L.

Crack Willow
Salix fragilis L.

Creeping Bent
Agrostis stolonifera L.

Creeping Cinquefoil
Potentilla reptans L.

Creeping Soft-grass
Holcus mollis L.

Creeping Thistle
Cirsium arvense (L.)

Cross-leaved Heath
Erica tetralix L.

Crown Vetch
Securigera varia (L.)

Cuckooflower
Cardamine pratensis L.

Curled Dock
Rumex crispus L.

Currant
Ribes spp.

Dame's Violet
Hesperis matronalis L.

Devil's-bit Scabious
Succisa pratensis Moench

Dog Rose
Rosa canina L.

Dove's-foot Cranesbill
Geranium molle L.

Dwarf Thistle
Cirsium acaule Scop.

Dyer's Greenweed
Genista tinctoria L.

Early Hair-grass
Aira praecox L.

Elm
Ulmus spp.

English Elm
Ulmus procera Salisb.

Evergreen Oak
Quercus ilex L.

Alphabetical list of foodplants

False Brome
Brachypodium sylvaticum (Hudson)

Fennel
Foeniculum vulgare Miller

Fescue
Festuca spp.

Field Maple
Acer campestre L.

Field Pansy
Viola arvensis Murray

Field Scabious
Knautia arvensis (L.)

Finger-grasses
Digitaria spp.

Garlic Mustard
Alliaria petiolata (Bieb.)

Geranium
Pelargonium spp.

Germander Speedwell
Veronica chamaedrys L.

Goat Willow
Salix caprea L.

Gorse
Ulex europaeus L.

Greater Bird's-foot Trefoil
Lotus uliginosus Schkuhr

Grey Willow
Salix cinerea L.

Hairy Violet
Viola hirta L.

Hare's-tail Cottongrass
Eriophorum vaginatum L.

Hawkweed
Hieracium spp.

Hawthorn
Crataegus monogyna Jacq.

Heath Dog Violet
Viola canina L.

Heather
Calluna vulgaris (L.)

Hedge Mustard
Sisymbrium officinale (L.)

Hemp Agrimony
Eupatorium cannabinum L.

Hogweed
Heracleum sphondylium L.

Holly
Ilex aquifolium L.

Honeysuckle
Lonicera periclymenum L.

Hop
Humulus lupulus L.

Horseshoe Vetch
Hippocrepis comosa L.

Ice Plant
Sedum maximum L.

Ivy
Hedera helix L.

Jointed Rush
Juncus articulatus L.

Kidney Vetch
Anthyllis vulneraria L.

Knapweed
Centaurea spp.

Alphabetical list of foodplants

Lavender
Lavandula x *intermedia* Lois

Lesser Trefoil
Trifolium dubium Sibth.

Lucerne
Medicago sativa L.

Mallow
Malva spp.

Mangetout Pea
Pisum sativum L.

Marsh Thistle
Cirsium palustre (L.)

Marsh Violet
Viola palustris L.

Mat-grass
Nardus stricta L.

Meadow Vetchling
Lathyrus pratensis L.

Michaelmas-daisy
Aster novi-belgii L.

Milk Parsley
Peucedanum palustre L.

Milkweed
Asclepias spp.

Mint
Mentha spp.

Narrow-leaved Everlasting Pea
Lathyrus sylvestris L.

Nasturtium
Tropaeoleum majus L.

Pansy
Viola spp.

Pedunculate Oak
Quercus robur L.

Pellitory-of-the-wall
Parietaria judaica L.

Poplar
Populus spp.

Primrose
Primula vulgaris Hudson

Purple Moor-grass
Molinia caerulea (L.)

Ragged Robin
Lychnis flos-cuculi L.

Ragwort
Senecio jacobaeae L.

Red Clover
Trifolium pratense L.

Red Fescue
Festuca rubra L.

Rest-harrow
Ononis repens L.

Ribwort Plantain
Plantago lanceolata L.

Sea Kale
Crambe maritima L.

Sea Radish
Raphanus raphanistrum L.

Sessile Oak
Quercus petraea (Matt.)

Sheep's Fescue
Festuca ovina L.

Sheep's Sorrel
Rumex acetosella L.

Alphabetical list of foodplants

Small-leaved Elm
Ulmus minor Miller

Small Nettle
Urtica urens L.

Small Scabious
Scabiosa columbaria L.

Snowberry
Symphoricarpos rivularis Suksd.

Spear Thistle
Cirsium vulgare (Savi)

Stonecrop
Sedum spp.

Thistle
Cirsium spp.

Thrift
Armeria maritima (Miller)

Tor-grass
Brachypodium pinnatum (L.)

Tormentil
Potentilla erecta (L.)

Tufted Hair-grass
Deschampsia cespitosa (L.)

Tufted Vetch
Vicia cracca L.

Turkey Oak
Quercus cerris L.

Violet
Viola spp.

Viper's Bugloss
Echium vulgare L.

Water Dock
Rumex hydrolapathum Hudson

Watercress
Rorippa nasturtium-aquaticum (L.)

Wavy Hair-grass
Deschampsia flexuosa (L.)

White Clover
Trifolium repens L.

Wild Cabbage
Brassica oleracea L.

Wild Cherry
Prunus avium (L.)

Wild Mignonette
Reseda lutea L.

Wild Pansy
Viola tricolor L.

Wild Privet
Ligustrum vulgare L.

Wild Strawberry
Fragaria vesca L.

Wild Thyme
Thymus praecox (Durland)

Willow
Salix spp.

Willowherbs
Epilobium spp.

Wood Millet
Millium effusum L.

Wych Elm
Ulmus glabra Hudson

Yorkshire Fog
Holcus lanatus L.

Appendix II: Useful contacts

Arisaig Marine
(passenger ferry to Isle of Rhum, Scotland)
Tel: 01687 450224

Ashberry Pasture
(site permit)
Yorkshire Wildlife Trust,
10 Toft Green, York, YO1 1JT.
(written request required)

Bird reports.
Birdguides
www.birdguides.com
or Birdline; Tel: 09068 700222

Butterfly Conservation
Manor Yard, East Lulworth, Wareham, Dorset, BH20 5QP.
Tel: 08707 744309
www.butterfly-conservation.org

Caledonian MacBrayne
Tel: 08705 650000
Online reservations: www.calmac.co.uk

Countryside Council for Wales
(site permit)
Plas Penrhos, Fford Penrhos, Bangor, Gwynedd LL57 2JA.

Gait Barrows
(site permit)
Natural England, Juniper House, Murley Moss, Oxenholme Road, Kendal, Cumbria, LA9 7RL.
Tel: 01539 792800

Islay Natural History Trust,
Port Charlotte, Isle of Islay, PA48 7TX.
Tel: 01496 850288

Isles of Scilly
(passenger ferry)
Isles of Scilly Travel
Tel: 08457 105555

Isles of Scilly
(helicopter)
British International Airways
Tel: 01736 368871

**DEFRA,
Department of the Environment, Food and Rural Affairs**
Tel: 08459 335577
www.defra.gov.uk

Muckle Moss
(site permit)
Natural England, Quadrant, Newburn Riverside, Newcastle, NE15 8NZ.
Tel: 01912 295500

Whixall Moss
(site permit)
Natural England, The Stable Block, Attingham Park, Shrewsbury, Shropshire, SY4 4TW.
Tel: 01743 282000

Appendix III: Table of flight periods (phenological table)

It is stressed that these are guidelines only. Flight periods may vary according to weather.
○ = usual flight period.
● = optimum period for seeing the butterflies in their peak condition.
▸ = partial second brood in favourable years but should not be relied upon.

Month	April				May				June				July				August				September			
Week	1	2	3	4	1	2	3	4	1	2	3	4	1	2	3	4	1	2	3	4	1	2	3	4
Chequered Skipper							○	○	●	●	○	○												
Small Skipper												○	○	○	●	●	○	○						
Essex Skipper													○	○	○	●	●	○	○	○				
Lulworth Skipper												○	○	○	○	○	○	●	●	●	○	○	○	
Silver-spotted Skipper																	○	○	●	●	○	○		
Large Skipper								○	○	○	○	○	●	●	○	○	○	○						
Dingy Skipper		○	○	○	●	●	○	○	○	○							▸	▸	▸	▸	▸			
(N. Scotland)						○	○	●	●	○	○													
Burren Dingy Skipper		○	○	○	●	●	○	○	○	○							▸	▸	▸	▸	▸			
Grizzled Skipper		○	○	○	●	●	○	○	○	○							▸	▸	▸	▸				
British Swallowtail							○	○	●	●	○	○	○				▸	▸	▸	▸				
Wood White								○	○	○	●	●	○	○	○									
(warm summers in south)						○	○	●	●	○	○	○				○	○	●	●	○	○			
Irish Wood White							○	○	●	●	○	○	○				▸	▸	▸	▸				
Réal's Wood White							○	○	●	●	○	○	○			▸	▸	▸	▸					
Clouded Yellow								○	○	○	○	○	○	○	●	●	●	●	●	●	●	●	●	●
Brimstone	●	●	●	●	●	●	●	●	○	○	○	○	○			○	●	●	●	●	○	○	○	○
Irish Brimstone	●	●	●	●	●	●	●	●	○	○	○	○	○			○	●	●	●	●	○	○	○	○
Large White			○	○	●	●	●	●	○	○			○	○	●	●	●	●	○	○				▸
Small White					○	○	●	●	●	○	○			○	○	●	●	●	○	○	▸	▸	▸	▸
British Green-veined White					○	○	○	●	●	○	○	○	○	○	○	●	●	○	○	○			▸	▸
(high altitude and parts of N. England)									○	○	●	●	●	○	○									
Irish Green-veined White					○	○	○	●	●	○	○	○	○	○	○	●	●	○	○	○			▸	▸
Scottish Green-veined White					○	○	○	●	●	○	○	○	○	○	○	●	●	○	○	○			▸	▸
(high altitude and extreme north)									○	○	●	●	●	○	○									
British Orange-tip				○	○	●	●	●	○	○							▸	▸	▸	▸	▸			
(Scotland)						○	○	○	●	●	○	○	○											
Irish Orange-tip				○	○	●	●	●	○	○														
Green Hairstreak				○	○	○	●	●	○	○	○													
(Mid- and Northern Scotland)						○	○	○	●	●	●	○	○	○										

Phenological table

Month	April				May				June				July				August				September			
Week	1	2	3	4	1	2	3	4	1	2	3	4	1	2	3	4	1	2	3	4	1	2	3	4
Brown Hairstreak																O	O	●	●	O	O	O		
Purple Hairstreak														O	O	O	●	●	O	O	O	O		
(Scotland)																O	O	O	●	●	O	O	O	
White-letter Hairstreak													O	●	●	O	O	O						
Black Hairstreak										O	●		O											
Small Copper				O	O	O	●	●	O	O	O			O	O		●	●	O	O		O	●	●
(Northern England; southern Scotland)					O	O	O	●	●	O	O	O			O	O	O	●	●	O	O	O		
(Northern Scotland)							O	O	O	●	●	O	O	O			O	O	O	●	●	O	O	O
Irish Small Copper					O	O	O	●	●	O	O	O				O	O	O	●	●	O	O	O	
Small Blue							O	O	●	●	O	O				▶	▶	▶	▶	▶				
(Northern Scotland)									O	O	●	●	O	O										
Silver-studded Blue													O	O	●	●	●	O	O					
(Eastern England)										O	O	●	●	●	O	O								
Southern Silver-studded Blue										O	O	●	●	●	O	O								
Northern Silver-studded Blue													O	O	●	●	●	O	O					
Western Silver-studded Blue										O	O	●	●	●	O	O								
Northern Brown Argus					O	O	O	●	●	O	O	O			O	O	O	●	●	O	O	O		
(North Wales; parts of Northern N. England)									O	O	O	●	●	O	O	O	▶	▶	▶	▶				
Brown Argus									O	O	●	●	●	O	O									
(North-east Scotland)												O	O	●	●	●	O	O						
Castle Eden Argus									O	O	●	●	●	O	O									
Common Blue					O	O	O	●	●	O	O	O			O	O	O	O	●	●	O	O	O	
(N. England; Scotland)										O	O	O	●	●	●	●	O	O	O	O	O			▶
Irish Common Blue					O	O	O	●	●	O	O	O				O	O	O	●	●	O	O	O	
(North and north-west)										O	O	O	●	●	●	●	O	O	O	O				
Chalkhill Blue														O	O	O	●	●	O	O	O			
Adonis Blue						O	O	●	●	O	O						O	O	●	●	O	O		
Holly Blue	O	O	O	O	●	●	O	O	O	O				O	O	O	●	●	O	O	O			
(North)		O	O	O	O	O	●	●	O	O	O	O	O				▶	▶	▶	▶	▶			
Large Blue										O	O	●	●	O	O									
Duke of Burgundy					O	O	●	●	O	O														
(Northern England)							O	O	●	●	O	O												
White Admiral											O	O	O	●	●	O	O	O						
Purple Emperor												O	O	●	●	O	O							
Red Admiral	O	O	O	O	●	●	●	●	●	●	●	●	O	●	●	●	●	●	●	●	●	●	●	●
Painted Lady	O	O	O	O	O	●	●	●	●	●	●	●	O	O	O	O	●	●	●	●	●	●	O	O
Small Tortoiseshell	●	●	●	●	●	O	O	O					O	●	●	●	●	O	●	●	●	●	O	O
(Scotland)	●	●	●	●	●	O	O	O								O	O	●	●	●	O	O	O	O
Peacock	●	●	●	●	O	O												O	O	●	●	O	O	

Phenological table

Month	April				May				June				July				August				September			
Week	1	2	3	4	1	2	3	4	1	2	3	4	1	2	3	4	1	2	3	4	1	2	3	4
Comma	O	O	O	O												O	O	O	●	●	●	O	O	O
Hutchinson's Comma												O	●	●	O	O								
Small Pearl-bordered Fritillary						O	O	●	●	O	O													
(Northern Scotland)											O	O	●	●	O	O								
(South-west England)					O	O	●	●	O	O							▶	▶	▶	▶				
Northern Small Pearl-bordered Fritillary									O	O	●	●	O	O										
Pearl-bordered Fritillary				O	●	●	●	O	O								▶	▶	▶	▶				
(Northern England)					O	O	●	●	O	O														
(Scotland)						O	O	●	●	O	O													
High Brown Fritillary											O	O	●	●	O	O	O							
(North-west England)													O	O	●	●	O	O	O					
Dark Green Fritillary										O	O	O	O	●	●	O	O	O	O					
(Northern Scotland)												O	O	O	O	●	●	O	O	O	O			
Scottish Dark Green Fritillary (W. Scotland)											O	O	O	O	●	●	O	O	O					
Silver-washed Fritillary											O	O	O	●	●	O	O	O	O					
Greenish Silver-washed Fritillary												O	O	O	●	●	O	O	O					
Marsh Fritillary						O	O	O	●	●	O	O	O											
(Scotland)								O	O	●	●	O	O											
Glanville Fritillary								O	●	●	●	O	O				▶	▶	▶					
Heath Fritillary									O	O	●	●	O	O	O	O	O		▶	▶	▶			
(Cornwall)									O	O	O	●	●	O	O									
Speckled Wood	O	O	O	O	●	●	O	O	O	O	O	O	O	O	●	●	O	O	O	O	●	●	O	O
Scottish Speckled Wood			O	O	●	●	O	O							O	O	O	●	●	O	O	O		
Isles of Scilly Speckled Wood	O	O	O	O	●	●	O	O	O	O	O	O	O	O	●	●	O	O	O	O	●	●	O	O
Wall						O	O	O	●	●	O	O	O				O	O	●	●	O	O	O	
(Northern England; Scotland)								O	O	O	●	●	O	O	O				O	O	●	●	O	O
English Small Mountain Ringlet												O	O	●	●	O	O							
Scottish Small Mountain Ringlet													O	O	●	●	O	O						
Scotch Argus																O	O	●	●	O	O			
Western Scotch Argus																O	O	●	●	O	O			
Marbled White											O	O	O	●	●	O	O	O						
Grayling													O	O	O	●	●	O	O	O	O			
Great Orme Grayling									O	O	●	●	●	O	O									
Scottish Grayling													O	O	O	●	●	O	O	O				
Atlantic Grayling													O	O	●	●	●	O	O	O				
Burren Grayling													O	O	O	●	●	●	O	O	O			

Phenological table

Month	April				May				June				July				August				September			
Week	1	2	3	4	1	2	3	4	1	2	3	4	1	2	3	4	1	2	3	4	1	2	3	4
Irish Grayling													O	O	O	●	●	●	O	O	O	O		
Gatekeeper																O	●	●	O	O				
British Meadow Brown										O	O	O	●	●	●	●	O	O	O	O	O	O	O	O
Irish Meadow Brown										O	O	O	●	●	●	●	O	O	O	O	O	O	O	O
Isles of Scilly Meadow Brown										O	O	O	●	●	●	●	O	O	O	O	O	O	O	O
Hebridean Meadow Brown										O	O	O	●	●	O	O	O	O						
Small Heath				O	O	O	O	●	●	●	O	O	O	O	O	●	●	●	O	O				
(Northern England; Scotland)											O	O	●	●	●	O	O	O						
Hebridean Small Heath								O	O	O	O	●	●	O	O	O								
Southern Large Heath											O	O	O	●	●	O	O							
Northern Large Heath											O	O	O	●	●	O	O							
Scottish Large Heath											O	O	O	●	●	O	O							
(Far north; high altitude)													O	O	●	●	O	O	O					
Ringlet												O	O	●	●	O	O	O						

Appendix IV: Index of butterflies found within each geographical region

The page number refers to the description of each butterfly; the section 'Regional Prime Sites' should be consulted for grid references and/or site directions. Species that are widespread and common are not included.

SCOTLAND
Chequered Skipper 43; Dark Green Fritillary 232; Dark Green Fritillary, Scottish 236; Dingy Skipper 57; Grayling, Scottish 282; Grayling, Atlantic 284; Green Hairstreak 113; Green-veined White, Scottish 103; Holly Blue 176; Large Heath, Northern 307; Large Heath, Scottish 309; Large Skipper 56; Marsh Fritillary 244; Northern Brown Argus 161; Orange-tip, British 106; Pearl-bordered Fritillary 222; Purple Hairstreak 121; Scotch Argus 269; Scotch Argus, Western 271; Small Blue 143; Small Heath, Hebridean 302; Small Mountain Ringlet, Scottish 265; Small Pearl-bordered Fritillary 217; Small Pearl-bordered Fritillary, Northern 221; Speckled Wood, Scottish 257; Wall 260.

NORTHERN ENGLAND
Brimstone 89; Brown Argus 157; Castle Eden Argus 163; Comma 209; Dark Green Fritillary 232; Dingy Skipper 57; Duke of Burgundy 183; Essex Skipper 49; Gatekeeper 289; Grayling 277; Green Hairstreak 113; High Brown Fritillary 228; Holly Blue 176; Large Heath, Northern 307; Large Heath, Southern 304; Marbled White 274; Pearl-bordered Fritillary 222; Purple Hairstreak 121; Scotch Argus 269; Silver-washed Fritillary 239; Small Skipper 46; Small Blue 143; Small Mountain Ringlet, English 263; Small Pearl-bordered Fritillary 217; Speckled Wood 255; Wall 260; White-letter Hairstreak 124.

CENTRAL ENGLAND
Black Hairstreak 127; Brown Argus 157; Brown Hairstreak 117; Chalkhill Blue 169; Dark Green Fritillary 232; Dingy Skipper 57; Grayling 277; Green Hairstreak 113; Grizzled Skipper 62; Large Heath, Southern 304; Marbled White 274; Pearl-bordered Fritillary 222; Purple Emperor 191; Purple Hairstreak 121; Silver-studded Blue, Northern 153; Silver-washed Fritillary 239; Small Blue 143; Small Pearl-bordered Fritillary 217; White Admiral 187; White-letter Hairstreak 124; Wood White 75.

EASTERN ENGLAND
Black Hairstreak 127; Brown Argus 157; Brown Hairstreak 117; Chalkhill Blue 169; Dark Green Fritillary 232; Dingy Skipper 57; Duke of Burgundy 183; Grayling 277; Green Hairstreak 113; Grizzled Skipper 62; Large Heath, Northern 307; Marbled White 274; Marsh Fritillary 244; Purple Hairstreak 121; Silver-studded Blue 149; Small Blue 143; Swallowtail, British 68; White Admiral 187; White-letter Hairstreak 124; Wood White 75.

Index of butterflies found within each geographical region

SOUTH-EAST ENGLAND
Adonis Blue 172; Black Hairstreak 127; Brown Argus 157; Brown Hairstreak 117; Chalkhill Blue 169; Dark Green Fritillary 232; Dingy Skipper 57; Duke of Burgundy 183; Glanville Fritillary 247; Grayling 277; Green Hairstreak 113; Grizzled Skipper 62; Heath Fritillary 250; Marbled White 274; Marsh Fritillary 244; Pearl-bordered Fritillary 222; Purple Emperor 191; Purple Hairstreak 121; Silver-spotted Skipper 53; Silver-studded Blue 149; Silver-washed Fritillary 239; Silver-washed Fritillary, Greenish 242; Small Blue 143; Small Pearl-bordered Fritillary 217; White Admiral 187; White-letter Hairstreak 124; Wood White 75.

SOUTH-WEST ENGLAND
Adonis Blue 172; Brown Argus 157; Brown Hairstreak 117; Chalkhill Blue 169; Dark Green Fritillary 232; Dingy Skipper 57; Duke of Burgundy 183; Essex Skipper 49; Glanville Fritillary 247; Grayling 277; Green Hairstreak 113; Grizzled Skipper 62; Heath Fritillary 250; High Brown Fritillary 228; Large Blue 179; Lulworth Skipper 51; Marbled White 274; Marsh Fritillary 244; Pearl-bordered Fritillary 222; Purple Emperor 191; Purple Hairstreak 121; Silver-spotted Skipper 53; Silver-studded Blue 149; Silver-studded Blue, Southern 152; Silver-washed Fritillary 239; Silver-washed Fritillary, Greenish 242; Small Blue 143; Small Pearl-bordered Fritillary 217; Speckled Wood, Isles of Scilly 258; White Admiral 187; White-letter Hairstreak 124; Wood White 75.

WALES
Brimstone 89; Brown Argus 157; Brown Hairstreak 117; Dark Green Fritillary 232; Dingy Skipper 57; Grayling 277; Grayling, Great Orme 281; Green Hairstreak 113; Grizzled Skipper 62; High Brown Fritillary 228; Large Heath, Northern 307; Marbled White 274; Marsh Fritillary 244; Pearl-bordered Fritillary 222; Purple Hairstreak 121; Silver-studded Blue 149; Silver-studded Blue, Western 156; Silver-washed Fritillary 239; Small Blue 143; Small Pearl-bordered Fritillary 217; White-letter Hairstreak 124.

WESTERN IRELAND
Brimstone, Irish 91; Brown Hairstreak 117; Dark Green Fritillary, Scottish 236; Dingy Skipper 57; Dingy Skipper, Burren 61; Gatekeeper 289; Grayling, Burren 286; Grayling, Irish 287; Green Hairstreak 113; Holly Blue 176; Large Heath, Northern 307; Marsh Fritillary 244; Pearl-bordered Fritillary 222; Purple Hairstreak 121; Réal's Wood White 80; Silver-washed Fritillary 239; Small Blue 143; Small Copper, Irish 134; Small Mountain Ringlet, Irish 266; Wall 260; Wood White, Irish 78.

EASTERN IRELAND
Brimstone, Irish 91; Dark Green Fritillary, Scottish 236; Dingy Skipper 57; Gatekeeper 289; Grayling, Irish 287; Green Hairstreak 113; Holly Blue 176; Large Heath, Northern 307; Marsh Fritillary 244; Purple Hairstreak 121; Réal's Wood White 80; Silver-washed Fritillary 239; Small Blue 143; Small Copper, Irish 134; Wall 260.

Appendix V: Vice-counties of Britain and Ireland

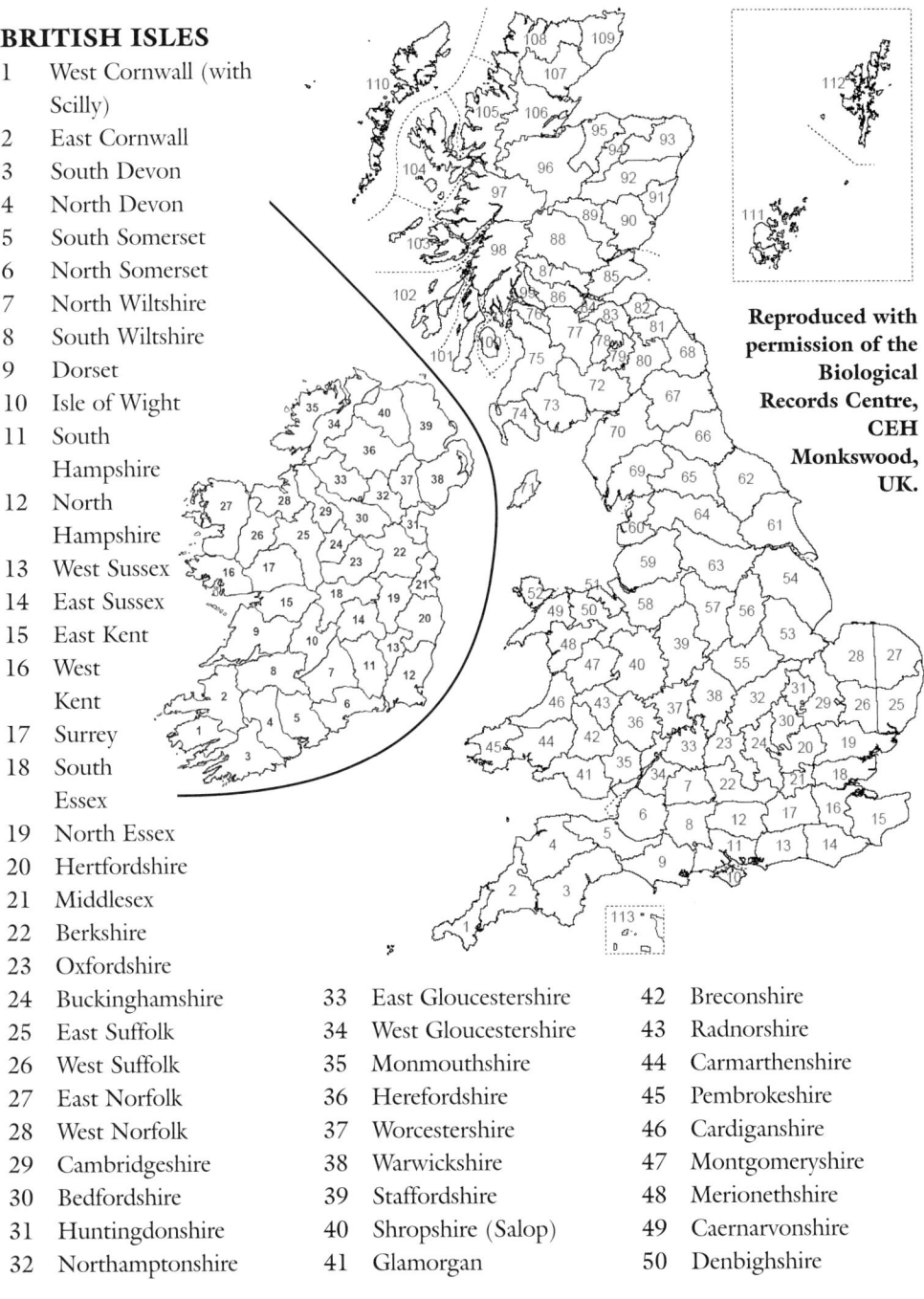

Reproduced with permission of the Biological Records Centre, CEH Monkswood, UK.

BRITISH ISLES
1. West Cornwall (with Scilly)
2. East Cornwall
3. South Devon
4. North Devon
5. South Somerset
6. North Somerset
7. North Wiltshire
8. South Wiltshire
9. Dorset
10. Isle of Wight
11. South Hampshire
12. North Hampshire
13. West Sussex
14. East Sussex
15. East Kent
16. West Kent
17. Surrey
18. South Essex
19. North Essex
20. Hertfordshire
21. Middlesex
22. Berkshire
23. Oxfordshire
24. Buckinghamshire
25. East Suffolk
26. West Suffolk
27. East Norfolk
28. West Norfolk
29. Cambridgeshire
30. Bedfordshire
31. Huntingdonshire
32. Northamptonshire
33. East Gloucestershire
34. West Gloucestershire
35. Monmouthshire
36. Herefordshire
37. Worcestershire
38. Warwickshire
39. Staffordshire
40. Shropshire (Salop)
41. Glamorgan
42. Breconshire
43. Radnorshire
44. Carmarthenshire
45. Pembrokeshire
46. Cardiganshire
47. Montgomeryshire
48. Merionethshire
49. Caernarvonshire
50. Denbighshire

Vice-counties of Britain and Ireland

51	Flintshire	72	Dumfriesshire	92	South Aberdeenshire
52	Anglesey	73	Kirkcudbrightshire	93	North Aberdeenshire
53	South Lincolnshire	74	Wigtownshire	94	Banffshire
54	North Lincolnshire	75	Ayrshire	95	Moray (Elgin)
55	Leicestershire (with Rutland)	76	Renfrewshire	96	East Inverness-shire (with Nairn)
		77	Lanarkshire		
56	Nottinghamshire	78	Peeblesshire	97	West Inverness-shire
57	Derbyshire	79	Selkirkshire	98	Argyll Main
58	Cheshire	80	Roxburghshire	99	Dunbartonshire
59	South Lancashire	81	Berwickshire	100	Clyde Isles
60	West Lancashire	82	East Lothian (Haddington)	101	Kintyre
61	South-east Yorkshire			102	South Ebudes
62	North-east Yorkshire	83	Midlothian (Edinburgh)	103	Mid Ebudes
63	South-west Yorkshire			104	North Ebudes
64	Mid-west Yorkshire	84	West Lothian (Linlithgow)	105	West Ross
65	North-west Yorkshire			106	East Ross
66	Durham	85	Fifeshire (with Kinross)	107	East Sutherland
67	South Northumberland	86	Stirlingshire	108	West Sutherland
68	North Northumberland (Cheviot)	87	West Perthshire (with Clackmannan)	109	Caithness
				110	Outer Hebrides
69	Westmorland with North Lancashire	88	Mid Perthshire	111	Orkney Islands
		89	East Perthshire	112	Shetland Islands (Zetland)
70	Cumberland	90	Angus (Forfar)		
71	Isle of Man	91	Kincardineshire	113	Channel Isles

IRELAND

1	South Kerry	14	Leix	28	Sligo
2	North Kerry	15	South-east Galway	29	Leitrim
3	West Cork	16	West Galway	30	Cavan
4	Mid Cork	17	North-east Galway	31	Louth
5	East Cork	18	Offaly	32	Monaghan
6	Waterford	19	Kildare	33	Fermanagh
7	South Tipperary	20	Wicklow	34	East Donegal
8	Limerick	21	Dublin	35	West Donegal
9	Clare	22	Meath	36	Tyrone
10	North Tipperary	23	West Meath	37	Armagh
11	Kilkenny	24	Longford	38	Down
12	Wexford	25	Roscommon	39	Antrim
13	Carlow	26	East Mayo	40	Londonderry
		27	West Mayo		

References and further reading

Allen, P.B.M. (1980) *Leaves from a Moth-hunter's Notebook.* Classey, Oxon.

Asher, J., Warren, M., Fox R. & Harding, P. (2001) *The Millennium Atlas of Butterflies in Britain and Ireland.* Oxford University Press.

Baynes, E.S.A. (1964) *A Revised Catalogue of Irish Macrolepidoptera.* Classey, Middlesex.

Beirne, B.P. (1952) *The Origin and History of British Fauna.* Methuen, London.

Berger, L.A. (1948) A *Colias* new to Britain (Lep. Pieridae). *The Entomologist* **81**: 129-131.

Blamey, M., Fitter, R. & Fitter, A. (2003) *Wild Flowers of Britain and Ireland.* A&C Black, London.

Bradley, J.D. (2000) *Checklist of Lepidoptera recorded from the British Isles* (Revised second edition). Private publication (ISBN 0-9532508-0-6).

Brower, L.P. (1995) Understanding the migration of the Monarch butterfly (*Nymphalidae*) in North America: 1875-1995. *Journal of the Lepidopterist's Society* **49**: 304-385.

Chalmers-Hunt, J.M. (1970) The Butterflies and Moths of the Isle of Man. *Transactions of the Society of British Entomology* **19**: 50-66.

Cooke, B.H. (1943) The Scottish race of *Erebia epiphron* Knoch. *The Entomologist* **76**: 105.

de Lattin, G. (1952) Two new subspecies of *Hipparchia semele*. *Entomologist's Records and Journal of Variation* **64**: 335-336.

Duffey, E. (1977) Re-establishment of large copper butterfly *Lycaena dispar batavus* Obth. on Woodwalton Fen National Nature Reserve, Cambridgeshire, England, 1969-73. *Biological Conservation* **12**: 143-158.

Emmet, J. & Heath, J. (1989) *The Moths and Butterflies of Great Britain and Ireland* Vol 7, part 1. Harley, Colchester.

Fabricius, J.C. (1777) *Genera Insectorum*: 259. M.F. Bartschii, Cologne, 310 pp.

Fabricius, J.C. (1793) *Entomologia Systematica* **3**: 297, Christ. Gottl. Proft, Hafniae. 519 pp.

Fabricius, J.C. (1798) *Supplementum Entomologiae Systematicae*: 430, Proft et Storon, Hafniae. 572 pp.

Fitter, R., Fitter, A. & Farrer, A. (1987) *Grasses, Sedges, Rushes and Ferns of Britain and Northern Europe.* Collins, London.

Ford, E.B. (1945) *Butterflies.* Collins, London.

Ford, H.D. & Ford, E.B. (1930) Fluctuation in numbers, and its influence on variation, in *Melitaea aurinia* Rott. (Lepidoptera). *Transactions of the Royal Entomological Society of London* **78**: 345-351.

References and further reading

Fox, R., Asher, J., Roy, D., Brereton, T. & Warren, M. (2006) *The State of Butterflies in Britain and Ireland*. Pisces, Oxford.

Frohawk, F.W. (1886) *Melitaea aurinia* in Shropshire. *The Entomologist* **91**: 41.

Godart, J.B. (1821) *Histoire naturelle des Lépidoptères ou papillons de France* **1**: 605.

Goodson, A.L. (1948) New varieties of *Argynnis cydippe* L. and *Lycaena phlaeas* L. *The Entomologist* **81**: 177-178.

Graves, P.P. (1930a) The British and Irish *Maniola jurtina*. *The Entomologist* **63**: 49-54.

Graves, P.P. (1930b) The British and Irish *Maniola jurtina*. *The Entomologist* **63**: 75-81.

Harmer, A.S. (1999) *Variation in British Butterflies*. Paphia, Hampshire.

Harrison, J.W.H. (1937) Rhapolocera on the Island of Scalpay, with an account of the occurrence of *Nymphalis io* on Raasay. *The Entomologist* **70**: 1-4.

Harrison, J.W.H. (1946) The Lepidoptera of the Hebridian Isles of Coll, Tiree and Gunna, with some remarks on the Biogeography of the Islands. *Entomologist's Record and Journal of Variation* **58**: 58.

Harrison, J.W.H. (1948) A new race of *Coenonympa pamphilus* L. from the Hebrides. *Entomologist's Record and Journal of Variation*. **60**: 111.

Harrison, J.W.H. (1949) Rhopalocera in the Scottish Western Isles in 1948, with an account of two new forms of *Pararge aegeria* L. (Lep. Satyridae). *Entomologist's Monthly Magazine* **85**: 25-28.

Haworth, A.H. (1803) *Lepidoptera Britannica*: part I, page 16.

Haworth, A.H. (1812) A brief Account of some rare Insects announced at various times to the Society, as new to Britain. *Transactions of the Entomological Society of London* **1**: 332-340.

Heslop, I.R.P., Hyde, G.E. & Stockley, R.E. (1964) *Notes and Views of the Purple Emperor*. Southern Publishing, Brighton.

Hickin, N. (1992) *The Butterflies of Ireland: A Field Guide*. Roberts Rinehart, Schull.

Hill, J., Thomas, C.D. & Huntley, B. (1999) Climate and habitat availability determine 20th century changes in a butterfly's range margin. *Proceedings of the Royal Society of London* (B) **266**: 1197-1206.

Hill, P. & Twist, C. (1998) *Butterflies and Dragonflies: A Site Guide*. Arlequin, Essex.

Howarth, T.G. (1971a) Descriptions of a new British subspecies of *Pararge aegeria* (L.) (Lep., Satyridae) and an aberration of *Cupido minimus* (Fuessly) (Lep., Lycaenidae) *Entomologist's Gazette* **22**: 117-118.

References and further reading

Howarth, T.G. (1971b) The status of Irish *Hipparchia semele* (L.) (Lep., Satyridae) with descriptions of a new subspecies and aberrations. *Entomologist's Gazette* **22**: 123-129.

Howarth, T.G. (1973) *South's British Butterflies*. Warne, London.

Huggins, H.C. (1956a) The Burren subspecies *Erynnis tages* Linn. *The Entomologist* **89**: 241-242.

Huggins, H.C. (1956b) The Irish race of *Gonepteryx rhamni* (Lep. Pieridae). *The Entomologist* **89**: 65-66.

Joy, J. (1995) *Heathland Management for the Silver-studded Blue Butterfly*. English Nature leaflet.

Kane, W.F. de Viesmes (1893) A catalogue of the Lepidoptera of Ireland. *The Entomologist* **26**: 240-244.

Lorkovic, Z. (1993) *Leptidea reali* Reissinger 1989 (=*lorkovicii* Réal 1988), a new European species (Lep., Pieridae). *Natura Croatica* **2**: 1-25.

Mitchell, A. & Wilkinson, J. (1989) *Trees of Britain and Northern Europe*. Collins, London.

Morley, A.M. & Chalmers-Hunt, J.M. (1959) Some observations on the crimson-ringed butterfly (*Parnassius apollo* L.) in Britain. *Entomologist's Record and Journal of Variation* **71**: 273-276.

Mouffett, T. (1634) *Insectorum sive minimorum animalium Theatrum*. **20**: 326 [4]. London.

Mouquet, N., Thomas, J.A., Elmes, G.W., Clarke, R.T. & Hochberg, M.E. (2005) Population dynamics and conservation of a specialised predator: a case study of *Maculinea arion*. *Ecological Monographs* **75**: 525-542.

Müller, L. & Kautz, H. (1939) *Pieris bryoniae* O. und *Pieris napi* L. *Abhandlungen des Österreichischen Entomologen-Vereines* **1**: 76.

Nash, R. & Samson, C. (1990) A fourth Irish specimen of the Small Mountain Ringlet *Erebia epiphron* Knoch (Lepidoptera). *Irish Naturalist's Journal* **23**: 339.

Nelson, B., Hughes, M., Nash, R. and Warren, M. (2001) *Leptidea reali* Reissinger, 1989 (Lep.: Pieridae): a butterfly new to Britain and Ireland. *Entomologist's Record and Journal of Variation* **113**: 97-101.

Newland, D.E. (2006) *Discover Butterflies in Britain*. Wildguides, Hampshire.

Pelham-Clinton, E.C. (1964) Comments on the supposed occurrence in Scotland of *Erebia ligea* (Linnaeus) (Lepidoptera, Satyridae). *Entomologist's Record and Journal of Variation* **76**: 121-125.

Porter, J. (1997) *The Colour Identification Guide to the Caterpillars of the British Isles*. Viking, Harmondsworth.

References and further reading

Pratt, C.R. (1983) A modern review of the demise of *Aporia crataegi* L.: the black-veined white. *Entomologist's Record and Journal of Variation* **95**: 45-52, 161-166 and 244-250.

Pratt, C.R. (1986) A history and investigation into the fluctuations of *Polygonia c-album* L.: the comma butterfly. *Entomologist's Record and Journal of Variation* **98**: 197-203 and 244-250.

Pratt, C.R. (1987) A history and investigation into the fluctuations of *Polygonia c-album* L, the Comma butterfly. *Entomologist's Record and Journal of Variation* **99**: 21–27, 69–80.

Ravenscroft, N.O.M. (1990) The ecology and conservation of the silver-studded blue butterfly *Plebejus argus* L. on the Sanderlings of East Anglia. *Biological Conservation* **53**: 21-36.

Riley, A.M. (1991) *A Natural History of the Butterflies and Moths of Shropshire*. Swan Hill, Shrewsbury.

Russwurm, A.D.A. (1978) *Aberrations of British Butterflies*. Classey, Oxon.

Saccheri, I., Kuussaari, M., Kankare, M., Vikman, P., Fortelius, W. & Hanski, I. (1998) Inbreeding and extinction in a butterfly metapopulation. *Nature* **392**: 491-494.

Salmon, M.A. (2000) *The Aurelian Legacy*. Harley, Colchester.

Seitz, A. (1907) 1. Gattung Papilio, Schwalbenschwänze. In: Seitz, A. (ed): *Die Groß-Schmetterlinge der Erde. I. Abteilung (Die Großschmetterlinge des Palaearktischen Faunengebietes). 1. Band: Tagfalter*. pp. 8-15; F. Lehmann, Stuttgart.

South, R. (1941) *The Butterflies of the British Isles* (revised third edition). Warne, London.

Staudinger, O. & Rebel, H. (1901) *Catalog der Lepidopteren des Palaearctischen Faunengebietes 1. Theil: Famil. Papilionidae - Hepialidae* **32**: 66

Stephens, J.F. (1827) *Illustrations of British Entomology* (Haustellata) **1**: 21. Baldwin and Cradock, London.

Stephens, J.F. (1828) *Illustrations of British Entomology* (Haustellata.) **1**: 235. Baldwin and Cradock, London.

Stephens, J.F. (1829) *A Systematic Catalogue of British Insects*. Baldwin and Cradock, London.

Thomas, C.D. (1985) The status and conservation of the butterfly *Plebejus argus* (Lepidoptera: Lycaenidae) in North West Britain. *Biological Conservation* **33**: 29-51.

Thomas, C.D. & Jones, T.M. (1993) Partial recovery of a skipper butterfly (*Hesperia comma*) from population refuges – lessons for conservation in a fragmented landscape. *Journal of Animal Ecology* **62**: 472-481.

Thomas, C.D., Glen, S.W., Lewis, O.T., Hill, J.K. & Blakeley, D.S. (1999) Population differentiation and conservation of endemic races: the butterfly *Plebejus argus*. *Animal Conservation* **2**: 15-21.

References and further reading

Thomas, J. & Lewington, R. (1991) *The Butterflies of Britain and Ireland.* Dorling Kindersley, London.

Thomas, J.A. (1983) The ecology and status of *Thymelicus acteon* (Lep. Hesperiidae) in Britain. *Ecological Entomology* **8**: 472-435.

Thomas, J.A., Thomas, C. D., Simcox, J.D. & Clarke, R.T. (1986) The ecology and declining status of the Silver-spotted Skipper butterfly (*Hesperia comma*), in Britain. *Journal of Applied Ecology* **23**: 365-380.

Thompson A. (1937) *A new subspecies of* Plebejus argus (*L.*): 3; privately published.

Thompson, A. (1944) A new subspecies of *Eumenis semele*, L. *Entomologist's Record and Journal of Variation* **56**: 65.

Thomson, G. (1969) *Maniola (Epinephile) jurtina* (L.) (Lep. Satyridae) and its forms. *Entomologist's Record and Journal of Variation* **81**: 1-58.

Thomson, G. (1970) The distribution and nature of *Pieris napi thomsoni* Warren (Lep., Pieridae). *Entomologist's Record and Journal of Variation* **82**: 255-261.

Thomson, G. (1980) *The Butterflies of Scotland.* Croom Helm, London.

Tolman, T. & Lewington, R. (2004) *Butterflies of Britain and Europe.* Collins, London.

Tutt, J.W. (1909) *Plebeius argus* var. *cretaceous*, n. var. *P. argus* var. *masseyi*, n. var., *P. argus* var. *corsica*, Bell, and *Plebeius argyrognomon* var. *corsica*, n. var. *Entomologist's Record and Journal of Variation* **21**: 58-59.

Urquhart, F.A. & Urquhart, N.R. (1977) Overwintering areas and migratory routes of the Monarch butterfly (*Danaus p. plexippus*, Lepidoptera: Danaidae) in North America, with special reference to the western population. *Canadian Entomologist* **109**: 1583-1589.

Verity, R. (1908) *Rhopalocera Palaearctica. Papilionidae et Pieridae* **1**: 190, Verity, Florence.

Verity, R. (1911) Races inédites de Satyridae européens [Lep. Rhopalocera]. *Bulletin de la Société Entomologique de France* (1911), 311-314.

Verity, R. (1913) Revisione dei Tipi Linneani dei Ropaloceri Paleartici. *Bollettino della Societa Entomologica Italiana* **44** (1912): 205.

Verity, R. (1915) Contributo allo studio della variazione nei Lepidotteri. *Bollettino della Societa Entomologica Italiana* **45** (1913): 220.

Verity, R. (1916) The British Races of Butterflies: their relationships and nomenclature. *Entomologist's Record and Journal of Variation* **28**: 79.

Verity, R. (1919) Seasonal Polymorphism and Races of some European Grypocera. *Entomologist's Record and Journal of Variation* **31**: 46

References and further reading

Verity, R. (1929) Races de l'Europe occidentale de l'*Argynnis phryxa* Bergstr., qu'on nomme, à tort, *adippe* L. [Lep. Nymphalidae]. *Bulletin de la Société Entomologique de France* (1929): 277.

Wacher, J., Worth, J. & Spalding, A. (2003) *A Cornwall Butterfly Atlas*. Pisces, Berkshire.

Warren, B.C.S. (1968) On an unstable race of *Pieris adalwinda*, located in Scotland. *Entomologist's Record and Journal of Variation* **80**: 299-302.

Warren, M.S. (1991) The successful conservation of an endangered species, the Heath Fritillary butterfly *Mellicta athalia*, in Britain. *Biological Conservation* **55**: 37-56.

Warren, M.S. (1994) Autecology and conservation needs of the High Brown Fritillary. *Butterfly Conservation Annual Report for 1993/1994*.

Warren, M.S. (1995) Managing local micro-climates for the High Brown Fritillary. In: *The Ecology and Conservation of Butterflies* (ed. A. S. Pullin), pp. 198-210. Chapman & Hall, London.

Warren, M.S. & Oates, M.R. (1995) The importance of bracken habitats to fritillary butterflies and their management for conservation. In: *Bracken: An Environmental Issue* (eds. Smith, R. T. & Taylor, J. A.), pp. 178-181. I. B. G. Aberystwyth.

Warren, M.S., Thomas, J.A. & Wilson, R.J. (1999) *Management Options for the Silver-spotted Skipper Butterfly: A Study of the grazing timings at Beacon Hill NNR, Hampshire, 1986-1998*. Butterfly Conservation, Wareham.

Watkins, H.T.G. (1923) A new *Argynnis* Race. *The Entomologist* **56**: 108.

White, F.B. (1871) The Lepidoptera of Scotland. *Scottish Naturalist* **1**: 200.

Williams, H.B. (1916) Notes on the life-history and variation of *Euchloe cardamines* L. *Transactions of City of London Natural History Society* [1915]: 62-84.

Williams, H.B. (1946) The Irish form of *Leptidea sinapis* L. *The Entomologist* **79**: 1.

General index

Aberdeenshire, North 238, 257, 270, 284, 309

Aberdeenshire, South 162, 224, 256, 270, 307

Adonis Blue 31, 166, 167, **172-174**

Aglais antiopa 204

Aglais polychloros 203

Aglais urticae 201

Agrimony 63

Agrimony, Hemp 119, 198, 199, 206, 208

Alder 122

American Painted Lady 199, **200-201**

Angelica 68

Anglesey 49, 136, 152, 220, 236, 307

Angus 145, 162, 207, 219, 238

Anthocharis cardamines ssp. *britannica* 106

Anthocharis cardamines ssp. *hibernica* 110

Antrim 242, 301

Apatura iris 191

Apatura iris f. *iole* 192

Apaturinae 191

Apanteles bignellii 245

Apollo 20, **67-68**

Apollos 67

Aporia crataegi 93

Aphantopus hyperantus 311

Aphantopus hyperantus f. *arete* 312

Aphantopus hyperantus f. *crassipuncta* 312

Aphantopus hyperantus f. *lanceolata* 312

Aphantopus hyperantus f. *pallens* 312

Araschnia levana 213

Araschnia levana f. *levana* 214

Araschnia levana f. *prorsa* 214

Argyll Main 103, 122, 207, 209, 265, 273

Argynninae 217

Argynnis adippe ssp. *vulgoadippe* 228

Argynnis aglaja ssp. *aglaja* 232

Argynnis aglaja f. *albescens* 233

Argynnis aglaja f. *wimani* 233, 234

Argynnis aglaja ssp. *scotica* 236

Argynnis niobe 226

Argynnis paphia 239

Argynnis paphia f. *valesina* 242

Aricia artaxerxes ssp. *artaxerxes* 161-163

Aricia artaxerxes ssp. *salmacis* 163-165

Aricia agestis 157

Armagh 301

Arran Brown 20, 270, **272-274**

Ash 33, 118, 121, 122, 128

Ayrshire 56, 115, 139, 219, 292, 308

Banffshire 257, 258, 270, 311, 313

Bartramia longicauda 317

Bath White 105-106, 108

Bedfordshire 31, 60, 64, 72, 116, 127, 146, 160, 171, 185, 276, 203

Bent, Black 260

Bent, Bristle 278

Bent, Common 260, 290, 300

General index

Bent, Creeping 312

Berger's Clouded Yellow 83, 84, **85-86**, 88

Berkshire 146, 172, 174, 175

Berwickshire 162, 211, 234, 284

Bilberry 114, 117, 251

Birch 204, 206

Bird's-foot Trefoil, Common 58, 61-63, 76, 79, 81, 87, 114, 145, 148, 150, 153, 156, 162, 166, 218

Bird's-foot Trefoil, Greater 76, 166

Black Hairstreak 35, 122, 125, **127-129**

Black-veined White 93-94

Blackthorn 73, 94, 118, 119, 128, 129

Bladder Senna 144

Blaeberry 114

Blind Ringlet 321

Bloxworth Blue 147

Blues 139

Bobolink 317

Boloria euphrosyne 222

Boloria selene ssp. *selene* 217

Boloria selene ssp. *insularum* 221

Bracken 36, 122, 218, 220, 223-225, 229, 231, 232, 253

Bramble 57, 68-70, 101, 119, 126, 177, 178, 187, 188, 229, 231, 240, 252, 256, 279, 290, 312, 313

Brimstone 31, 37, **89-91**, 96

Brimstone, Irish 89, **91-93**

Broom 114, 140

Brome, False 43, 56, 256, 260, 292

Brown Argus 30, 31, 36, 151, **157-161**, 164, 166, 167

Brown Hairstreak 32, **117-121**

Browns 255

Brussels sprout 95, 97

Buckinghamshire 8, 35, 60, 86, 117, 120, 123, 129, 189, 195, 226, 235, 241, 276

Buckthorn 90, 92

Buckthorn, Alder 90, 92

Buddleia 72, 91, 96, 98, 198, 199, 202, 206, 208

Buff-breasted Sandpiper 317

Bugle 63, 184, 218, 224

Bugloss, Viper's 199

Bullace 73, 118, 128

Burnet Companion moth 58, 59, 184

Burren 20, 21, 32, 60-62, 75-80, 92, 93, 118, 120, 135, 146, 222, 225, 238, 278, 281, 286, 301

Buttercup 63, 218, 224, 252

Butterfly Conservation 7, 13, 17, 26, 28, 45, 153, 324

Cabbage 95, 97, 100

Cabbage White 95

Cacyreus marshalli 241

Caernarvonshire 21, 32, 83, 91, 139, 149, 156, 157, 161, 278, 281, 282

Caithness 103, 104, 145, 310

Callistege mi 63,

Callophrys rubi 113

General index

Camberwell Beauty 67, **204-207**, 215, 228

Cambridgeshire 123, 127, 129, 134, 136, 137, 145, 160, 171, 188, 226, 227, 274

Cardiganshire 117, 120, 124, 220, 225, 236, 241

Carmarthenshire 65, 83, 117, 118, 242, 277

Carrot 68, 71

Carterocephalus palaemon 43

Castle Eden Argus 32, 159, 161, **163-165,** 166, 167

Celastrina argiolus ssp. *britanna* 176

Chalkhill Blue 31, 86, 159, 166, 167, **169-172**, 173

Channel Isles 24, 45, 49, 70, 71, 90, 96, 105, 113, 121, 132, 140, 148, 157, 176, 198, 204-207, 210, 226, 227, 229, 232, 248, 255, 260, 274, 277, 289, 292

Charlock 97

Chequered Skipper 29, **43-45**

Cherry 207, 210

Cheshire 89, 123, 126, 139, 214, 280

Cinquefoil, Creeping 62

Clare 32, 57, 60, 61, 75, 78, 81, 93, 118, 120, 135, 146, 222, 225, 238, 242, 262, 278, 286, 301

Clover 83, 84, 87-89, 106, 175

Clover, Red 148, 176

Clover, White 166

Clouded Yellow 20, 83, **86-88**

Clouded Yellow, Helice, 20, 25, 83, 84, 86, **88-89**

Clyde Isles 105, 256, 273, 298, 309

Cock's-foot 50, 56, 260, 292, 312

Coenonympha pamphilus spp. *pamphilus* 299

Coenonympha pamphilus ssp. *rhoumensis* 320

Coenonympha tullia 304

Coenonympha tullia f. *cockaynei* 306

Coenonympha tullia f. *lanceolata* 306

Coenonympha tullia ssp. *davus* 304

Coenonympha tullia ssp. *polydama* 307

Coenonympha tullia ssp. *scotica* 309

Colias alfacariensis 85

Colias croceus 86

Colias croceus f. *helice* 88

Colias hyale 82

Comma 209-211, 212, 213, 230

Comma, Hutchinson's 20, 25, 210, **211-213**, 230

Common Blue 30, 141, 151, 159, 164, **165-168**, 169, 170, 173, 177

Common Blue, Irish 32, 165, 166, **168-169**

Compositae 133, 200

Coppers 131

Cork, East 289

Cork, Mid 179, 200

Cork, North 82,

Cork, West 83, 112, 200, 239, 291

Cornwall 51, 152, 236, 250, 251

General index

Cornwall, East 49, 51, 60, 67, 85, 86, 105, 116, 148, 152, 157, 175, 200, 203, 225, 241, 246, 250, 252, 277, 289, 296

Cornwall, West 51, 60, 65, 105, 116, 124, 142, 148, 152, 157, 161, 200, 220, 236, 259, 260, 277, 280, 296, 297

Cottongrass 29, 305, 306

Cottongrass, Common 305

Cottongrass, Hare's-tail 305

Countryside Council for Wales 18, 247

Cow-wheat, Common 25, 251, 252, 253

Cowslip 183

Crane's-bill 158

Crane's-bill, Dove's-foot 158

Crimson-ringed Butterfly, see Morley and Chalmers-Hunt (1959), p. 335 (Refs.)

Cuckooflower 100, 107

Cumberland 46, 96, 110, 118, 145, 246, 263, 265, 289, 307, 313

Cupido minimus 143

Currant 210

Cyaniris semiargus 175

Daisy 133

Daisy, Michaelmas 206

Danainae 315

Danaus plexippus 315

Dark Green Fritillary 24, 30, 32, 36, 228, 230, **232-236**, 237, 240

Dark Green Fritillary, Scottish 232, 234, 235, **236-239**

DEFRA 142, 324

Denbighshire 60, 65, 83, 124, 127, 161, 220, 222, 225, 236

Derbyshire 115, 137, 139, 148, 157, 159, 160, 235

Devon 51, 146, 250, 251

Devon, North 36, 73, 78, 117, 124, 146, 157, 160, 200, 220, 225, 228, 231, 236, 246, 280

Devon, South 24, 34, 60, 65, 71, 73, 78, 86, 116, 117, 120, 124, 127, 136, 146, 152, 157, 160, 189, 200, 214, 220, 225, 227, 228, 231, 236, 241, 277, 280

Dingy Skipper 21, 31, **57-60**, 61

Dingy Skipper, Burren 21, 32, 58, 60, **61-62**

Dock, Broad-leaved 132, 134

Dock, Curled 132, 134

Dock, Water 137

Dogwood 177

Dolichonyx oryzivorus 317

Donegal, East 117, 289, 308

Donegal, West 60, 135, 239, 262

Dorset 37, 48, 51-53, 55, 85, 86, 105, 116, 120, 124, 140, 142, 146-149, 152, 153, 160, 172, 174, 175, 185, 189, 200, 203, 227, 236, 241, 243, 246, 277, 280, 331

Down, Co. 30, 82, 93, 117, 135, 179, 211, 239, 247, 289, 301

Dublin 60, 147, 179, 211, 262, 289, 301

Dutch Elm disease 124, 126,

Duke of Burgundy 31, 33, **183-185**

Dumfries-shire 272

Durham 59, 103, 163, 164, 165, 176

Durham Argus 163

General index

Ebudes, Mid 238, 246, 273, 285, 310

Ebudes, North 221, 222, 256, 257, 285, 299, 302, 303

Ebudes, South 311, 313

Elm 122, 125-127, 204, 206, 210,

Elm, English 125

Elm, Dutch 125

Elm, Small-leaved 125

Elm, Wych 125, 204

England, Central see 329

England, Eastern see 329

England, Northern see 329

England, South-east see 330

England, South-west see 330

Emperors 191

Erebia aethiops ssp. *aethiops* 269, 272

Erebia aethiops f. *ochracea* 270

Erebia aethiops ssp. *caledonia* 271, 272

Erebia epiphron 262

Erebia epiphron f. *nelamus* 267

Erebia epiphron ssp. *mnemon* 263

Erebia epiphron ssp. *scotica* 265

Erebia epiphron ssp. *aetheria* 262, 266, 267

Erebia ligea 272

Erynnis tages ssp. *tages* 57

Erynnis tages ssp. *baynesi* 61

Essex Skipper 30, 47, 48, **49-51**

Essex, North 116, 188, 203, 227

Essex, South 34, 67, 73, 82, 105, 176, 214, 252, 289,

Euclidia glyphica 58

Euphydryas aurinia 244

Euphydryas aurinia f. *anglicana* 245

Euphydryas aurinia f. *hibernica* 245

Euphydryas aurinia f. *scotica* 245

European Map 213-215

Everlasting Pea, Broad-leaved 140

Everlasting Pea, Narrow-leaved 140

Everes argiades 147

Fennel 72

Fescue, Red 275, 278

Fescue, Sheep's 54, 275, 278, 290, 292, 300

Fifeshire 103, 104, 115, 209, 238, 256

Finger-grasses 274

Fleabane, Common 119, 206

Fritillaries 217

Galway, South-east 58, 60, 61, 75, 78, 81, 82, 93, 118, 120, 135, 146, 222, 225, 238, 242, 247, 278, 286, 301

Galway, West 91, 93, 308

Gatekeeper 289-291

Geranium 142

Geranium Bronze 20, **141-142**

Glamorgan 60, 83, 91, 116, 124, 127, 146, 161, 175, 315, 200, 220, 231, 236, 247, 277, 281

Glanville Fritillary 34, 218, **247-250**, 251

Gloucestershire, East 105, 116, 146, 160, 172, 185, 277, 280, 225, 236

General index

Gloucestershire, West 65, 73, 169, 189, 220, 241

Gonepteryx rhamni ssp. *rhamni* 89

Gonepteryx rhamni ssp. *gravesi* 91

Gorse 114, 150, 154, 177,

Granulosis 95

Grayling 30, 35, **277-281**, 282, 283, 284, 286, 288, 289

Grayling, Atlantic 36, 278, 279, **282-284**

Grayling, Burren 32, 278, 281, **286-287**

Grayling, Great Orme 32, 278, **281-282**

Grayling, Irish 278, 281, **287-289**

Grayling, Scottish 36, 278, 279, **282-284**

Greasy Fritillary 245, 246

Great Orme 32, 91, 149, 156, 157, 161, 278, 281, 282

Great White Butterfly 95

Green Hairstreak 31, **113-117**

Green-veined White 30, 37, 76, 80, 82, 97, 98, 103, 108

Green-veined White, British **99-101**, 102, 104

Green-veined White, Irish **101-103**

Green-veined White, Scottish 99, 101, **103-105**

Greenweed, Dyer's 114

Grizzled Skipper 21, 25, 31, **62-65**

Guernsey 157, 248,

Hairstreaks 113, 141, 142, 177

Hair-grass, Early 278

Hair-grass, Tufted 278, 312

Hair-grass, Wavy 260

Hamearis lucina 183

Hampshire, North 116, 120, 172, 185, 189, 195, 203, 227, 241, 276

Hampshire, South 34, 55, 60, 65, 85, 87, 93, 105, 116, 120, 123, 140, 146, 147, 148, 151, 160, 172, 174, 189, 200, 214, 225, 227, 228, 235, 241, 243, 246, 248, 249, 252, 280

Hawthorn 94, 114-116, 184

Hazel 62, 79

Heath Fritillary 25, 34, 36, 218, 248, 249, **250-253**

Heath, Cross-leaved 150, 154, 305, 306

Heather 150, 151, 177, 279, 306

Heather, Bell 150

Hebrides, Outer 96, 107, 113, 271, 284, 285, 299

Hebrides, Inner 285

Hedge Brown **289-291**

Herefordshire 73, 93, 212, 213, 214, 225, 231

Hertfordshire 123, 146, 172, 191, 194, 205, 226, 227

Hesperia comma 53

Hesperiidae 43

Heteropterus morpheus 45

High Brown Fritillary 35, **228-231**, 233, 235, 240

Highlands 67, 96, 98, 115, 256

Hipparchia semele ssp. *semele* 277

Hipparchia semele ssp. *atlantica* 284

General index

Hipparchia semele ssp. *clarensis* 286

Hipparchia semele ssp. *hibernica* 287

Hipparchia semele ssp. *scota* 282

Hipparchia semele ssp. *thyone* 281

Hogweed 126

Holly 177, 178

Holly Blue 141, 151, 167, 169, **176-179**

Honeydew 118, 122, 126, 128, 188, 193, 256

Honeysuckle 187

Hop 198, 208-210, 212

Huntingdonshire 136, 142

Ice Plant 198, 199, 202

Inachis io 207

Inverness-shire, East 59, 115, 131, 145, 162, 209, 219, 257, 258, 270, 271, 284

Inverness-shire, West 29, 37, 43, 104, 109, 115, 131, 222, 224, 238, 246, 258, 266, 286, 310, 311

Iphiclides podalirius 72, 226

Ireland, Eastern, see 330

Ireland, Western see 330

Islay Natural History Trust 246, 324

Isle of Man 24, 62, 89, 100, 107, 110, 111, 132, 134, 135, 176, 205, 207, 210, 232, 235, 237, 260, 277, 298, 299

Isle of Wight 67, 85, 87, 146, 172, 174, 200, 235, 248, 249, 251, 292

Isles of Scilly 24, 176, 200, 227, 255, 257-260, 292, 294, 296, 315, 317

Issoria lathonia 226

Ivy 177, 178, 197, 198

Jersey 45, 46, 56, 107, 124, 175, 248, 274

Kale, Sea 95

Kent, East 55, 60, 64, 127, 67, 72, 73, 82, 85, 93, 105, 116, 124, 146, 152, 160, 172, 174, 185, 189, 200, 203, 214, 227, 252, 273, 276

Kent, West 65, 82, 85, 86, 105, 106, 235

Kerry 134, 294, 200

Kerry, South 105, 117, 121, 135, 289

Kerry, North 287

Kildare 78, 91, 93, 239, 242, 247, 309

Kilkenny 211, 242

Kincardineshire 162

Kirkcudbrightshire 36, 59, 122, 162, 176, 178, 219, 224, 234, 261, 284, 308

Knapweed 48, 91, 101, 233, 276

Lake District 96, 110, 115, 263

Lampides boeticus 139

Lancashire, South 235, 280, 313

Lancashire, West 89, 189, 147, 159, 164, 200, 222, 224, 231, 239, 240, 280, 306, 313

Large Blue 25, 31, **179-181**

Large Chequered Skipper 19, **45-46**

Large Copper 15, 19, 20, 33, **136-137**, 176

Large Heath 24, 300, 304, 306

Large Heath, Northern 29, **307-309**, 310

Large Heath, Scottish 37, 300, 308, **309-311**

General index

Large Heath, Southern 29, **304-306**, 307, 308, 310
Large Skipper 54, **56-57**
Large Tortoiseshell 202, **203-204**
Large White 90, **95-96**, 97
Lasiocampa quercus 233
Lasiommata megera 260
Lavender 72
Leicestershire 105, 126, 184
Leptidea lorkovicii 80
Leptidea reali 80
Leptidea sinapis ssp. *sinapis* 75
Leptidea sinapis ssp. *juvernica* 78
Limenitinae 187
Limenitis camilla 187
Limenitis camilla f. *nigrina* 187
Limenitis camilla f. *obliterae* 187, 189
Limerick 60, 124
Lincolnshire Fritillary 247
Lincolnshire, North 60, 64, 77, 93, 116, 118, 120, 123, 127, 128, 129, 160, 175, 188
Lincolnshire, South 127, 134, 136, 171, 185
Long-tailed Blue 139-141
Lothian, East 103, 256
Lothian, Wet 256
Louth 301
Lucerne 83, 84, 87, 106
Lulworth Skipper 47, 48, 50, **51-53**, 56

Lycaena dispar 136
Lycaena dispar ssp. *batavus* 136, 137
Lycaena dispar ssp. *rutilus* 136, 137
Lycaena phlaeas f. *caeruleopunctata* 133
Lycaena phlaeas f. *fuscae* 133
Lycaena phlaeas f. *schmidtii* 132
Lycaena phlaeas ssp. *eleus* 131
Lycaena phlaeas ssp. *hibernica* 134
Lycaenidae 113, 139, 183
Lycaeninae 131
Lysandra bellargus 172
Lysandra coridon 169
Maculinea arion ssp. *arion* 179
Maculinea arion ssp. *eutyphron* 179
Mallow 199
Maniola jurtina 292
Maniola jurtina ssp. *cassiteridum* 296
Maniola jurtina ssp. *iernes* 294
Maniola jurtina ssp. *insularis* 292
Maniola jurtina ssp. *splendida* 298
Maple, Field 128
Marbled White 31, **274-277**
Marsh Fritillary 218, **244-247**, 248
Mat-grass 263, 266
Mayo, East 91
Mayo, West 91, 262, 266, 268, 289
Mazarine Blue 19, **175-176**
Meadow Brown 30, 118, 119, 176, 270, 290, 292, 312, 313

General index

Meadow Brown, British **292-294**, 296-299

Meadow Brown, Hebridean 36, 292-294, **298-299**

Meadow Brown, Irish 32, 292, **294-296**

Meadow Brown, Isles of Scilly 9, 292-294, **296-297**

Meadow-grass, Annual 290, 292, 300

Meath 289

Melanargia galathea

Melanargia galathea ssp. *serena* 274

Melitaea athalia 250

Melitaea cinxia 247

Merionethshire 83, 96, 116, 236, 247, 280, 308

Metalmarks 183

Middlesex 67, 99, 127

Midlothian 161, 211, 256

Mignonette, Wild 95, 97, 106

Milkweed 315-317

Millet, Wood 274

Mint 101

Monarch 24, 315-317

Monarchs 315

Monmouthshire 117, 214, 281

Montgomeryshire 83, 96, 124, 220, 225, 231, 236, 241

Moor-grass, Blue 270

Moor-grass, Purple 43, 44, 46, 270, 271

Moray 59, 145, 257, 270

Mother Shipton moth 63, 64

Mr Howard's White Butterfly 97

Mustard, Garlic 97, 100, 107

Mustard, Hedge 100, 106

Myrmica sabuleti 181

Myxomatosis 53, 169, 172, 180, 184

Nasturtium 95, 97, 100, 101

Natural England 28, 55, 165, 306, 324

Neozephyrus quercus 121

Nettle 208

Nettle, Common 198, 199, 202, 208-210, 214

Nettle, Small 198, 202, 208, 214

Niobe Fritillary 226

Norfolk Broads 15, 68, 70, 136

Norfolk, East 33, 70, 105, 116, 123, 136, 137, 151, 168, 188, 235, 280

Norfolk, West 30, 60, 64, 71, 116, 123, 127, 136, 160, 168, 188, 235, 280

Northamptonshire 43, 60, 64, 77, 105, 106, 115, 123, 126, 160, 171, 180, 184, 188, 194, 276

Northern Brown Argus 36, 158, 159, **161-163**, 164

Northumberland, North 46, 56, 280, 307

Northumberland, South 262, 307, 308, 313

Nottinghamshire 126

Nymphalidae 187, 191, 197, 217, 255, 315

Nymphalinae 197

Nymphalis 203, 204

Oak 15, 33, 121, 122, 123, 124

General index

Oak Eggar moth 233
Oak, Evergreen 122
Oak, Pedunculate 122
Oak, Sessile 121
Oak, Turkey 122
Ochlodes faunus 56
Offaly 60, 309
Orange-tip 100, 111
Orange-tip, British **106-110**
Orange-tip, Irish 107, 109, **110-111**
Orkney 103, 104, 205, 232, 294, 309
Outer Hebrides 96, 107, 113, 271, 284, 285, 299
Oxfordshire 55, 78, 117, 120, 146, 160, 172, 191, 195
Painted Lady 198-199
Pale Clouded Yellow 82-84, 85, 86, 88
Pansy, Field 227
Pansy, Wild 227
Papilio machaon ssp. *britannicus* 68
Papilio machaon ssp. *gorganus* 70
Papilionidae 67
Pararge aegeria ssp. *insula* 258
Pararge aegeria ssp. *oblita* 257
Pararge aegeria ssp. *tircis* 255
Parnassius apollo 67
Parsley, Milk 68, 69
Pea, Mangetout 139
Pea, Sweet 141
Peacock 207-209

Pearl-bordered Fritillary 33, 36, 218, **222-225**, 251
Pelargonium 142
Pellitory-of-the-Wall 198
Pembrokeshire 105, 120, 152, 200, 220, 236, 280
Perthshire, East 163, 224, 256, 270
Perthshire, Mid 104, 219, 238, 265, 266
Perthshire, West 103, 122, 209
Pieridae 75
Pieris brassicae 94
Pieris napi 98
Pieris napi f. *fasciata* 100
Pieris napi f. *flava* 100
Pieris napi f. *sulphurea* 100
Pieris napi ssp. *britannica* 101
Pieris napi ssp. *sabellicae* 99
Pieris napi ssp. *thomsoni* 103
Pieris rapae 96
Plantain, Buck's-horn 248
Plantain, Ribwort 248, 251
Plebejus argus 148
Plebejus argus ssp. *argus* 149
Plebejus argus ssp. *caernensis* 156
Plebejus argus ssp. *cretaceus* 152
Plebejus argus ssp. *masseyi* 153
Polygonia c-album 209
Polygonia c-album f. *hutchinsoni* 211
Polyommatus icarus ssp. *icarus* 165
Polyommatus icarus ssp. *mariscolore* 168

General index

Pontia daplidice 105

Poplar 194, 204, 206

Primrose 183

Privet 126-129, 313

Purple Emperor 15, 33, 122, 187, 188, **191-195**

Emperors 191

Purple Hairstreak 33, **121-124**, 125, 128

Pyrgus malvae 62

Pyrgus malvae f. *taras* 25, 63, 65

Pyronia tithonus ssp. *britanniae* 289

Queen of Spain Fritillary 226-228

Radish, Sea 106

Radnorshire 96

Ragged Robin 68, 69, 70, 218

Ragwort 229, 231, 240, 256, 279, 290

Rape, Oilseed 95, 97

Réal's Wood White 30, 34, 76, 78, **80-82**

Red Admiral 197-198, 211, 214

Red-eyed Vireo 317

Renfrewshire 209

Rest-harrow 52, 166

Ringlet 30, 293, **311-313**

Riodininae 183

Rockrose, Common 114, 150, 153, 156-158, 162, 164

Rose, Dog 128

Ross, East 109, 257, 258, 270

Ross, West 222, 224, 298, 310

Roscommon 214

Roxburghshire 211, 217, 226

Rush, Jointed 218, 305

Sapporo Autumn Gold 125

Sark 149, 232

Satyrinae 255

Satyrium pruni 127

Satyrium w-album 124

Scabious, Devil's-bit 244

Scabious, Field 244

Scabious, Small 54, 244

Scarce Silver-Y moth 67

Scarce Swallowtail 72-73, 226

Scotch Argus 29, **269-271**, 272-274

Scotch Argus, Western 269, **271-272**, 274

Scotland see 329

Selkirkshire 271, 273

Sheep's Fescue 54, 275, 278, 290, 292, 300

Shetland 198, 201, 205, 206, 207, 236

Short-tailed Blue 147-148

Shropshire 29, 50, 59, 62, 64, 72, 73, 77, 105, 115, 123, 126, 149, 151, 154, 155, 160, 188, 220, 224, 235, 241, 244, 276, 280, 305, 306,

Silver-spotted Skipper 31, **53-55**, 56

Silver-studded Blue 20, 35, **148-152**, 153, 156, 166, 177

Silver-studded Blue, Northern 149, 151, **153-155**

General index

Silver-studded Blue, Southern 149, **152-153**

Silver-studded Blue, Western 149, 150, 152, **156-157**

Silver-washed Fritillary 33, 233, **239-242**, 243

Silver-washed Fritillary, Greenish 20, 25, 240, **242-243**

Skippers 43

Sligo 117, 247, 268

Small Blue 31, **143-147**, 148

Small Copper 15, **131-134**, 135

Small Copper, Irish 32, 132, **134-135**

Small Heath 299-301, 303

Small Heath, Hebridean 9, 20, **302-304**

Small Mountain Ringlet 15, 262

Small Mountain Ringlet, English 37, **263-265**, 266, 268

Small Mountain Ringlet, Irish 265, **266-268**

Small Mountain Ringlet, Scottish 37, 264, **265-266**, 268, 310, 311

Small Pearl-bordered Fritillary 33, 36, 37, **217-220**, 222, 224

Small Pearl-bordered Fritillary, Northern 29, 217, 218, **221-222**

Small Skipper 46-49, 50, 52

Small Tortoiseshell 30, **201-202**, 203, 204, 210

Small White 96-98, 100

Snowberry 177, 178

Speedwell, Germander 251

Soft-grass, Creeping 50

Somerset, North 51, 65, 67, 85, 116, 127, 146, 147, 172, 189, 220, 226, 236, 248, 249, 251, 280

Somerset, South 31, 53, 60, 78, 117, 120, 124, 127, 136, 160, 181, 185, 228, 231, 246, 252, 277

Sorrel 132, 133

Sorrel, Common 132

Sorrel, Sheep's 132

Speckled Wood 255-257, 258, 259

Speckled Wood, Isles of Scilly 9, 255-257, **258-259**

Speckled Wood, Scottish 255, 256, **257-258**

Stirlingshire 104, 122, 209, 219, 308

Stonecrop 68

Stork's-bill, Common 158

Strawberry, Wild 62

Suffolk, East 67, 71, 105, 116, 136, 151, 160, 175, 188, 227, 203

Suffolk, West 89, 280

Sutherland, East 115, 257, 284

Sutherland, West 236, 286

Surrey 35, 55, 77, 99, 116, 117, 120, 123, 127, 140, 143, 146, 151, 152, 160, 172, 174, 191, 195, 214, 220, 225, 227, 235, 241, 280

Sussex, East 82, 85, 86, 106, 123, 140, 142, 148, 152, 160, 172, 174, 175, 189, 200, 203, 220, 235, 241, 274, 276

Sussex, West 105, 117, 120, 148, 172, 175, 191, 203

Swallowtail 15, 68, 69, 70

Swallowtails **67**

General index

Swallowtail, British **68-70**, 71, 72

Swallowtail, Continental 68, **70-72**

Syngrapha interrogationis 67

Thecla betulae 117

Theclinae 113

Thistle 44, 48, 57, 68, 69, 91, 101, 119, 199, 201, 229, 231, 233, 240, 276, 312, 313

Thistle, Creeping 126, 199

Thistle, Dwarf 54

Thistle, Marsh 199

Thistle, Spear 199

Thrift 249

Thyme, Wild 162, 180, 181

Thymelicus acteon 51

Thymelicus lineola 49

Thymelicus sylvestris 46

Tipperary 90-92, 136, 137

Tipperary, South 301

Tor-grass 52, 260

Tormentil 115, 184, 218, 252, 264

Tryngites subruficollis 317

Upland Sandpiper 317

Vanessa atalanta 197

Vanessa atalanta f. *bialbata* 198

Vanessa cardui 198

Vanessa virginiensis 200

Vanessids 197

Vetch 48, 77

Vetch, Crown 86

Vetch, Horseshoe 58, 61, 84, 86, 145, 150, 170, 173, 174

Vetch, Kidney 144, 145

Vetch, Tufted 76, 81, 148

Vetchling, Bitter 76

Vetchling, Meadow 76, 81

Violet 227, 228, 229

Violet, Common Dog 217, 221, 223, 229, 232, 240

Violet, Dame's 107

Violet, Heath Dog 223

Violet, Hairy 229, 232

Violet, Marsh 217, 221, 223, 232, 237

Vireo olivaceous 317

Wales see 330

Wall 260-262

Warwickshire 105, 123, 126, 145, 148, 160, 276

Watercress 100

Waterford 262, 301

Western Isles 98, 131, 218, 237, 271, 283, 299

Westmorland 46, 49, 53, 59, 83, 89, 91, 96, 103, 110, 115, 118, 123, 179, 184, 153, 164, 211, 219, 222, 224, 231, 235, 239, 240, 241, 257, 261, 263, 269, 271, 272, 280, 291, 306, 313

Wexford 34, 81, 82, 135, 147, 211, 239, 289, 291, 301

White Admiral 33, **187-189**, 192, 215

White Admirals 187

White-letter Hairstreak 122, **124-127**

General index

Whites 75, 76

Wicklow 117, 121, 124, 179

Wigtownshire 57, 123, 219

Willow 195, 199, 202, 204, 206, 207, 210

Willow, Crack 191

Willow, Goat 191

Willow, Grey 191

Willowherbs 233

Wiltshire, North 67

Wiltshire, South 33, 51, 85, 127, 189, 195, 220, 225, 231, 241, 243, 277

Wood White 33, 34, 129, **75-78**, 80, 81,129, 195

Wood White, Irish 32, 75, 76, **78-80**, 82

Worcestershire 60, 77, 93, 120, 160, 188, 214, 226, 241, 276

Yellows 75

Yorkshire 160, 307

Yorkshire Fog 47, 48, 50, 256, 260

Yorkshire Wildlife Trust 324

Yorkshire, Mid-west 91, 115, 123, 126, 163, 165, 179, 291

Yorkshire, North-east 53, 59, 83, 103, 115, 160, 175, 184, 219, 235, 274, 307, 308

Yorkshire, South-east 50, 59, 115, 123, 160, 227, 255, 276, 280

Yorkshire, South-west 50, 126, 160, 257

Swallowtail garden at Strumpshaw Fen, Norfolk